The first phrase in brackets after the number 1 is an example of the word you looked up, and the words following it in dark letters are other words for 'important'. The phrase in brackets after the number 2 is a slightly different meaning of the word you looked up. It too is followed by other words in dark letters that relate to this slightly different meaning.

Small figures in front of an entry word, as in ¹pack and ²pack, show separate meanings or uses of the word 'pack'.

As soon as you've tried it once or twice, you'll see how easy it is to find the best way of saying what you want to say.

*It's often difficult to think of exactly
the right word to use – or a different word
when you've used the same word more than once.
That's when your thesaurus will come in handy,
with several alternatives for each of 2000 words.
And just browsing through it will give you
lots of new ideas – try it!*

A catalogue record for this book is available
from the British Library

Published by Ladybird Books Ltd
A subsidiary of the Penguin Group
A Pearson Company

THE LADYBIRD THESAURUS

by Clare Vickers
with Della Summers

illustrations by Peter Massey

Aa

abandon *(They abandoned the sinking ship.)* The older boys **left** the younger ones in the park. I **gave up** my tap classes. Has Sean **quit** school? We **evacuated** the burning house. Cora was **deserted** by her husband. The king **forsook** his palace and went on a quest. The farm was **derelict**.

ability *(the ability to read)* musical **talent**, an **aptitude** for art, the **skill** of sailing, the **knack** of making friends

able 1 *(able to swim)* **knowing how** to play, **capable** of winning **2** *(able to come)* **allowed** to go, **free** to come **3** *(an able swimmer)* a **skilful** player, **intelligent**, **clever**, a **talented** musician, a **capable** woman

about 1 *(about two o'clock)* **around** ten, **approximately** a litre, **roughly** five hours, **more or less** done **2** *(a book about dogs)* a talk **on** cats, **concerning** crime, **relating to** computers

above 1 *(above the window)* **over** the door, **higher than** the trees **2** *(above average)* **over** 80%, **more than** half marks, **better than** the pass mark, **superior to** last term's result

abroad *(working abroad)* going **overseas**, **foreign** food, **exotic** holidays

absent *(absent today)* Dan's **away**, Jim's **missing**, and Dad's **off**.

absolute *(an absolute idiot)* a **total** write-off, a **complete** disaster, **utter** chaos

absolutely *(He's absolutely useless!)* **totally** hopeless, **completely** destroyed, **thoroughly** fed up

abuse *(child abuse)* doing **harm**, causing **injury**, **molesting** children, **damage** to phones, **misuse** of money, **mistreatment** of animals

accept 1 *(accepting money)* **saying yes to** the party, **taking** a lift **2** *(accepting that you are wrong)* **admitting** stealing, **agreeing** she could work harder, **realising** I've made mistakes

accident 1 by accident *(doing something bad by accident)* pushing me **by mistake**, **accidentally** dropping the tray, **not** doing it **on purpose 2** *(a road accident)* a **crash** outside our house, a **pileup** on the motorway, a **collision** at the crossroads

a **shipwreck**

account *(an account of a long journey)* the **story** of her life, a **description** of a holiday, a **report** from Birmingham, the **history** of the Jews, an **explanation** of electricity, the **narration** of a story

accurate *(an accurate throw)* the **right** way to do it, a **correct** description, the **exact** time, a **precise** answer

accuse *(I accused her of taking the ring.)* I **said** she'd **done it**. The police **charged** her with the crime. Dad was **blamed** for the accident.

ache *(Her head ached.)* My arm **hurts**. The broken bone **was** very **painful**. My leg was **throbbing**. I've **got a pain** in my chest.

achieve *(We achieved the highest score.)* We **got** a silver cup. He **did** what he was asked. We've **carried out** some improvements. We **succeeded in** finishing on time. Has she **gained** the prize?

achievement *(a great achievement on the sports field)* **success** in exams, the **attainment** of a prize, a **feat** of courage, a daring **deed**

acquire *(He managed to acquire 20 games.)* Where did you **get** that game? How did you **come by** this medal? I **found** it on the ground. Can you **buy** me one?

¹**act 1** *(She's acting strangely.)* **behaved** sensibly, **carrying on** as if she'd really hurt herself **2** *(acting a part)* **performing** the play, **playing the part** of the mum

²**act 1** *(an act of kindness)* a good **deed**, a thoughtless **action 2** *(putting on an act)* She's not really ill – it's a **pretence**.

action 1 *(Do the actions while I say the words.)* quick **movements 2** *(an action-packed film)* endless **activity**, **drama** and **excitement**

active *(active games)* **energetic** kids, **lively** songs, **agile** dancers

activity *(outdoor activities)* a rewarding **hobby**, a **craze** for stamps, a boy with lots of **interests**, **pastimes** for wet days

actually 1 *(He's actually here!)* **really** leaving, **truly** amazing **2** *(Actually, I haven't finished.)* **In fact**, you're already too late.

adapt *(Joy adapted the play from a story.)* I **changed** the ending. She **altered** the names. Can you **adjust** this seat? He **modified** his story. **Vary** your cooking to suit the people eating it.

add *(Add biscuits to your list.)* **Put** coffee **on** the list, and **join** the lists together. **Combine** yellow and blue to make green.

addicted *(addicted to drugs)* She's **got** a drug **habit**. He's **hooked** on them. She's **dependent** on tranquillisers. He's a **junkie**.

additional *(additional time)* **extra** ice, a **spare** pen

a clean T-shirt
in reserve

a

admiration *(looking at the acrobats with admiration)* He treated the old man with **respect**. They clapped to show **approval**.

admire *(I admire her singing.)* I **respect** your honesty. She **looks up to** her grandmother.

admit 1 *(admitting to a crime)* **confessing** to it, **owning up** to it **2** *(admitting her to a film)* **letting** me **in**, not **allowed in**

adult *(an adult and two children)* Here come the **grown-ups**!

advantage *(an advantage to be tall)* One of the **benefits** of old age is that you see your grandchildren. It's a great **help** to have a calculator. Knowing how to use a computer is a **plus**, too. One of the **good things** about this house is the sea view.

adventure *(the adventures of a space crew)* a lot of **excitement** on our journey, the **experiences** of a pilot, a boy seeking his **fortune**, the explorer's daring **exploits**

adventurous *(an adventurous person)* a **daring** journey into the desert, an **audacious** plan

advertisement *(a toothpaste advertisement)* a TV **commercial** for a car, an **ad** in the paper for a secondhand computer

advice *(advice about choosing a school)* some **suggestions** about the project, asking for your doctor's **help** with your diet, **hints** on writing a good story, **tips** about the game, **guidance** on what toys to make

advise *(I advise you to leave.)* He **suggested** that I go to the library. Kevin **recommended** the game. 'Be careful,' he **warned**.

afraid 1 *(afraid of spiders)* **frightened** of that dog, **scared** of the dark, **terrified** when he's driving **2** *(I'm afraid I can't eat this.)* I'm **sorry**, but I can't come tomorrow. I **regret** not being able to come.

age 1 *(What age is he?)* **How old** is Jane? She's ten years **of age**. The parrot's 30 **years old**. **2** *(the age of steam)* in past **times**, the Victorian **period**, the war **years**

the start of the space **era** –

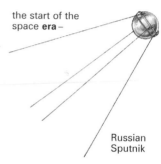

Russian Sputnik

ages *(He's been waiting ages.)* It takes **a long time** to cook. I haven't seen him **for weeks**. She takes **forever** in the shower.

agree 1 *(I agree with you.)* I **think the same** as Jo. She **admitted** I was right. **2** *(She agreed to let us go.)* Lucy **accepted** my idea. The king **consented** to his daughter's marriage. **3** *(Their stories did not agree.)* His story didn't **match** Jim's. Their stories didn't **correspond** at all.

agreement *(an agreement about pocket money)* I thought we had a **deal**! Keep your side of the **bargain**. He made a **promise** to feed the cats. The two generals signed a **treaty**. There was a peace **settlement**.

¹aim *(the aim of the game)* What is the **object** of chess? Your **goal** is to become the richest player. The **target** is 900 points. My **ambition** is to be a doctor. The **objective** is to capture the castle.

²aim 1 *(aiming the ball at the goal)* **Take aim** before you throw. He **trained** the gun on the running man. The police cars **zeroed in on** the fight. Jan **pointed** the arrow at the target. **2** *(aiming for the highest prize)* **Go for** it! Sean's **trying for** a hat trick.

air 1 *(the air we breathe)* the earth's **atmosphere**, giving a patient **oxygen**, improving **ventilation 2** *(the fresh air)* The sheets caught the **breeze**. The **wind** dried them. There's a cold **draught!** **3** *(The birds rose into the air.)* The **sky** was full of them.

alarm 1 *(The alarm went off when the prisoner escaped.)* a **warning signal**, a **fire bell**, **sirens** for a bombing raid **2** *(He stopped in alarm.)* to run off in **fear**, to cry out in **shock**

alert *(Keep alert!)* I hope you're **awake** and **on your toes** for the quiz. Be **prepared!** An **observant** policeman had noticed something wrong. Keep **wide awake** to win at this game!

alike *(The sisters were alike.)* Jenny's **very like** her mother. All the Smiths have **similar** noses. The twins are **identical**. They're **as alike as two peas in a pod**. Choose **matching** colours.

all *(all the king's horses; plenty for all)* Let's welcome **everyone**. **Everybody** sang. **Everything** worked out well. **Every** child has a medal. The **whole** class laughed. He got a **complete** set of CDs.

all right 1 *(I'm all right.)* Isn't Robert feeling **well**? He's **fine**. The tyre burst but the driver's **safe**. The passenger was **unhurt**. **2** *(This book's all right.)* It's **not bad**. The new teacher's **OK**. This story's **satisfactory** but you could do better.

allow *(He allowed me to play.)* She **let** me stay. Miss Grant **gave** me **permission** to go. He **permitted** me to go. He **said** I **could** go.

almost *(almost ten years old)* **nearly** home, **not quite** ready

alone *(Home Alone!)* having tea **by myself**, going **on your own**, working **separately**, living **apart** from his family – see also LONELY, ONLY

also *(She's a teacher and also a writer.)* Debbie **and** I go to the park after school. Her sister goes **as well**. My brother goes **too**. The two girls **plus** the dog live next door. **In addition**, they learn judo.

alter *(altering a dress)* **changing** the story, **adjusting** the lamp to read in bed, **converting** the loft into a playroom

altogether *(It's 35 altogether.)* It's £3 **in total**.

always *(always late)* mean to me **all the time**, happy **forever**, to live happily **ever after**

amazing 1 *(amazing stories)* a **surprising** win, an **astonishing** fact, phoning someone **out of the blue 2** *(We had an amazing time.)* a **wonderful** new band, a **great** time, a **sensational** computer game

amount *(a small amount of sugar)* a large **quantity** of white paper, a great **deal** of work, a **number** of children learning the guitar

amusing *(an amusing show)* a **funny** film, a **comic** actor, some **entertaining** jokes. Tom's stories always **make** me **laugh**.

anger *(white with anger)* Mr Gibson's in a **temper**. The child screamed with **rage**. Jo roared in **fury**. He stamped in **annoyance**.

angry *(angry with Sam)* Dad gets **cross** if I'm late. He was **furious** with me yesterday. Mum's **mad** with the cats. He was **wild** when I jumped on him. Mrs Nixon's **steamed up** about something.

animal *(a farmyard animal)* warm-blooded **creatures**, wild **beasts** like lions and tigers, a great **brute** of a dog

announcement *(announcements about Sports Day)* a **notice** banning ball games, a **poster** about the sale, a **sticker** with the price on it, an **advertisement** for old toys, a royal **proclamation**, a **declaration** of war

No smoking **sign**

annoy *(annoyed by her rudeness)* Noise from the building site **irritated** me. The dog's **pestering** Ben again. Stop **bothering** your father. It **gets on her nerves**. Your music's **driving me up the wall**. It's **driving** Mr Jones **crazy**, too. Her questions are **driving** the teacher **round the bend**. My little brother **bugs** me! He's trying to **wind** me **up**.

annoying *(annoying sounds)* **irritating** habits, a **pain in the neck**

¹**answer 1** *(an answer to my question)* a **reply** to your letter, no **response** from Jack **2** *(the answer to a sum)* a **solution** to a problem

²**answer** *(Answer me!)* **replying** at once, **responding** to an order

anxious *(an anxious moment)* The teacher's **worried** about Julia. Your parents are **concerned** about you. She was **unhappy** about Emma going home alone. She got **uptight** about the school play. She felt she was **under pressure** to do well. I'm getting **nervous** about the swimming gala. That ghost story made me **uneasy**.

apartment *(a New York apartment)* I live in a **flat**.

apologise *(apologising for being rude)* **Say** you're **sorry**!

appear 1 *(appearing without warning)* Mike **arrived** unexpectedly. Kevin **turned up** a bit later. Did anyone else **show up** at the party? The outline of a ship **materialised** out of the mist. **2** *(appearing rather sleepy)* Tim **seems** rather tired. You **look** hot.

8

appearance *(his strange appearance)* I don't like the **look** of those clouds. Pay attention to the **presentation** of your work.

applause *(the applause of the audience)* We heard **clapping** and **cheering**. A **big hand** for our winners! **Three cheers** for Joe!

approve **1** *(approve of someone's choice)* Mr Wells **is in favour of** spelling tests. She's **pleased with** our hard work. He **believes in** taking exercise. I **support** what you say about cruelty to animals. **2** *(approve a plan officially)* The council **authorised** plans for the bypass. He got planning **permission** for a new garage.

area *(a woodland area)* the biggest park in this **district**, the wettest **region** of Britain, the oldest school in the **neighbourhood**, a **patch** of ground, the wizard's **territory**

argue *(arguing about money)* Tim and Kitty are **quarrelling** about whose turn it is. They **squabbled** over the sweets. They **fight** a lot.

argument *(an argument over money)* The brothers had a **quarrel** last night. Meryl had a **row** with Mum. Don't pick a **fight** with me.

army *(joining the army)* The **forces** are divided into the **army**, the **navy** and the **air force**. British **troops** were fighting in North Africa in 1942.

arrange **1** *(I've arranged to see your teacher.)* Bob **planned** to go to the match. Rachel's **organised** a meeting of the chess club. They **decided** to get married in July. **2** *(arranging furniture)* We had **put** all the

chairs **in the right place** for the play. Vivien **put** the books **in order** in her new bookcase. Have you **laid** the table yet? I've **set out** the cakes on our stall. **Sort** the CDs into different piles.

arrangement **1** *(an arrangement to meet)* We haven't got any **plans** for Sunday. I have an **appointment** with Dr Taylor. The companies reached an **understanding** so they could work together. **2** *(a flower arrangement)* Change the **position** of those chairs. The **layout** of the hospital is very good. **3** *(an arrangement about pocket money)* I've got an **agreement** with Max about using the computer.

Japanese flower **arrangement**

arrest *(arresting a robber)* They've **caught** the man who killed her. The man was **captured** last night. The enemy **took** him **prisoner**.

arrive *(arriving at midday)* The next patient's just **come**. This train **reaches** Plymouth at 12.40. We **got there** by bus. When do you think they'll **get here**? They didn't **appear** till midnight. He **turned up** late for the match. The plane's **landing**. The ship **docked** at 3.30.

a

art *(good at art)* Here's some of their **artwork**. I love **drawing** and **painting**. **Illustrations** in this book look like computer **graphics**.

artificial *(artificial flowers)* Lycra is a **man-made** material but cotton is natural. A **synthetic** substance is made from chemicals. It's **fake** fur.

ashamed *(ashamed of yourself)* She **feels bad** about breaking your watch. He's got a **guilty conscience** about being mean. I'm **embarrassed** by Mum's hat!

ask 1 *(asking for something)* I **demand** to see the manager! The children **begged** for some sweets. They **nagged** their mother to buy some. Her parents **requested** to see the teacher. Police **questioned** three suspects. **2** *(asking the way)* I don't know – you'd better **inquire** at the desk. I'll **consult** Dr Cooper about the injections.

asleep *(She's fast asleep.)* He tripped over the **sleeping** dog. Charlie's **dead to the world** on Saturday mornings. Grandpa was **snoozing** in the chair. She **dozed off** again after the alarm went off.

assistant 1 *(a shop assistant)* The **check-out** operator gave me 37p change. She gave the money to the **cashier**. **2** *(Dr Green's assistant)* I'm Miss Lee's **helper** this week. The **deputy** head is Mrs Muscroft.

attach *(He attached a note to the fridge.)* Kate **fastened** a bell to her bike. He **hung** a picture on the wall. She **stuck** up a poster. Can you **fix** the legs to the table? We **connected** the video to the TV.

¹**attack** *(an attack by a fierce dog)* a recent **mugging**, a bank **raid**, an **ambush** on the soldier's camp, an enemy **invasion**

²**attack** *(attacking the enemy)* Dan's gang **set on** us. My dog **went for** Dan. He **picked a fight** with Sam. Thieves **raided** the bank. The soldiers **ambushed** the camp and **stormed** the castle. Japan **invaded** China.

attempt *(an attempt to climb Everest)* Have another **try**. I've had a **go** – you try. That's a good **effort**. Arsenal's **bid** for the Cup failed.

attractive *(an attractive dress)* a **pretty** garden, a **beautiful** view, a **lovely** idea, a **good-looking** woman, a **handsome** man, an **appealing** puppy

average *(An average family has two children.)* **normal** weather for May, my **usual** way home, a **typical** lazy Sunday afternoon

avoid *(avoiding the wasps' nest)* Dennis **dodged** the stone Sally threw. Rick **kept clear of** Mrs Evans after she shouted at him. You children should **keep out of my way**! Chris **went round** the puddle.

award *(a science award)* an art **prize**, a **medal** for running, the winner's **badge**, a bronze **shield**, the FA **Cup**, a **rosette** for Best Dog

awful *(an awful day)* a **bad** cold, **nasty** smells, **terrible** weather, **dreadful** traffic, **horrible** people

awfully *(awfully cold)* **very** smelly, **terribly** hot, **dreadfully** late, **horribly** ugly

awkward *(an awkward fall)* a **clumsy** kid, a **bungling** idiot, a **gawky** lad

Bb

baby *(a newborn baby)* a little **child**, **toddlers** at playgroup, her **infant** son

¹**back** *(the back of the chair)* the **tail** of the queue, the **rear** of the train, the **end** of the story, the sea in the **background**, the **other side** of the page

²**back** **1** *(back down the drive)* **reversing** out of the garage, **retreating** to base **2** *(back a plan)* We **support** your idea.

bad **1** *(a bad thing to do)* a **nasty** person, a **mean** woman, a **cruel** man, a **horrible** thing to say, **unkind** treatment, a **baddie** **2** *(a bad day at school)* an **awful** time, **terrible** weather, a **hopeless** mess, **lousy** marks, an **unpleasant** smell **3** *(bad for you)* **serious** accidents, **dangerous** drugs, **harmful** to pets **4** *(The meat's bad.)* **rotten** eggs, **mouldy** cheese, **sour** milk. That fish is **off**. **5** *(bad work)* **poor** spelling, **faulty** brakes, **defective** workmanship

bag

bake *(bake a cake)* I **cooked** the buns. He **roasted** a chicken.

bald *(a bald head)* Grandad's getting **thin on top**. He's got a **bare** patch on his head. The palm of your hand is **hairless**.

ban *(banning cigarettes)* Alcohol is **prohibited** at football matches. Smoking is **not permitted**. Walking on the grass is **not allowed**.

band **1** *(the band's latest CD)* The Beatles were the most famous **group** in the 1960s. The **orchestra** needs a drummer. **2** *(a band of robbers)* Jason's got a **gang**. The girls go out in a **group**. **3** *(an elastic band)* She's wearing a **hairband**. He tied a **sweatband** round his head. She put **ribbons** on her plaits. He tied up his hair with a **strip** of cotton. **4** *(a red shirt with blue bands)* Her dress had pink **stripes**, a **line** of white round the neck, and a lace **border**. The post had red **rings** round it.

handbag

purse

satchel

backpack

carrier bag

luggage

b

bang *(the bang of a gun)* the **slam** of a door, the **crash** of breaking glass, the **crack** of a bullet, the **thump** of Simon falling out of bed, the **boom** of thunder, the **thud** of his feet on the floor, the **thunder** of the waterfall, the **clatter** of Dad dropping the gardening tools, the **explosion** of a bomb

bank 1 *(a bank account)* a **building society** savings account, savings in the **Post Office 2** *(a river bank)* a grassy **hillside**, a slippery **slope**, a **mound** of earth, a sand **dune**

bar 1 *(a bar of chocolate)* a **chunk** of meat, a **hunk** of bread, a **slab** of toffee, a **lump** of sugar **2** *(a snack bar)* a **café** at the station, the local **pub**, a small **restaurant 3** *(Press the space bar.)* the letter **keys**

bare *(bare legs)* get **undressed**, in the **nude**, a **naked** baby

base *(the naval base)* an enemy **camp**, army **headquarters**, a **branch** of the bank

basin *(a basin of water)* Put the dishes in the **sink**. Mix the pudding in a **bowl**. There's a sparrow in the **birdbath**.

bat *(a cricket bat)* a tennis **racket**, a hockey **stick**

battle *(the battle of Hastings)* The two gangs had a **fight**. There was **fighting** in the streets. A man was killed in the **crossfire**. No further **exchanges** have been reported.

bay *(a sandy bay)* a rocky **cove**, an **inlet** of the sea

be *(being alive)* Do you think ghosts **exist**? The house has **remained** empty. Nothing **lives** on the moon. You can't **survive** without air. He **seems** tired. You **appear** surprised.

beach *(a sandy beach)* a visit to the **seaside**, a dangerous **coast**, golden **sands**, a rocky **shore**

beam 1 *(a beam of light)* the sun's **rays**, a **shaft** of sunlight **2** *(a beam holding up the roof)* a bird's nest in the **rafters**

bear 1 *(I can't bear her!)* She can't **stand** cabbage. Don't **put up with** the neighbours being nosy. I won't **take** his rudeness any longer. Some people can't **tolerate** hot weather. **2** *(bear a weight)* They **carried** the winner on their shoulders.

hanging basket **supported by** a bracket

beat 1 *(beating the other team)* We **thrashed** King's Park 5–0. Arsenal **defeated** Leeds at home. We'll **slaughter** them! **2** *(beating a dog)* He **hit** the robber. I would never **smack** a child. Jo got **beaten up** at school. Teachers used to **cane** children. The jockey **whipped** his horse. Slaves were **flogged** if they tried to escape. Your Dad'll **thrash** you! She **slapped** his face. **3** *(beating eggs)* He **whipped** the cream, **whisked** the eggs, and **stirred** them into the mixture.

beautiful *(a beautiful beach)* **pretty** flowers, a **lovely** day, an **attractive** house, a **good-looking** boy, a **handsome** man, a **nice-looking** girl, a **gorgeous** costume

bedcover

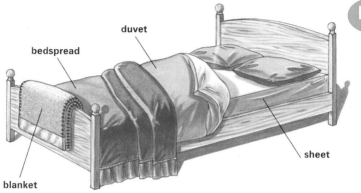

duvet

bedspread

sheet

blanket

before *(the day before)* We came an hour **ago**. Can you start **earlier**? Ask your Mum **first**. I knew her **previously**.

beg 1 *(begging in the street)* **cadging** a few pounds **2** *(beg for more time)* **plead** for another chance, **nag** Mum for a drink

begin *(begin to run)* It's **starting** to rain. Let's **kick off** with an easy question. We must **get** things **moving**. Let's **get going**. The play **opens** with a song. **2** *(He began a new school.)* It was **founded** in 1993. A drama department was **set up**.

beginning *(the beginning of the day)* the **start** of the race, the **first part** of the song, the **origin** of life, the **opening** of the film, the **commencement** of World War II

behave *(behaving badly)* You're **acting** like a spoilt child. Don't **be** silly. He's **on his best behaviour**.

believe *(believing something is true)* I **think** Paul's ill. He **feels** you don't trust him. I **take your word for it**. I'll **give you the benefit of the doubt**. **Trust** me! He **fell for** that one – I said we were late and he started running! I don't **buy** that excuse! I **suspect** him of lying.

belong 1 *(belonging to Kit)* These socks **are yours**. This book is **owned by** Wayne Hawkins. This is **part of** your puzzle. **2** *(I belong to the fan club.)* Jody's **a member of** the Drama Club.

belongings *(Where are your belongings?)* Collect your **things** and come with me. Where's all your PE **stuff**? It's in Lost **Property**. All her precious **possessions** were in the box.

below 1 *(below the clouds)* **under** the bed, **underneath** him, **beneath** the sea **2** *(below 15)* **less than** 20, **lower than** 100

13

b

¹**bend** *(a bend in the road)* lots of **twists and turns**, a sharp **corner**, a slow **curve**

²**bend** *(bending to one side)* The road **turns** to the right and **curves** round the bay. Her hair **curls** round her ears. He **twisted** the dog's lead round his hand.

bend down *(Stand up – don't bend down!)* We **crouched** down. She **stooped** to look at it. **Get down!** I **ducked** as the bullets flew by.

best *(the best player)* the **greatest** boxer, the **top** scorer, the **star** performer, a **record-breaking** jump. He's **number one**! She's **unbeatable**!

better 1 *(You're doing better than me.)* You're **making** good **progress**. Your work's **improving**. Things are **looking up**! **2 Get better** *(He got better quickly.)* Has Gran **recovered**? She's still **convalescing**.

big *(a big house)* a **large** box, a **huge** man, an **enormous** tree, a **gigantic** spaceship, a **massive** amount of work

bin

biscuit *(a sweet biscuit)* chocolate **cookies**, lemon **wafers**, fudge **brownies**, cheese and **crackers**, **crispbread**

bit *(bits of cheese)* a **piece** of cake, a **slice** of bread, a **lump** of sugar, a **chunk** of coal, a **hunk** of bread, a **scrap** of meat, a **sheet** of paper, a **dollop** of cream

¹**bite** *(bite an apple)* I **bit off** a piece of meat. He **chewed** the gum. The dog **nipped** my ankle. Kate **munched** her cereal. Birds **pecked** at the nuts. The wolf **gnawed** the bone. A rabbit **nibbled** the grass.

²**bite 1** *(a bite out of my leg)* You can see the **toothmarks**! **2** *(a bite to eat)* a quick **snack**, a **mouthful** of cake, a **morsel** of cheese

blame *(blaming someone for doing something)* He **said** it **was your fault**. He **picks on** you. You always **put the blame on** Jim. Mr Haines **criticises** everyone. Maria **accused** him of stealing.

skip

wastepaper basket

wheelie bin

dustbin

bottle bank

14

blanket *(a warm blanket)* a pretty **duvet**, a double **quilt**, a cotton **bedspread**, striped **sheets**

¹**block** *(a blocked sink)* a **clogged** drain, a **bunged up** nose. Tea leaves **stopped up** the pipe. This lane's **coned off**. The barrier **held back** the flood. Don't **obstruct** the traffic.

²**block** *(a block of flats)* an office **building**, a **shopping centre**, new **high-rise** flats, a huge **skyscraper**, a gigantic **construction**

blonde *(blonde curls)* a **fair-haired** boy, a man with a **yellow** beard, a girl with **sandy** hair, a **golden-haired** retriever

blouse *(a cotton blouse)* a striped **shirt**, a black **top**

blow *(blowing bubbles)* **breathing out** noisily, **puffing** smoke in my face, wind **fanning** the forest fire, a storm **howling** round the house

blow it *(You've blown it!)* He's **ruined his chances**. I've **missed out on** the hot dogs. You've **spoilt your chance** of winning.

blow up 1 *(blowing up balloons)* **Put** more **air in** the airbed. Let's **pump up** the tyres. **2** *(blowing up a building)* The bomb **went off** just now. The army **bombed** the town. They **set off** dynamite under the mountain. The fireworks **exploded**. They **let off** some rockets.

blue *(a blue jacket)* **sky blue**, **royal blue**, **navy blue**, **indigo**, **turquoise**

blush *(blushing in confusion)* She **went red** when Ken came in. She **gets embarrassed** easily. She **flushed** to the roots of her hair.

boast *(boasting too much)* Stop **bragging**! He **shows off** a lot.

boat

b

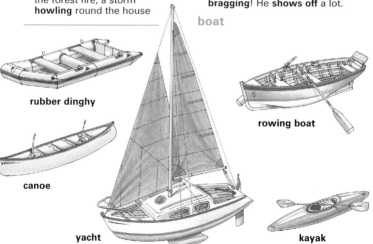

rubber dinghy

rowing boat

canoe

yacht

kayak

body 1 _(a fat body)_ a slim **figure**, a good **physique**, a heavy **build** **2** _(a dead body)_ a man's **corpse**, a deer's **carcass**, the **remains** of the enemy soldier

border _(the Welsh border)_ the **frontier** between France and Italy

boring _(a boring programme)_ an **uninteresting** book, a **dull** person, a **dreary** subject, a real **drag**

bottom _(the bottom of the well)_ the **base** of a triangle, the **lower** lip, the **foot** of a tree, the **depths** of the ocean

bound to _(bound to fall)_ **going to** rain, **sure to** go, **certain to** win

¹**bow** (_say like_ so) _(a ribbon tied in a bow)_ tied in a fancy **knot**

²**bow** (_say like_ cow) _(bowing low)_ **kneeling** before the king, **curtseying** gracefully

box

boy _(a tall boy)_ a nice **lad**, a fat **guy**, a tough **kid**, a skinny **youth**

brain _(Use your brain!)_ She's got the **brains** in the family. Use some **intelligence**. He can't get it into his **head**. Show some **sense**.

brainy _(a brainy kid)_ an **intelligent** girl, a **clever** boy, a **bright** child, a **brilliant** scientist

brake _(The bus braked suddenly.)_ It **stopped** at the lights. He **pulled up** beside the postbox. The car **slowed down** by the school.

branch _(an oak branch)_ Put **twigs** on the fire. Here's a long **stick**. She swung from the **bough** of the tree.

brave _(a brave rescue)_ a **courageous** man, a **fearless** knight, a **heroic** escape, a **gutsy** kid, a **daring** adventure

carton

treasure chest

packet

container

bread

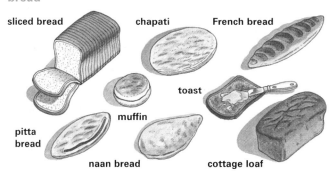

sliced bread

chapati

French bread

toast

muffin

pitta bread

naan bread

cottage loaf

break *(breaking a window)* The glass **cracked** when I put hot water in. The handle **came off**. It just **came apart** in my hands! The cake **fell to bits** as I lifted it. He **smashed** a cup and **chipped** a plate. A pen **snapped** under my foot. The glass **splintered** into tiny pieces. The conker **split** open. Sam **fractured** his arm. The computer **crashed**.

breathe *(breathing fast)* Chris was **puffing** as he walked up the hill. The dog **panted** in the heat. When Grandad had a cold, he **wheezed** at night. She **gasped** with surprise. He **sighed** loudly.

bright 1 *(a bright light)* a **good** light for reading, **blinding** floodlights, **dazzling** headlights, a **blazing** fire, a **light** classroom, a **sunny** kitchen, **sparkling** Christmas lights, **brilliant** sunlight **2** *(a bright idea)* an **intelligent** girl, a **clever** boy, a **brainy** person, a **brilliant** answer, a **smart** suggestion **3** *(a bright smile)* a **happy** face, a **cheerful** look, a **lively** expression

brilliant 1 *(a brilliant solution)* a **clever** idea, a **brainy** child, an **intelligent** woman **2** *(What a brilliant band!)* They're just **great**! That's an **excellent** new video. That's really **cool**. **3** *(a brilliant light)* **dazzling** headlights, the **blinding** light of the sun

bring *(bringing him home)* They **delivered** the TV. Can you **fetch** me some milk? No – I've already **got** you the cake! **Carry** them in.

bring up *(bringing up children)* a baby to **look after**, **taking care of** the children, **raising** their family in the country

broken *(a broken doll)* a **cracked** glass, a **chipped** plate, a **smashed** vase, a **split** nail, a **fractured** arm. The computer's **down**. There's **something wrong** with it. It's **not working**.

brown *(brown eyes)* **chocolate**, **coffee colour**, **chestnut**, **rust**, **tawny**

brush *(brushing your hair)* **Sweep** the steps and **scrub** the floor. **Mop** up the mess. **Sponge** his face.

b

build *(building a house)* They're **putting up** a new block. We **constructed** a model of the airport.

The birds are **making** a nest.

¹**bump** *(a bump on the head)* a big **bruise**, a bad **swelling** **2** *(drop with a bump)* stop with a **crash**, fall with a **thump**, land with a **thud**

²**bump** *(bumping into a wall)* Dad **hit** the door when he drove in. The bike **crashed** into her. We **smashed** into a bus. Joshua **collided** with Mrs Lamb. The moth **knocked** against the lamp. We **thumped** into the wall. The ball **thudded** into the net. The horse **jolted** against the fence.

bump into *(I bumped into Gary outside the school.)* Mum **met** Mrs Harris on the bus. She **came across** Katie waiting at the bus stop.

bunch 1 *(a bunch of primroses)* a **bouquet** of red roses **2** *(a bunch of problems)* a **lot** of trouble, **plenty** of hassles, a **group** of friends

bundle *(a bundle of old clothes)* a **pile** of papers, a **heap** of socks, a **mass** of washing

burglar *(A burglar climbed through the window.)* A **thief** stole his money. An **intruder** took our video. **Robbers** broke in at night.

burgle *(burgling a house)* He **broke in** while I was out. He was arrested for **breaking and entering**. She **stole** £10 from my purse.

burn 1 *(burning wood)* The house is **on fire**. The wood **caught fire** and **blazed** up. The roof **burst into flames**. Can you **light** a fire? He **set fire to** the paper. The gas **ignited**. It **went up in flames**. **2** *(I burnt myself!)* The water **scalded** me. I **scorched** the sheet.

burrow *(an animal's burrow)* a rat's **hole**, a rabbit **warren**

burst 1 *(A balloon burst.)* A bomb **exploded** by the hotel. It **went off** at 12. **2** *(The dam burst.)* A wall **caved in**. My jeans **split open**.

business *(running a business)* a building **company**, a **firm** that makes clothes, the computer **industry**, banking and **commerce**

businessman *(a businessman's suit)* She's a **businesswoman**. His father's a car **dealer**. The **merchants** were selling gold cloth. They were fur **traders** from the Canadian forests.

busy 1 *(a busy person)* Joanna's **got lots to do** today. She'll be **rushed off her feet**. Mr King is **engaged** with a client. He's **occupied** now, can you call again? **2** *(a busy station)* a **bustling** town, a **frantic** rush

buy *(buying a ruler)* He **got** a paper. Mum **stocked up** on biscuits. She **goes shopping** on Thursdays. We **shop** at the supermarket. The government **purchased** land for the bypass. I **paid for** your ticket.

Cc

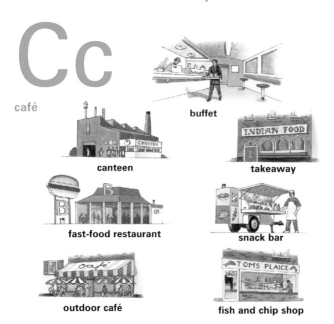

café

buffet

canteen

takeaway

fast-food restaurant

snack bar

outdoor café

fish and chip shop

calculate *(Calculate what you owe me.)* **Work out** how much the box weighs, then **estimate** its length.

call 1 *('John!' I called.)* 'I'm home!' she **shouted**. 'Help!' she **cried**. 'Oh no!' I **exclaimed**. 'Come here,' **yelled** Dad.
2 *(She's called Kay.)* His **name** **is** Neil. The **title** of the film **is** 'The Wizard of Oz'. Doris **refers to** her husband as 'Big Ben'.
3 *(call home)* Peter **rang** – can you **phone** him back? I'll **call** him **up** after tea.

calm *(a calm sea)* a **peaceful** walk, a **quiet** life, a **placid** man, a **tranquil** scene

calm down *(Calm down and be quiet!)* Try and **control yourself**. **Don't get excited. Don't panic!**

¹can 1 *(She can juggle.)* The little boy **is able to** read now. Ruth **knows how to** play chess. This dog **is capable of** winning the race. **2** *(Can Sophie come too?)* Lee **is allowed** to stay out late. You're **free to** go if you want to. Yes, you **may** have a biscuit.

²can *(a can of pop)* a **tin** of peas

cancel *(The match was cancelled.)* The play has been **called off**. The sports centre has **dropped** tennis coaching. They've **stopped** judo classes too. The project to build a new jet was **scrapped**.

cap 1 *(the cap of the toothpaste)* the **lid** of a jar, the **top** of a bottle, the **ring-pull** from a can **2** *(a baseball cap)* a straw **hat**, a soldier's **beret**

¹care *(I don't care!)* She never **worries** what clothes she wears. Do you **mind** which colour you have?

²care 1 *(Take care!)* **Be careful! Look out! Mind it! Watch it! Pay attention! 2** *(in the care of her aunt)* She's left in the **charge** of her aunt. Eva's under the **protection** of the court. He got **custody** of the children.

care for *(caring for your pet)* Mandy's **looking after** my hamster.

carpet *(a fitted carpet)* a fluffy **rug**, a **mat** just inside the door

carry *(carrying a suitcase)* **Pick up** your case. **Lift** the box and **bring** it here. We've got to **move** these books. **Take** this box away. I **fetched** the papers. Ian **brought** some cakes with him. He has to **lug** his football boots round all day.

carry on *(carrying on with the lesson)* **Go on** reading. She **continued** sewing. I hope this rain doesn't **last** all day. We have to **stick at** that project all term.

castle *(Windsor Castle)* a Roman **fort**, an old **fortress**

¹catch 1 *(catch a ball)* **grab** the cup as it falls, **snatch** it in midair **2** *(catch the thief)* The killer was **captured** last night. The police **arrested** him. Quick, **grab** the cat before it goes out! I've **got** it! The hunters **trapped** a tiger. Grandad's **hooked** a huge fish.

²catch 1 *(the catch on a door)* the **hook** on her dress, the **fastening** on the suitcase **2** *(a catch in the question)* There's a **trick** in the way it's asked.

¹cause *(What caused the fire?)* The rain's **made** the pitch all soggy. The cat's fur **brought on** Mum's asthma. A road accident **led to** huge traffic jams. The arrival of the Addams family **set off** some very strange happenings. The referee's decision **produced** an argument and **resulted** in a player being sent off.

²cause *(the cause of the argument)* the **reason** for the noise, the **root** of the trouble

central *(the central square)* the **main** office, the **middle** shelf

centre *(the centre of the field)* the **middle** of the room, the **heart** of the jungle, the Earth's **core**

certain *(Are you certain?)* Yes, I'm **sure**. Are you **positive** it's Amy's? He's **definitely** coming.

chain 1 *(a gold chain)* a silver **necklace** with a matching **bracelet 2** *(prisoners in chains)* a broken **link** in the chain **3** *(a chain of events)* a **series** of disasters, a **string** of coincidences, alphabetical **order**, a **course** of injections, a **sequence** of numbers, a **succession** of crashes

challenge *(challenge to a fight)* She **dared** us to climb in. He **took on** the bully. Jack **defied** the giant.

chance 1 *(a chance to play)* an **opportunity** to meet a champion, a **risk** of snow, the **possibility** of rain **2 by chance** *(I met him by chance.)* I **happened to** meet Sue. What a **coincidence** – so did I! I trod on a frog **by accident**. I called Mrs Lee 'Mum' **by mistake**. The goal was a **fluke**. You **got lucky**.

change *(change schools)* **altering** the end of a story, **adjusting** a reading light, **transforming** yourself into a monster, **swapping** your stickers for some sweets, **exchanging** seats for the next game

¹**channel** *(a TV channel)* a radio **station**. What's on the other **side**?

²**channel**

canal

moat

character *(the main character in the film)* the **part** of the baddie, the **role** of the king

charge 1 *(charging a lot of money)* They're **asking** £300 for that sofa. They **make you pay** more if it's delivered. The CDs **cost** too much. The petrol station's **put up its prices**. 2 *(They charged out of the door.)* They **attacked** the castle. They **rushed** the door. **3 in charge of** *(Mrs Watt is in charge of 1C.)* Who **looks after** the kids? Sal **takes care** of them. Give me your money for **safekeeping**. I'll be **responsible for** it.

chase *(chasing the cat)* **Run after** Maggie with the key. **Try and catch up with** her before she reaches the gate. Sam **went after** Maggie. The police are **following** that truck. They're **hunting** the bank robbers.

chat *(chatting away to Mum)* **having a chat** about your holidays, **talking** to her at the bus stop, **gossiping** over the hedge, **nattering** for hours

cheap *(cheap pens)* The carpet was quite **inexpensive**. The CDs are **reduced**. £2 is **reasonable**. She bought a **cut-price** dress. She got a **discount** on the computer. Dad likes a **bargain**. He paid a **low price** for the flat.

cheat *(cheating someone)* She **tricked** me out of 50p. Matt **did** his sister **out of** their parents' house. I was **swindled** out of £100. He **deceived** his teacher. He **conned** his friends into paying for him. He **fooled** me into signing the letter. The salesgirl **shortchanged** me.

check *(Check your answers.)* Just **go over** your work and **make sure of** the spellings. Let's **examine** the answers. She **made certain** she had her key. Jan wants a radio so I'm going to **check out** prices. I'm going to **test** your memory.

cheeky *(a cheeky face)* Don't be **rude**! What **insolent** remarks! Don't be **disrespectful**. You shouldn't **talk back**.

cheer up *(cheer someone up)* Mrs West tried to **make** the losers **feel better**. The sunny weather **put** Mum **in a good mood**. The class **brightened up** when he said they could play a game.

cheerful *(a cheerful person)* a **happy** face, **in a good mood**, a **jolly** time

chew *(I chewed the meat.)* Tim **munched** an apple. The pony **nibbled** the grass. The dog **gnawed** the bone.

¹**chief** *(the pirate chief)* the gang **leader**, the tribal **headman**

²**chief** *(the chief reason)* the **main** point, the **most important** question, the **basic** problem, **essential** foods, **key** facts

child *(a child of eight)* Line up, **girls** on the right and **boys** on the left. My **son** is twelve and my **daughter** is nine. three **kids**, a little **toddler**, a tiny **baby**, **youngsters** of school age, her **infant** son

choice *(You've got a choice of vanilla or chocolate.)* your **pick** of the magazines, my **selection** of games, an **alternative** appointment, the **option** of learning French

choke *(choking on a fish bone)* **coughing** and **spluttering**, nearly **suffocating**, **stifling** heat, **smothered** by fumes

choose **1** *(choosing a baby's name)* **Select** an animal name for your team. We've **picked** the name 'Wolves'. They **went for** 'Cats'. They **decided on** pink for the walls. **2** *(choosing a leader)* Our team must **elect** a captain.

circular **1** *(a circular brooch)* a **round** face, a **rounded** cheek **2** *(a circular route)* a **ring** road, going in a **loop**, an **elliptical** orbit

city *(the city centre)* a small **town**, schools in **urban** areas, **inner-city** schools, the **Metropolitan** Police

clap *(clapping the clowns)* The audience **applauded** the play. We **cheered** the song. A **big hand** for the winner! **Three cheers** for Sarah!

class **1** *(in Class 3D)* in the first **year**, in seventh **grade**, the Sixth **Form** college, the top maths **set** **2** *(an English class)* a science **lesson**, second **period** after lunch

¹**clean** **1** *(a clean shirt)* Have my shorts **been washed**? This place is **spotless**! **2** *(clean water)* **clear** liquid, **fresh** water, **pure** juice

²**clean** *(clean the brushes)* **Wash** your socks, **brush** your teeth, **scrape** the mud off your boots, **wipe** the table, **dust** the ornaments, **sweep** the kitchen, **scrub** the floor, **spring-clean** the whole house, and **swill** out the bins.

¹**clear** **1** *(clear glass)* a **see-through** saucepan, a **colourless** liquid, **transparent** plastic **2** *(clear writing)* It's **easy to read**, and the pictures are **easy to see**. **3** *(Is that clear?)* It's quite **plain** she likes him. Do you **understand**? It's **obvious** you don't like her.

²**clear** *(clear the table)* It's time to **clear up** now. Can you **put away** your books? We need to **tidy up** the classroom. **Take away** those papers. **Remove** all your things. Please **leave** the bin **empty**.

clever *(She's the clever one.)* an **intelligent** girl, a **brainy** boy, a **bright** idea, a **brilliant** answer, a **smart** move, a **cunning** plan

climb *(climbing the hill)* **Go up** the steps. The plane **rose** into the sky. Warm air **ascended** from the valley. Birds **soared** above us. The price **increased**.

¹**clip** *(clipping a dog)* They're **shearing** the sheep. He's **shaved** his hair off. She's **cut** the lawn.

²**clip**

closed 1 *(closed windows)* His door's **shut** and **locked**. The curtains are **drawn**. My laces are **done up**. **2** *(The bank's closed.)* It's **not open**.

cloth 1 *(a cleaning cloth)* a **tea towel**, a **duster**, a polishing **rag 2** *(a cloth cap)* soft **material**, shiny **fabric**

club *(the chess club)* the drama **society**, a charity **organisation**, the Football **Association**

clue *(a clue to the killer)* a **suggestion** about the game, a **hint** about where to look, some helpful **tips**, no **sign** of an intruder

clumsy *(a clumsy throw)* an **awkward** movement, a **hamfisted** person

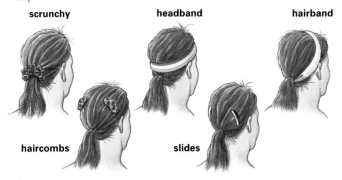

scrunchy   headband   hairband

haircombs   slides

¹**close** (*say like* **doze**) *(Close the window.)* **Shut** the door and **lock** it. Don't **slam** it! The road's **blocked** by snow.

²**close** (*say* **klose**) *(close to Mum)* **near** the supermarket, **next door** to John, **handy** for the shops, **convenient** for school

coach 1 *(a coach journey)* We went by **bus**. **2** *(a football coach)* the team **trainer**, a music **teacher 3** *(the king's coach)* a horse-drawn **carriage**

coast *(the Devon coast)* a wild **coastline**, a rocky **shore**, a sandy **beach**, golden **sands**

23

coat

jacket   anorak   bomber jacket   parka

overcoat   cloak   raincoat

coil *(coiling a rope)* **rolling up** string, **curling** hair, **looping** a rope round a post, **twisting** ribbons

¹cold *(cold weather)* a **freezing** night, a **chilly** morning, a **nippy evening**, an **icy** day, **wintry** weather, an **unheated** classroom, a **cool** drink

²cold *(blue with cold)* feeling **stone cold, frozen, chilly, shivering, chilled to the bone**

coldhearted *(a coldhearted man)* an **unkind** remark, a **hardhearted** jailer, a **mean** woman, a **cruel** king

collect 1 *(collect stickers)* Can you **get** your things **together**? Have you **got all your bits and pieces**? I'm **finding** shells **for my collection**. He was **gathering** firewood. **2** *(collect someone from school)* Can you **pick** me **up**? Kerry **fetched** me from the bus. I must **go and get** Sam. Can you **bring** the cake?

come 1 *(come at teatime)* When's he **arriving**? The train **gets here** at four. He should **turn up** soon. Did Tanya **show up** yesterday? Yes, she **appeared** after tea. She **came round** with her Dad. **2** *(Christmas is coming.)* The end of term's **getting nearer**. The train now **approaching** is the 2.15 for Leeds.

comedian *(The comedian told lots of jokes.)* a **comic**, a **funny man**, a **joker**, a **clown**, a **real laugh**, a **hoot**

comfort *(comforting a crying child)* Nana **sympathised** with me. She **cheers** me **up**. He **made** me **feel better**.

comfortable *(comfortable clothes)* a **comfy** chair, a **soft** carpet, a **cosy** room, a **luxurious** house

command *(give a command)* Here are your **orders**. Obey the **rules**.

common *(a common flower)* David is an **ordinary** name. **There are lots** of Davids in our school. That's not the **usual** way to do it!

company 1 *(a building company)* a **firm** of lawyers, running a **business**, the computer **industry 2** *(keep someone company)* Would you like to **come with me**? I like going out **with friends**.

compare *(comparing two dogs)* I **checked** my answer **against** yours. Can you **tell the difference** between the twins?

competition *(a crossword competition)* a **match**, a **knockout**, a **game**, a **championship**, a **tournament**, a **challenge**, a **contest**

complain *(complain about the food)* Katy's **grumbling**. She's **whining** about the chips. Jim's **fussing** about something. He's always **making a fuss**. Mum **moans** about the weather. My parents **protested** about the expensive uniform. Don't **whinge** all the time!

complete *(a complete set of CDs)* the **whole** world, the **entire** day, the **total** amount, a **full** week's holiday, **all the** words in the dictionary

concentrate *(Concentrate on your work.)* **Pay attention**, Carl! Kim tried to **focus** on what the teacher was saying.

condition 1 *(a car in good condition)* in a bad **state**, in poor **health**, improving **fitness 2** *(on condition you come too)* I'll go **if** you do.

confess *(confess to a murder)* **admitting** to the robbery, **owning up** to stealing

confident *(a confident girl)* **self-confident** at school, **happy about** singing in public

confused *(confused about what we're doing)* a **puzzled** look, **mixed up** about the dates, **in a muddle** with this sum. I **can't think straight** with that music on!

conjuror *(The conjuror made a rabbit disappear.)* a **magician**, an **illusionist**, a **wizard**, a **witch**, a **sorcerer**

connect *(connecting two wires)* **joining** the handle onto the cup, **putting** the parts of the radio **together**, **attaching** a label to the picture, **fixing** the bumper onto the car, **plugging** the lamp **into** the socket, **linking** the computer to the weapons system

conscious *(The patient was conscious.)* He was **aware** of a dull pain. The fainting girl **came round** when I threw cold water over her.

consider *(considering giving a party)* They're **thinking about** it. Mum's **thinking over** their offer. I **wondered** what to do.

considerate *(a considerate woman)* a **kind** remark, a **thoughtful** person

contain *(The drink contains fruit juice and water.)* What's this pie **got in it**? The jug **holds** a litre.

container *(a container of frozen food)* a wooden **box**, a **carton** of milk, a **case** for floppy disks, a treasure **chest**, a **packet** of sweets

continue *(continuing the story)* **Go on** reading. **Carry on** with your drawings. **Don't stop** running. What **happens next**?

c

control *(control the robot)* Tom's **in charge of** the company but Jim **runs** the factory. Mum **manages** a shop. **Make** the dog **do what you want**. **Make** him **obey** your commands. He **told** us **what to do**.

convenient *(convenient for shopping)* **handy** for the shops, **near** our house, **close to** home, just **next door**, a **useful** gadget

conversation *(a long conversation)* a serious **talk**, a friendly **chat**, a good **natter**, a **gossip** with friends

cook *(cooking dinner)* You **bake** bread or **roast** chicken in an oven. You **boil** eggs in boiling water. You **stew** meat for a long time. You **simmer** rice. You **fry** chips. You **grill** steak. You **barbecue** sausages over a fire. You **toast** bread.

cool **1** *(a cool wind)* a **refreshing** drink, **iced** lemonade, a **chilly** day **2** *(a cool haircut)* an **excellent** tape, **trendy** boots, a **great** disco

cooperate *(Cooperate with her.)* **Work together**. **Help each other**.

cope *(coping with a new school)* Our teacher has 36 children to **deal with**. He couldn't **manage** to do everything on his own. Lisa **organised** the concert. Mrs Sykes **handles** all the letters.

copy **1** *(Stop copying me!)* He **imitated** my angry voice. The parrot can **mimic** a phone ringing. **2** *(copying the stories)* Mrs Jones **made copies** of our best work. Can you **photocopy** this poem? The school secretary **Xeroxed** it.

¹**correct** *(the correct result)* the **right** answer, the **exact** number, an **accurate** watch, the **precise** time

²**correct** *(correcting the sums)* You haven't **put** it **right**. **Improve** the spelling. Can you **edit** it?

corridor *(a long corridor)* the side **passage**, a **passageway** between the houses, a dark **hallway**

cost *(costing too much)* The **price is** 89p. The sofa's **worth** £300 but he's **asking/charging** £400.

cosy *(a cosy room)* a **comfy** chair, a **warm** bed, a **comfortable** home

couch *(Grandad's couch)* a big old **sofa**, a new **settee**

cough *(coughing and sneezing)* She **choked** on a bone. **Clear your throat** before you read. He **wheezed** and **spluttered** because of his cold.

count **1** *(counting the children)* **Add up** the beads in the box. They **total** 28 red and 22 green. **2** *(Your marks won't count If you've cheated.)* They won't **mean anything**. They won't **be included**.

country **1** *(Canada is a big country.)* the American **nation**, an independent **state**, the **Republic** of South Africa, the cleverest witch in the **land** **2** *(They live in the country.)* pretty **countryside**, the **rural areas**

couple *(a couple of pounds)* **two** friends, a **pair of** robins

courage *(It takes courage to stand up to a bully.)* She won an award for **bravery**. He's got **guts**, jumping out of a plane like that!

course 1 *(an art course)* **classes** in German, Spanish **lessons 2** *(a course of injections)* a **series** of programmes **3 of course** *(Of course I am.)* He's **definitely** late. You can **certainly** sit next to Jason. **Naturally** I'm meeting the teacher. **4** *(Of course not!)* **No way! You must be joking! Not on your life! Never!**

cover *(cover the cake with icing)* snow **hiding** the ground, a sheet **masking** his face, **putting a lid on** a pan, **coated** with plastic, **roofed** with thatch

¹**crack** *(cracking a nut)* **breaking** glass, **splitting** open an old cut, **chipping** a plate, **slitting** an envelope, **snapping** a biscuit, **splintering** glass

²**crack** *(a crack in the window)*

a **chip** in the glass

a **split** in the jeans

²**crash 1** *(The plane crashed into the sea.)* A car **smashed** into the tree and **knocked** down a fence. A bus **collided** with a van. The toy car **bumped** into a chair. A moth **banged** into the light. **2** *(Stop crashing about!)* The car **smashed** into the van. Simon **thumped** onto the floor. A door **slammed**. Tools **clattered** to the floor.

crawl *(crawling under the desk)* I **wriggled** through the bushes. Adam **wormed his way** to the front. I **crept** into bed.

crazy 1 *(a crazy thing to do)* a **silly** noise, a **senseless** remark, a **stupid** idea, a **dumb** dog **2** *(a crazy person)* going **mad**, an **insane** woman

a **slit** in paper

¹**crash 1** *(the crash of breaking glass)* the **bang** of a gun, the **crack** of a bullet, the **slam** of a door, the **thump** of Simon falling out of bed, the **boom** of thunder, the **thud** of feet on the floor, the **thunder** of a waterfall, the **clatter** of plates, the **explosion** of a bomb **2** *(a car crash)* a road **accident**, a motorway **pileup**

¹**creak** *(a creaking gate)* The door **squeaked** open. The floorboards **groaned** when he trod on them.

²**creak** *(the creak of the gate)* **squeak** of the door, **groan** of the floorboards

creased *(a creased skirt)* a **crumpled** collar, **crinkly** paper, a **scrunched-up** letter, **wrinkled** hands, a **lined** face

27

c

creature *(a sea creature)* a warm-blooded **animal**, a wild **beast**

creep *(creeping along)* **slipping** away, **slithering** through the window, **worming his way** forward, **moving silently** past the machines, **wriggling** through the bushes, **prowling** through the woods, **skulking** past, **crawling** by

creepy *(creepy stories)* a **scary** film, a **spooky** old house, a **frightening** sound, a **ghostly** laugh, a **weird** dream

criminal *(The criminal was sent to prison.)* The man who sold us the car was a **crook**. The **culprit** was a cat!

crisp *(crisp biscuits)* a **crunchy** cereal, a piece of **crackly** toffee, **fresh** lettuce leaves

¹**cross** *(crossing the road)* Don't **go across** yet. The railway **passes over** the road. It's hard to **bridge** a powerful river.

²**cross** *(feeling cross)* an **angry** shout, a **bad-tempered** man, feeling **annoyed**, a **grumpy** mood

crowd *(a crowd of people)* a **big group** of people, a **mass** of children, a **gang** of boys, an **army** of schoolchildren, a **herd** of cows, a **flock** of birds, a **swarm** of bees, **millions** of them

cruel *(a cruel laugh)* **unkind** men, a **mean** girl, a **vicious** dog, a **merciless** act

¹**cry** **1** *(crying children)* She was **in tears**. He **burst into tears**. **2** *(cry out in pain)* **scream** loudly, **yell** out, **squeal** with surprise, **shriek** with pain, **screech** out loud. Wind **howled** in the trees, **wailed** in the telephone wires and **moaned** round the house.

²**cry** *(a loud cry)* a **scream**, **shriek**, **squeal**, **screech**, **shout**, **yell**, **howl**, **wail**, **moan**, **whine**

¹**cuddle** *(Mum gave me a cuddle.)* Dad gave Ann a **hug**. They had a **snuggle**. Mum gave Dad a **kiss**.

²**cuddle** *(I cuddled the puppy.)* Dad **hugged** Mum. Sam **clung to** his Dad. The twins **snuggled up to** each other. She **kissed** him. Mark **clasped** her in his arms. The couple **embraced**.

cupboard

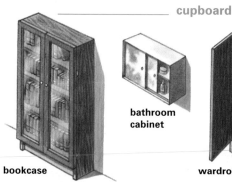

bathroom cabinet

bookcase

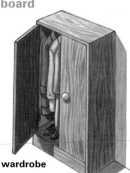

wardrobe

cure *(cure a disease)* **treating** a burn, **recovering from** an illness. The cut has **healed**.

curious 1 *(curious to see what was inside)* an **inquisitive** boy, **interested in** everything, a **nosy** neighbour, **prying** eyes **2** *(What curious writing!)* a **strange** story, a **weird** plant, a **peculiar** smell, an **odd** remark, a **funny** noise

¹**curl** *(His hair curled over his collar.)* Her hair **waved** round her face. The road **curved** to the right. Jess **twisted** the ribbon round her hair. The river **wriggles** through the town. The path **spiralled** up the hill. The wires **snaked** across the floor.

²**curl** *(golden curls)* A **wave** of hair fell into his eyes. The model's hair was done in **ringlets**.

curly *(curly hair)*

¹**cut 1** *(I cut up the apple.)* **Chop** the onion. **Slice** the bread. I **carved** the chicken. He **sawed** up the branches. She **hacked** down the brambles. They **slashed** at the nettles. I must **mow** the lawn and **prune** the roses. **2** *(Neil cut his hand.)* **gashed** in the leg, **wounded** by a sword, **stabbed** in the back, **knifed** by a gangster **3** *(Ryan cut my hair.)* He **trimmed** the top, **snipped** an inch off the back, then he **shaved** the sides. We picked out Danny's **cropped** head in the photo. **4** *(He cut open the parcel.)* Can you **slit** this envelope? **5** *(I cut off 6cm of string.)* The surgeon **amputated** his leg. **6** *(She cut a hole in the fence.)* She **made a hole** with a knife. The knife **pierced** the wood. **7** *(Dad cut Steve's pocket money.)* He **took £4 off** to mend the broken window, and then **subtracted** £1 for a raffle ticket.

ringlets

curly

wavy

frizzy

¹**curve** *(a curving road)* roads **twisting** and **turning** up the hill, hair **waving** round her face, trees **bending** in the wind, a **crescent** moon

²**curve** *(Draw a curve here.)* a **bend**, a **twist**, a **turn**, a **wave** in her hair

²**cut** *(a cut on your hand)* a **wound**, a **gash**, a **scratch**, a **graze**

Dd

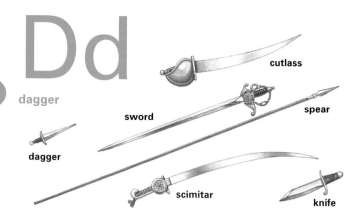

dagger

cutlass

sword

spear

dagger

scimitar

knife

¹**damage** *(I've damaged my knee.)* You've **broken** the toy and **torn** the book. That dog won't **harm** you. Tom's **injured** his elbow. The cat was **hurt**. You mustn't **ill-treat** animals. The radio's **not working properly**. Reading in a bad light can **impair** your sight. He **spoilt** his chances of being on the team.

²**damage** *(The rain did some damage to the roof.)* Using chemicals can do **harm** to the Earth. Her **injury** has healed.

damp *(damp clothes)* **wet** socks, **moist** skin, **dewy** grass, a **waterlogged** field, **watery** eyes, a **humid** day. My shirt's **soaking**.

¹**dance 1** *(a new dance)* Mike and Karen go **ballroom dancing** on Wednesdays. They know all the old dances: **waltz**, **fox-trot**, **tango**, **jive**, **rock 'n' roll** and **twist**. Helen prefers **ballet**, but she also does **folk dancing**, **country dancing** and **square dancing**. **2** *(a dance in the village hall)* Cinderella went to the **ball**. There's a **rave** on. Let's go to the **disco**.

²**dance** *(Phil's dancing with Tracy.)* We started **jigging** to the music. The children **pranced** around pretending to be horses. Tara and Zoë **skipped** along. Lambs were **frisking** in the fields.

danger 1 *(a danger of floods)* a **risk** of fire, the **threat** of losing your job, the **hazards** of sailing, a **chance** of hurting yourself **2** *(put someone in danger)* put them **at risk**, **endangering** wild animals, fire **threatening** to destroy the house

dangerous *(a dangerous road)* a **risky** jump, a **high-risk** sport, a **perilous** journey, **hazardous** to your health, a wall that's **unsafe**, **unreliable** brakes, a **dodgy** bike, **dicey** driving on icy roads, **touch and go** whether he'll live

dare *(dare to cross the rope bridge)* She **braved** the rapids in a canoe. He **risked his life** to save the child. Kate **accepted the challenge** of rock climbing.

dark 1 *(a dark night)* a **gloomy** building, a **black** tunnel, a **shadowy** figure, a **shady** garden, a **dim** light, a **murky** pond, a **moonless** night **2** *(dark hair)* a **black-haired** boy, a **brunette**, a **tanned** face **3** *(a dark colour)* **deep** blue, a **rich** brown

dash *(dash to the shops)* **hurry** along the road, **rush** to school, **run** for the bus, **sprint** down the steps, **dart** behind the door, **speed** away, **race** upstairs, **zoom** down the hill, **charge** into the room, **tear** along the path

dawn *(a beautiful dawn)* He was up at **daybreak**. **Sunrise** is at 6.45. The ship left at **first light**. The farmer woke at **cockcrow**.

dawn on *(It dawned on me that I was lost.)* I **realised** he was talking to me. Emily explained the problem but he didn't really **take it in**. Richard **became aware** that we were talking about him.

dead *(a dead animal)* He's as **dead as a doornail**. Her **late** husband built this house. My aunt's been **six feet under** for twenty years. The dodo is an **extinct** bird. The **deceased** man left his money to a cats' home. *See also* DIE.

deal 1 *(I thought we had a deal!)* an **agreement** about pocket money, keeping your side of the **bargain**, a **promise** to tidy your room **2** *(a great deal of work)* a **lot** of money, a **large amount** of water, **masses** of time

deal with *(Mum deals with all the bills.)* **handling** the sports fixtures, **seeing to** the baby, **sorting out** what we're doing, able to **cope with** a young family, **managing** a company, **organising** a raffle

¹**dear 1** *(a dear little puppy)* What a **sweet** baby! Isn't she a **lovely** little girl? Look at those **adorable** kittens. She's got a **darling** little brother. **2** *(£50 – that's too dear!)* **a lot** for such an old bike, an **expensive** watch

²**dear** *(Yes, dear!)* **love**, **duck**, **darling**, **sweetie**, **honey**, **babe**

decay *(His tooth has decayed.)* The fish will **go bad** if you don't put it in the fridge. The fallen apples **rotted** on the ground. The milk **went sour** and the bread **went mouldy**.

deceive *(trying to deceive someone)* He **tricked** me into buying a fake watch. He **conned** her into paying for him and **fooled** her into lending him her bike. Mr Ellis **did** his sister **out of** their parents' house. You **lied** to me and **kidded** me into believing you! She deliberately tried to **mislead** me.

decide *(decide what to buy)* I can't **make up my mind**. Have you **chosen** what to give Matt yet? **Pick out** something he'd really like. Sara's **opted for** French instead of German. David **thinks it's best** to sell the house. Only you can **judge** if you've done your best work. We **settled on** Spain for our holidays.

decision *(Think carefully before making a decision.)* You've got a difficult **choice** to make. What **options** has Hayley chosen for GCSE?

decorate *(decorate your bedroom)* The cake was **ornamented** with roses. The sundae is **garnished** with nuts. Her ball gown was **adorned** with lace. The skirt was **trimmed** with silk flowers. We **decked** the tree with lights.

d

deep 1 *(a deep voice)* a **low** rumble **2** *(How deep is the lake?)* the **profound** depths of the ocean

delay *(delay someone from leaving)* Miss Luke **made** me **late**. She **prevented** me getting my bus. Don't let me **hold** you **up**. He **kept** me **behind** after class. We had to **put** our holiday **off** because Mum got ill. **Postpone** the match till the 15th. We were **slowed down** by heavy traffic.

delicate *(a delicate skin)* a **fragile** vase, lace that is **easily damaged**, **breakable** cups, **brittle** icicles

delicious *(a delicious cake)* a **scrumptious** tea, **yummy** ice cream, a **succulent** roast turkey, a **tasty** meal. Those strawberries look **good to eat**.

delighted *(I'm delighted to meet you at last.)* **pleased** you're coming, **glad** you asked me, **thrilled** to meet a real rock star, **over the moon** when I won

delightful *(delightful children)* He's a **lovely** dad. We had a **nice** time. It was very **pleasant**. The staff were **friendly and helpful**. There's a **great** view.

deliver *(to deliver the letters)* He **distributed** the sweets. Jane **gave out** the pencils. **Hand over** the presents. Kindly **convey** a message to your mother.

depend *(depend on someone to help you)* I can always **rely on** her for some money. We **need** your **support**!

describe *(describe a friend)* **Tell** me **about** your holiday. Write a story **giving an account of** a frightening night. The film **shows** the life of a caveman. This painting **depicts** the sea at sunset.

deserve *(He deserves a round of applause.)* You've **earned** a rest. You **merit** a place in the team next term. Olly stole the money and now he's **got it coming to him**. He's **only got himself to blame**.

destroy *(destroying enemy ships)* They've **demolished** the old house. I **knocked down** the shed. He **smashed up** the base we made. The aliens were **annihilated**. Antiseptic **exterminates** germs in hospitals. We **made mincemeat of** their team. They're **history**!

determined *(a determined person)* a **stubborn** child, an **obstinate** character, a football fan with a **one-track mind**, a **committed** social worker. My **mind is made up**.

develop *(A caterpillar develops into a moth.)* The kitten **grew** every day. You're **becoming** better at art. You're **growing up** fast! The plans for the tree house began to **take shape**. Humans **evolved** from tiny life forms. Our plans **progressed** quickly.

diary *(keeping a diary)* a **calendar** on the wall, keeping a **journal** about your holidays

die *(His grandmother has died.)* Five people **were killed** in the accident. Two men **lost their lives** in the crash. The old lady **passed away** last week.

different 1 *(He's very different from his brother.)* They are **like chalk and cheese**. They're complete **opposites**. Rod's **unlike** his father. These two weights are **unequal**. Those cards **aren't a pair**. They **don't match**. **2** *(six different football shirts)* **various** kinds, **assorted** sweets, **varied** scenery

difficult *(a difficult sum)* a **hard** decision, a **tough** test, **uphill** work, a **puzzling** problem, an **impossible** task, a **stiff** question. It's **easier said than done**. **2** *(a difficult child)* Don't be **awkward** – do what I say. He's very **touchy**.

dig *(dig a hole)* They're **mining** for gold. The company **excavates** oil in the North Sea. The prospectors **bored** a hole in the sea bed. We **hollowed out** a sort of cave. The cat **scooped out** a hole in the flowerbed. A mole **burrowed** under the lawn. Worms **tunnel** through the soil.

dip

dirty *(a dirty jacket)* a **filthy** face, **grimy** hands, **muddy** boots. You always look **grubby** after school. Your clothes are **messy**. The shirt's **stained** with red ink.

disappear *(My money's disappeared.)* The cat **vanishes** as soon as Val walks in. He's **done the vanishing trick** again!

disappointed *(disappointed fans)* I felt **let down** when I did so badly. The girls were **heartbroken** when the concert was cancelled. His **hopes** of scoring **were dashed**. Don't get **discouraged** if your diet doesn't work straightaway.

d

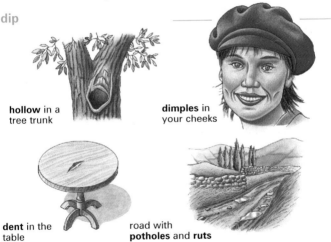

hollow in a tree trunk

dimples in your cheeks

dent in the table

road with **potholes** and **ruts**

direction *(Which direction is the sea?)* Mrs Earp showed me **the way** to the office. The plane is **on course**.

directly *(Go directly to the gym.)* The bus goes **straight** to the station. It's a **nonstop** bus.

discover *(discover buried treasure)* He **found** a puppy under the hedge. Jody **found out** who had taken the money. They **detected** blood on the floor. She **unearthed** an old map. A scandal was **uncovered** when they checked the books.

disease (*heart disease*) a long **illness**, a chest **infection**, 15 days lost through **sickness** this term, an **allergy** to cats. I'm **allergic** to them.

dish 1 (*a dish of vegetables*) a **plate** of biscuits, a **bowl** of fruit salad, a **platter** of cold meat 2 (*We ordered six dishes at the Chinese restaurant.*) a three-**course** meal, a new **recipe**

dishonest (*a dishonest way to make money*) **untrustworthy** neighbours, **untrue** statements, a **crooked** businessman, **illegal** activities, **criminal** behaviour, a **deceitful** person

dislike (*She dislikes Ian.*) Darren **hates** sport. Miss Vernon **can't stand** people who **don't like** sport. She's **got a down on** Darren. Darren **loathes** her, too. Mum **doesn't care for** shellfish. Lots of children **detest** cabbage. I **can't bear** it either.

distance 1 (*the distance from London to Perth*) It's **a long way** from here. It isn't **in walking distance**. It's too **far** to walk. 2 (*in the distance*) on the **horizon**, on the **skyline**

dive (*I dived into the sea.*) I **went headfirst** into the water. The dog **plunged** in too. The plane **plummeted** into the sea.

divide (*Divide the cake into six.*) Here's a cake to **share** with Claire. Mr Day **doled out** our new books. **Halve** the pie between you.

do 1 (*Do your sums.*) Try and **get them done** before break. When you've **finished** them you can go. See what you can **achieve** if you try. 2 (*Don't just stand there, do something!*) **Get going**! **Get busy**! Dan never **lifts a finger** when his wife's there. I'm going to **take action** on this.

do up 1 (*do up a parcel*) **Fasten** your coat, it's raining. **Tie up** your shoelaces. **Button up** your shirt and **zip up** your jacket. 2 (*They did up the house.*) **decorating** the kitchen, **painting** the hall, **renovating** the house

do well (*Anna's doing well at her new school.*) Chris **succeeded** in getting a job. Joanne's **thriving** at school. Mum's **doing a roaring trade** in secondhand toys. She's **making a fortune**. Business is **booming**!

do without (*Mrs Weeks can't do without her guide dog.*) He **gave up** sweets and **cancelled** the papers to save money. I can't **spare** the cash yet. I can't **deny myself** chocolate.

dodge (*dodge the arrows*) He **avoided** the oncoming car. The car **swerved**. Ken **sidestepped** the punch. I **ducked** the cricket ball. **Keep out of the way**!

dot (*a blue tie with red dots*) a dog with **spots**, a tiny **mark**, a **speck** of dirt, a **full stop**, a **point** of light

doubt 1 (*I doubt that Rob will keep his promise*) She **doesn't believe** you were ill on Monday. She **suspects** you of lying. 2 (*I doubt if I'll be back by ten.*) I **shouldn't think** she's there. I **don't expect** I'll have time. I **don't suppose** you're interested in cars.

drag (*drag the box outside*) We **pulled** the boat to the bank. I **hauled** the wet dog into the boat. She **drew** the table towards her. He **tugged** his toy truck along. The truck **towed** the car to the garage. Magnets **attract** iron.

¹**drain** *(a drain for water)*

manhole

gutter

drainpipe

sewers

ditch

²**drain** *(Water's draining out of the basin.)* The water's **run away** now. Milk's **leaking out** of the bottle. They've **emptied** the swimming pool.

¹**draw** *(draw a boat)* The artist **sketched** the view from the cliffs. Just **copy** this diagram from the board. **Trace** the map of Ireland.

²**draw** *(the game was a draw)* The teams **tied**. Their scores were **equal**.

¹**dress** *(dressing in the morning)* **Put on** your jacket. He was **wearing** a tie. The prince was **clothed** in silk.

²**dress** **1** *(a red dress)* a ball **gown**, a pretty **frock** **2** *(national dress)* historical **costume**

¹**drink** *(drink some water)* The baby was **sucking** his milk. The cat **laps** milk from a saucer. I **gulped** the water. I **swallowed** my lemonade quickly. She **guzzled** the water thirstily.

²**drink** *(a drink of milk)* a **swallow**, a **gulp**, a **guzzle**, a **swig**, a **suck**, a **lap**

drip *(water dripping from the trees)* Rain **splashed** into the pool. Spilt lemonade **dribbled** onto the floor. Dirty water **seeped** out of the gutter. He felt blood **trickle** down his arm.

drive *(driving a car)* He **steered** the boat well. She was **piloting** a light plane. He **operates** a crane.

¹**drop** **1** *(drop a cup)* **Let** the ball **go**, Lucky! She **let** the book **fall** onto the bed. The phone **fell** on her toe. It **slipped** out of her fingers. He **spilt** his drink. Juice **slopped** out of his glass. **2** *(He dropped his art lessons.)* Tess **stopped** learning ballet. The school has **discontinued** judo classes.

²**drop** **1** *(a drop of water)* a **bit** of butter, a **trickle** of blood **2** *(a drop of kindness)* a **small amount** of patience, a **bit** of fear

dry **1** *(dry feet inside your boots)* You're **not** at all **wet**! I've got a **waterproof** jacket and a **watertight** watch. **2** *(a dry country)* a **waterless** desert, a **dusty** path, an **arid** plain, **drought** conditions **3** *(a dry throat)* I'm **thirsty**. The garden's **parched**.

dull *(a dull class)* a **boring** film, **drab** walls, a **dreary** day, a **stodgy** book, a **colourless** girl

duty *(on duty)* It's her **responsibility** to lock up. We all have **jobs** to do. Your **task** is to put the rubbish out.

Ee

eager *(eager to play)* **keen** on sailing, **crazy** about dogs, **enthusiastic** about sport

early 1 *(arriving early)* He got there **in good time**. Get there **promptly**. **2** *(an early type of adding machine)* an **antique** typewriter, an **ancient** drinking cup, a **classic** car

earn *(earning a living)* How much does Mum **get**? She **makes** £166 a week. She**'s paid** £166. Her **wages** are £166. She **takes home** £140 after tax. She **deserves** more!

easy *(an easy game)* a **simple** sum, a **childish** reading book, an **effortless** dive

eat *(eating chocolate)* They **devoured** the cake. The kids **consumed** all the crisps. Here's a sandwich to **chew**. She **nibbled** a biscuit. I can't **swallow** this meat. You **scoffed** the lot! Don't **bolt** your food. He **munched** an apple. Here's your tea, **tuck in**! Cows and sheep **feed** on grass. Budgies **live on** seeds.

edge *(the edge of the table)* on the **fringe** of the crowd, on the **brink** of war, on the **verge** of leaving, on the **point** of crying, **about to** go to bed

effort *(Make an effort!)* This needs **hard work**. **Try harder** and you'll succeed. **Do your best**. **Put your heart and soul into it!** It's worth the **struggle**.

embarrass *(Don't embarrass me!)* You made me **go red**. I was **blushing** when I went up on stage. I felt **self-conscious**. Miss King looked **flustered** when Mr Lyons told us she was getting married. I was **ashamed** of my old coat.

employ *(The school employs two caretakers.)* We have thirty teachers **on the staff**. We're **taking on** two more. He **appointed** a drama teacher. They're **hiring** waiters at the café. The police **recruit** school leavers.

[1]**empty** *(an empty box)* The bathroom's **vacant**. The town's **deserted** on Sundays. The spooky house is **unoccupied**. This is an **uninhabited** island. Leave the form **blank**.

a country's **border**

hem

rim

outskirts of a town

²**empty** *(empty your pockets)*
Tip out your belongings. **Take everything out** of your desk. **Pour out** the milk. He **vacated** the house after he saw the ghost.

encourage *(She encouraged me to play chess.)* They **support** United. Mr Best **urged** me to try again. The programme about animal rights **prompted** several children to write letters. The beautiful day **cheered** us **up**, and **inspired** us to go out for a picnic. The referee's decision **provoked** a fight in the crowd.

¹**end** **1** *(the end of term)* the **finish** of the race, a happy **ending**, the **close** of play, the **conclusion** of her talk, the **closing scene** of the film, the **final part** of the course, the **last moments** of the play **2** *(the end of a line)* the **back** of a bus, the **tail end** of a train, the **rear** of a plane, the **tip** of a pencil

²**end** *(ending at 4.30)* It **stops** at two. The races **finish** by the post. The film **closes** with a wedding. Her talk **concluded** with a joke. The game is **over**.

energetic *(an energetic game of netball)* **vigorous** exercise, a **lively** discussion, a **dynamic** teacher, an **active** mind, a **brisk** walk

energy **1** *(children full of energy)* She's an athlete of great **power**. I haven't the **strength** to lift that box. She spoke with great **force** against the nuclear test. **2** *(energy from the sun)* the Earth's **resources**, **power** from electricity

enjoy *(enjoy the picnic)* We're **having fun**. I **like** swimming but I **love** riding. The old couple **took pleasure** in our visit. The dog **revelled in** the sunshine. I **appreciate** classical music. She **relishes** a day with a good book. Sam **gets a kick out of** making models.

enter **1** *(entering the classroom)* **Come in**, children. **Go in** and take off your wet clothes. The thieves **broke in** through the window. **2** *(entering a contest)* Mark wants to **join in** the race. Why don't you **put your name down for** the club? You can **enrol in** our next class. Anyone can **take part in** our carnival. **3** *(Enter your name on the screen.)* **Input** your data now. **Type in** the password first.

entertaining *(an entertaining film)* an **amusing** story, an **interesting** speech, a **fascinating** show, a **wonderful** pantomime

entire *(the entire school)* the **whole** world, **everybody** and **everything**, the **full** price, the **complete** set

entrance **1** *(the staff entrance)* The **door** opened. The **gate** closes at ten. He stood in the **doorway**. He carried the bride over the **threshold**. I'll wait in the **porch**. **2** *(Entrance to the museum is free.)* **Admission** is £4. It's easy to **get in**.

equal *(equal in height)* Simon's **the same** weight as his brother. They are **even** in weight. Their weights are **identical**. The twins are **alike**. They like **similar** things. The length of the room is **equivalent** to a cricket pitch. The teams are **level**.

equipment *(sports equipment)*
gym **apparatus**, garden **tools**,
sailing **supplies**, a model **kit**,
your school **stuff**, sports **gear**,
diving **paraphernalia**

escape *(escape from prison)*
The thief **broke out** of jail! He
bolted last night. He **gave** the
warders **the slip**.

especially *(I love fruit,
especially pears.)* Wash your
hands – **in particular**, do your
nails! I like Georgia **most of all**.
She's **specially** nice. She's
particularly good at maths.

even 1 *(an even surface)* a
smooth pitch, a **level** field, **flat**
country **2** *(getting even)* We've
got to **get our own back**. I'm
going to **pay** Sam **back** for
smashing my work. The army
retaliated by bombing them.

even so *(Jim came but even so
there was plenty of food.)* He
came **but still** there was lots of
food. **Even though** Jim came,
there was lots of food. **Despite**
Jim coming, there was lots of
food. **In spite of** Jim coming,
there was lots of food.

event *(a sporting event)* a funny
incident in the train, a
wonderful **occasion**, **fixtures**
every Saturday, a frightening
experience at the fair

evil *(an evil wizard)* a **wicked**
witch, a **bad** woman, a **cruel**
man, doing **wrong**

exact *(the exact number)* the
right size, the **precise** time, the
correct money, an **accurate**
answer

examine *(examining a leaf in
detail)* Mrs Binks **inspected** my
model carefully. Dad **looked
over** my work. **Study** this
picture. **Scan** the list for your
name.

example 1 *(an example of your
best work)* a **case** of chicken
pox, an **instance** of someone
dying for their beliefs **2 for
example** *(You can use any
filling, for example beef or
chicken.)* Many cities, **for
instance** Beijing and Tokyo, are
bigger than London. Drinks
such as beer and wine will go
up in price. Some people, **like**
Jim and Mike, really love
sailing.

excellent *(an excellent cook)*
first-rate results, **outstanding**
bravery, **brilliant** work,
exceptional talent, a **wonderful**
show, an **extraordinary** actor, a
magnificent house, a **stunning**
garden, a **superb** painting, a
great idea, a **sensational** match,
tremendous skill, a **marvellous**
time, a **fabulous** meal

exciting *(an exciting book)* a
film that **keeps you on the edge
of your seat**, **thrilling** rides,
daring stunts, **heart-stopping**
danger, **action-packed** drama

exclaim *('You're injured!' he
exclaimed.)* 'I'm home!' she
shouted. 'John!' I **called**. 'It's
wonderful!' she **cried**.

¹**excuse** *(say eks-kyoose)*
*(You've no excuse for this
messy work.)* What **reason** did
she give for being late? You
have no **grounds** for hitting
him. Have you any **basis** for
saying so? Helen didn't kill
him – she has an **alibi**. You
seem to fight on any **pretext**.

²**excuse** *(say eks-kyooz)*
*(excusing someone's
behaviour)* I'll **let** it **go** this time,
but don't do it again. Don't
make excuses for your sister.
You have to **make allowances
for** the younger children. I can't
forgive him for what he did.

exercise *(exercise your legs)*
taking exercise, **practising** your
judo, **training** for the team,
coaching us to win

aerobics

**step
aerobics**

weight training

yoga

expand *(The school's expanding.)*
The town's **getting bigger**. The
balloon **increased** in size. This
machine **enlarges** photos.
Computer games **took off** in the
1980s. Her knee **swelled up**.

expect *(expecting you to ring)*
I **suppose** you'll lend me the
book. I **believe** he's still in bed.
I **imagine** you'll be coming to
parents' evening. Yes, I **think**
so. I **presume** you know
Dr Livingstone. He **assumes**
everyone likes his stories.

expensive *(an expensive ring)*
Raspberries are **dear** this week.
That shop has some **high-
priced** stereos. They're
overpriced. The CD was a bit
pricey. The princess wore
costly jewels.

experience *(a frightening
experience)* a strange **incident**,
an exciting **event**

explain *(explaining why you're
late)* Can you **tell me why**
leaves are green? He **told me
how** to load the game. She
took Casey **through** the
instructions. She **cleared up** her
difficulties. She **simplified** the
problem.

explode *(exploding fireworks)* A
balloon **burst**. A bomb **went
off**. They **set off** a bomb. The
kids **let off** some fireworks.
Terrorists **blew up** the building.

expression 1 *(a friendly
expression)* an angry **look**, to
pull a silly **face 2** *(a slang
expression)* an unusual **phrase**,
a technical **term**, a good **way to
say something**, a new **word**

extra *(an extra box)* **additional**
information, **some more** help,
another set of plates, a **backup**
disk, a can of petrol **in reserve**

Ff

¹**face 1** *(He had a really nice face.)* pleasant **features**, an ugly **mug 2** *(She made a face.)* a bored **expression**, an angry **look**

²**face 1** *(Face me!)* **Look at** me when I'm talking to you. **2** *(The house faces the street.)* The store **opens onto** the square. The school **overlooks** the field. **3** *(to face an unpleasant fact)* to **face up to** difficulties, to **stand up to** a bully. Sir Lancelot **confronted** the dragon. The papergirl had to **brave** two fierce dogs. City **meet** United next Saturday.

fact *(some facts about computers)* **information** about riding classes, a lot of **data** on giant pandas, **statistics** from around the world, phoning for **details** about the offer. Tell us the **truth** about John and Hilary!

factory *(a huge factory)* a glass **works**, a repair **workshop**, the nuclear **plant**, an **industrial estate**

fail *(He failed his driving test.)* He **didn't pass**. I was **not successful** either. He **missed** getting into college.

faint 1 *(a faint pencil line)* a **dim** light, an **unclear** sign, **indistinct** writing **2** *(a faint sound)* a **slight** pain, a **weak** cry, a **feeble** mew

¹**fair 1** *(fair hair)* Claire's got **blonde** curls. the man with the **yellow** beard, a boy with **sandy** hair, a **golden-haired** retriever **2** *(a fair hearing)* a **just** decision, a **reasonable** punishment, an **unbiased** referee, an **impartial** judge, the **right** thing to do **3** *(fair weather)* a **fine** day, a **sunny** period, a **warm** afternoon

²**fair** *(a Christmas fair)* a church **fête**, a **carnival**, a **funfair**, a charity **bazaar**, a swimming **gala**, a county **show**, an **amusement park**, a big **theme park**

¹**fall 1** *(The vase fell off the table.)* Shari **tumbled** from the tree. The phone **dropped** on her toe. It **slipped** out of her fingers. The building **collapsed** in the earthquake. The car **plunged** over the side of the cliff. The plane **crashed** in the desert. Fruit juice **poured** out of the jug. It **slopped** onto the floor. The tea leaves **settled** at the bottom of the pot. **2** *(The child fell over in the street.)* Alan **missed his footing** and **tripped** over the cat. He **stumbled** over the step and **lost his balance**. His house of cards **toppled** over. Lara tried to stand on one leg but she **overbalanced**. **3** *(House prices have fallen.)* They have **dropped** by half. The company's profits **decreased** last month. The number of children learning the violin has **declined**. **4** *(Hopes of saving the child's sight fell.)* Her heart **sank** as she read the letter. His hopes of a job **were dashed** when the firm closed.

²**fall 1** *(a fall in house prices)* a **drop** in the price, a **decrease** in profits, a **decline** in numbers **2** *(a bad fall)* He **plunged** into the icy river. Sara's had a **tumble**.

false 1 *(a false statement)* That's **a lie**. What it says is **untrue**. It's **made up**. **2** *(a false beard)* a **fake** Swiss watch, **forged** money, a **counterfeit** coin

famous *(a famous show-jumper)* a **well-known** TV presenter, a **celebrated** artist, a **noted** scientist, a **distinguished** actor, an **eminent** historian, a **notorious** murderer, a **familiar** face, a **big name** in athletics

fan *(a rugby fan)* a **supporter** of the team, a computer **freak**, a film **buff**, a TV **addict**, a **follower** of fashion

fancy *(a fancy restaurant)* a **posh** wedding, an **expensive** holiday, a **luxury** car, a **high-class** resort, a **five-star** hotel, a **fashionable** dress

far 1 *(too far to walk)* **a long way**, a **distant** village, a **remote** farm, **farther** than I thought **2** *(far better)* **much** better, **a lot** better

fashion *(a new fashion)* sixties-**style** jeans, a new **way** of doing your hair, a **craze** for war games, the latest **trend**

fashionable *(a fashionable new disco)* the **in** place to go, a **hot** new band, **cool** sunglasses, **stylish** clothes, **modern** **contemporary** music

¹fast 1 *(a fast car)* a **quick** look, a **speedy** getaway, a **swift** kick, a **hurried** wave, a **hasty** goodbye, a **rapid** exchange of fire, a **brisk** walk, an **express** letter, a **high-speed** train **2** *(fast colours)* **indelible** ink, **permanent** dye

²fast 1 *(driving fast)* looking **quickly**, kicking **swiftly**, saying goodbye **hastily**, eating **hurriedly**, walking **briskly**, firing **rapidly**, riding **at breakneck speed 2** *(stuck fast)* wedged **firmly** between the branches, **tightly** screwed, tied **securely**

fasten *(fastening a bell on the bike)* Jonah **did up** his belt. **Fix** the shelves on with screws. Kate **attached** a note to the fridge. She **stuck** a poster behind the door. **Glue** the legs onto the table. He **hung** his pictures on the wall. She **pinned** his photo to the door. I **nailed** a horseshoe over the door. Let's **screw** the mirror to the bathroom wall. Stacey **tacked** down the carpet. We **connected** the TV up. Brian **secured** the loose tiles on the roof. Jade **put** her hair **back** with a slide.

fastener

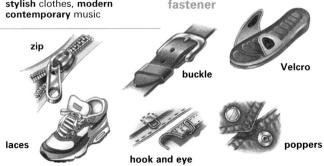

zip

buckle

Velcro

laces

hook and eye

poppers

¹fat *(a fat cat)* an **overweight** singer, a **chubby** baby, a **plump** dentist, a **stout** woman, a **podgy** child, a **tubby** teddy bear, a **dumpy** man, a **paunchy** policeman, an **obese** child

²fat *(fat on the meat)* **grease** on the plates, vegetable **oil**

fault 1 *(It's Sasha's fault.)* She **failed to do** her job. She should **take the blame**. It was her **mistake**. This robbery's **down to** the Fraser gang. **2** *(a fault on the computer)* a computer **error, something wrong with** it, a **glitch** on the computer, a **hitch** in our plans

favour 1 *(in favour of starting a computer club)* We **support** their idea. The head **approves of** the idea. I'm **on the side of** the teachers. The parents **back** it too. **2** *(Do me a favour.)* Give me **some help** with my project. My boss has done me **a good turn**.

favourite *(your favourite ice cream)* my **best** colour, wearing her **nicest** dress, a **popular** singer

¹fear *(fear of spiders)* The boys gave Mum a **fright**. I had a **scare** when the spider dropped off the wall. The TV presenter promised the audience a night of **terror**. a **horror** film, a feeling of **dread**, in a **panic** when she heard a cough upstairs

²fear *(fearing a bully)* to be **afraid of** horses, to **be frightened of** the dark, to **dread** the exam, to lie awake **worrying about** it. Stella **panicked** when she heard a cough upstairs.

feel 1 *(He felt the smooth fur of the rabbit.)* to **touch** the rough wall, a rash from **handling** the cat. Don't **finger** the ornaments! **2** *(feeling dizzy)* They **experienced** a sudden fear. He **sensed** my anger. **3** *(I feel you should apologise.)* Mum **thought** we'd be late. I **believe** you're right. I **found** her very helpful.

feeling *(angry feelings)* strong **emotion**, a strange **sensation**

fence

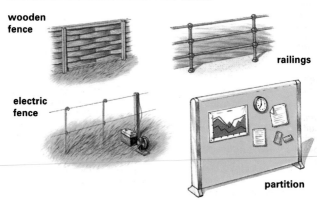

wooden fence

railings

electric fence

partition

fetch *(fetching him home)* Can you **bring** me a biscuit? No – I've already **got** you a cake! Can you **pick** me **up** after school? Kerry was **collected** from the bus. I've got to **go and get** Sam.

fête *(a church fête)* a Christmas **fair**, a town **carnival**, a visiting **funfair**, a charity **bazaar**, a swimming **gala**, a county **show**

few *(a few people)* **a handful of** children, **not many** schools with a theatre like ours, **hardly any** biscuits left, only **one or two** pages to go

field *(a grassy field)* a **meadow** by the river, a **paddock** with horses in it, a **pasture** for the cows, a cricket **ground**, a football **pitch**

fierce *(a fierce lion)* a **ferocious** dog, a **vicious** tiger, a **brutal** attack, a **violent** battle, **cruel** revenge

¹fight 1 *(Those two are fighting again.)* The dogs were **attacking** each other. The two sides have been **at war** for years. I certainly wouldn't **take on** a karate expert! The cats were **scrapping** on our roof. **2** *(fighting over whose turn it was)* Terry and Kitty are **quarrelling** about it again. Stop **arguing**! Stop **squabbling**, there's enough for everyone.

²fight 1 *(a fight between the two giants)* the **Battle** of Hastings, a **scuffle** between rival gangs, a **boxing match** on TV, the cats having a **scrap** outside **2** *(a fight about money)* a **quarrel** about the game, a **row** with Mum, too many **arguments**. I heard the **squabble** from downstairs.

fighting *(The fighting lasted for three days.)* casualties in the **conflict**, a woman killed in the **crossfire**, a hero in the **struggle** for freedom

fill *(Fill this jug with water, please.)* **pack** the boxes, **stuff** the cushion with foam, **cram** your mouth full of toast, **load up** the car, smoke **spreading through** the room. Just **top up** my glass.

filthy *(a filthy sports shirt)* **dirty** hands, a **grimy** face, **muddy** football boots, looking **grubby** after school, a shirt **stained** with red ink, **mucky** kids

final *(the final day of term)* the **last** minutes of the lesson, the **closing** scene of the film

find 1 *(Try and find that other sock!)* You might **come across** it under your bed. I **turned** it **up** in the washing. You have to **locate** the enemy ships. **Find out** where they are. Can you **discover** the buried treasure? **2** *(I find he talks too fast.)* He **feels** you should learn chess. Rob **thinks** I'm angry with him. We **believe** you know this man.

fine 1 *(a fine morning)* a **lovely** day, a **sunny** afternoon, a **cloudless** sky, **nice** weather **2** *(I'm fine.)* I feel **very well**. I feel **great**. Are you **OK**?

¹finish *(Just finish your picture, Amy.)* The lesson **ends** at 12.20. We **stop** serving lunch at 2.30. The film **closes** with a wedding. Her talk **concluded** with a joke. The lesson **is over**. Make sure you have **completed** your work.

²finish *(the finish of the race)* the **end** of term, the happy **ending** of the book, the **close** of play, the **conclusion** of her talk, the **closing scene** of the film

¹**fire 1** *(firing a gun)* The farmer **took aim** and **shot** the pigeon. The soldiers **opened fire** on the camp. **2** *(Mum's been fired from work.)* She's been **sacked**. The man was **dismissed** for stealing. They **gave** him **the sack**.

²**fire 1** *(a forest fire)* a big **blaze**, throwing branches into the **flames**, a **bonfire** in the garden **2** *(an electric fire)* a gas **heater**, **radiators** in all the rooms

¹**firm 1** *(a firm promise)* a **definite** plan, a **fixed** appointment, a **reliable** friend, a **steady** relationship **2** *(a firm handshake)* a **steady** ladder

²**firm** *(a computer games firm)* a sportswear **company**, a transport **business**, the computer **industry**

¹**first 1** *(my first day at school)* His **earliest** memory was feeding the ducks on the pond. The **original** inhabitants of America were the Native Americans. the **introductory** pages of a book, the **maiden** voyage of the first hovercraft in 1959 **2** *(I came first in the 100 metres!)* I was **the winner**. He's the **champion** swimmer. She's **the best** at drama. It's the **most important** day in my life. They're the **leading** software company in the world.

²**first** *(First, deal seven cards to each player.)* **At first**, I didn't like school very much. **Firstly**, let's welcome our speaker, Judy Moore. **To start with**, draw a head. Derek didn't see me **to begin with**. **In the first place**, everyone knows lying is wrong. **First of all**, we decided who should be in charge. **Originally**, Mark was going to play Aladdin, but now Anil's doing it.

¹**fit 1** *(Sport keeps you fit.)* a very **athletic** girl, **in training** for the interschools gala, **in top condition**, very **healthy** **2** *(These apples aren't fit to eat.)* They aren't **good enough**. The shoes are not **suitable**.

²**fit** *(Those jeans don't fit me any more.)* Are these jeans **the right size**? Are they **big enough**?

fit in 1 *(Can you fit any more children into your car?)* We can **squeeze in** one more. Now they're **packed in** like sardines. The hotel can **accommodate** 30 people. **2** *(How's David fitting in at school?)* He doesn't feel he **belongs** yet. It takes a while to **feel at home**. He's got to **adapt to** the new school.

fix 1 *(Jane fixed the hooks on the wall.)* Kate **attached** a note to the fridge. She **stuck** a poster behind the door. **Fasten** the legs onto the table. Sara **glued** a photo into her folder. He **hung** his pictures on the wall. I **nailed** a horseshoe over the door. Let's **screw** the mirror to the bathroom wall. Stacey **tacked** down the carpet. We **connected** the TV to the socket. Brian **secured** the loose tiles on the roof. **2** *(Can you fix the radio?)* We **mended** the hole in the roof. I can't **repair** the toaster. **3** *(Chris fixed us a quick meal.)* Jonah **cooked** the steak while I **prepared** the vegetables.

¹**flap 1** *(The budgie flapped its wings.)* The butterfly **fluttered** away. The flag was **waving** in the wind. There was no wind so the sails didn't **stir**. Spot **wags** his tail when we come home. **2** *(Don't flap! Everything's OK!)* Kit **panicked** when he lost his wallet. Lee **gets in a state** if he's late.

²**flap**

cat flap

envelope flap

shutters

kitchen hatch

car bonnet

¹**flash** *(The torch flashed three times.)* Far away she saw it **flickering**. The Christmas lights **twinkled**. The sun **glittered** on the sea. The match **sparked** and went out.

²**flash** *(a flash of lightning)* a **flicker**, a **twinkle**, a **glitter**, a **spark**

¹**flat** *(a flat field)* a **level** garden, a **smooth** lawn, a **calm** sea, a **horizontal** position

²**flat** *(a block of flats)* a holiday **apartment**, a **penthouse** on the roof

flavour *(a fruity flavour)* a **taste** of vanilla, spicy **seasoning**

flight *(The flight to Delhi leaves at 9 p.m.)* a nine-hour **journey**, ready for the **departure**

float *(floating in the sea)* A lifebelt makes you **stay up** in the water. The boat was **afloat**.

flow *(water flowing across the road)* The river **runs** under the railway. Tears **welled up** in her eyes and **streamed** down her face. The stream **rippled** over the stones and **swirled** under the bridge. Big waves **rolled** onto the beach, **surged** over the rocks and **dashed** against the cliffs. The waterfall **cascaded** down the hillside, **splashed** into the pool and **washed** into the stream. The **spilt** orange juice **trickled** across the table, **poured** over the edge and **dribbled** onto the floor.

fly *(The birds flew away.)* The eagle **rose** in the air, **soared** above the cliffs and **hovered** high above us before **gliding** away. The plane **took off**, **climbed** to 30,000 feet and **cruised** at 480 miles an hour. A feather **drifted** past and **floated** down to earth.

focus 1 *(Focus on what I'm saying. Don't stare out of the window.)* They **paid attention** to the head's speech. It's difficult to **concentrate** when there's lots of noise. **2** *(She focussed the camcorder on Rowena's face.)* The TV cameras **zoomed** into a close-up.

f

fog *(We couldn't see the end of our road because of the fog.)* a **mist** covering the cliffs, a **haze** over the coastline, a cloud of brown **smog** over the town, **clouds** covering the mountain tops

fold *(He folded the letter and put it in the envelope.)* The paper was **doubled over** so they couldn't read it. The children **rolled up** their sleeping bags. He **tidied away** the washing. You've **creased** your shirt – the collar's **crumpled**! It's a **pleated** skirt.

follow *(Don't follow me!)* The little kids always **come after** us. They like **running after** the big children. Our dog **chased** the cat up a tree. **Tail** the girl when she leaves the club. A detective has been **shadowing** her for hours. He **trailed** her to an address in King Street. The detective **tracked** down some drug dealers. The police car **pursued** the stolen van. That green car's been **sitting on our tail** for the last hour!

fond *(fond of horses)* Peter **enjoys** running. Nan's **affectionate** to all her grandchildren. She **thinks the world of** them. She **cares about** her whole family.

foot *(the foot of the tree)* at the **bottom** of the steps, something carved on the **base** of the statue

forbid *(I forbid you to go.)* Smoking is **prohibited**. You are **not allowed** to bring food in here. Selling drugs is **against the law**. It's **illegal**. They've **banned** drinking at all matches.

¹force *(forcing her to eat more cabbage)* Dad **makes** me do my homework before I watch TV. The alien captain **compels** you to surrender! The salesman **pressurised** us into buying the most expensive microwave. The music **drove** him out into the garden. You've **given** me **no choice** – I must tell the police.

²force *(The ball hit me with such force that it broke my finger.)* He used all his **strength** to pull up the tree. They committed robbery with **violence**. I don't think **aggression** helps win an argument. Mum's putting **pressure** on me to work harder.

foreign *(a foreign country)* working **abroad**, going **overseas**, **distant** lands, an **alien** country, **exotic** holidays, **imported** fruit

foreigner *(Viktor's a foreigner.)* a **stranger** in this town, an overseas **visitor**, an illegal **immigrant** without a proper passport, a Vietnamese **refugee**, an **alien** from outer space

forget *(Don't forget your lunchbox!)* He did **not remember** it. You **missed out** a sum on this page. Don't **leave out** any of the questions. He **neglected** to do his homework. She **overlooked** an important instruction.

¹form *(Form two teams.)* **Make** a circle, children. He **shaped** the clay into a bird. The chair was **moulded** from plastic. In early spring, buds **grow** on the trees.

²**form 1** *(in sixth-form college)* in the first **year**, in seventh **grade**, in **Class** 5, in the top **set** for maths **2** *(In some places, shells were a form of money.)* Owls and ducks are **sorts** of bird. A poodle is a **kind** of dog. What **type** of car has she got? **3** *(The ghost took the form of his dead father.)* Jade wore a brooch in the **shape** of a butterfly. He saw the **outline** of a man against the light. Then he saw the **figure** of a boy.

fortune 1 *(Bruce won a fortune on the lottery.)* The millionaire spent his **wealth** on building hospitals in poor countries. The king refused to share his **riches** with anyone. The pirates quarrelled over the captured **treasure**. **2** *(The fortune teller predicted that he would go abroad.)* Your **fate** is an unhappy one!

forward *(walking forward)* moving **onward**, running **ahead**

uncooked fruit

fraction *(A half is a fraction of one.)* a small **part** of the problem, a large **section** of the computer's memory, another **portion** of pie, my **share** of the cake

free 1 *(This game came free with the magazine.)* Under-tens get in **for nothing**. Mum's got **complimentary** tickets for the play. Here's your **bonus** gift. Your first ride is **on the house**. **2** *(They set the birds free.)* The prisoners were **released**. He **let** the wild duck **go**. **3** *(Is Mr Henderson yet?)* I'm sorry, he's not **available** now, but he **isn't busy** after three o'clock. **4** *(You're free to choose your own games.)* I'm **allowed** out at three o'clock. Rae's **able to** come camping next week. Her sister **can** come too.

freeze *(Water freezes at 0 degrees C.)* The puddles had **turned to ice**. You should **put** this ice cream **in the freezer**.

fresh 1 *(fresh raspberries, not frozen)* **unpreserved** meat **2** *(fresh plans for the school fair)* **new** games, an **original** idea **3** *(fresh drinks)* **refreshing** lemonade, a **cool** glass of water, some **chilled** apple juice

raw vegetables

friend *(my best friend)* a **mate** of hers, one of her **pals**, **chums** since the first year, only an **acquaintance**, a cat for a **companion**

friendly *(a friendly smile)* a **nice** neighbour, a **sociable** woman, a **hospitable** man, a **helpful** nurse, a **tame** lion

frighten *(Don't frighten the children.)* **afraid** of that dog, **scared** of the dark, **terrified** when he's driving, **nervous about** going home alone, **worried about** the maths test, **petrified** of spiders. Children **fear** the dark. She **panicked** when she heard the cough. I **dreaded** the exam.

frightening *(a frightening scream)* a **scary** movie, a **terrifying** experience, a **horrifying** story, a **nightmarish** journey, a **ghostly** voice, an **alarming** noise. It **made** me **jump**! The ghost **gave** him a **fright**. The explosion **gave** her a **shock**. She tried to **give** me a **scare**. The sight of the knife **made** my **blood run cold**. The creaking door **made** her **blood turn to water**. The ghostly moaning **made** his **hair stand on end**. I've got a story to **make** your **flesh creep**.

front *(the front of the classroom)* the **head** of the queue, a horse in the **foreground** of the painting, the **nose** of the plane

prow of boat

full *(My bag's full of books.)* a box **crammed** with presents, a mug **brimming** with hot chocolate, a bag **stuffed** with paper, a truck **loaded** with logs. The suitcase was **bursting** – it was **full to the brim**. See that the vase is **topped up** with water.

fun 1 *(Miranda had fun at the party.)* She **enjoyed herself**. I was remembering the **good times** we had at Christmas. We could hear them **playing** in the attic. They loved the **amusement** park. We had a **great time**. **2 make fun of** *(Don't make fun of her.)* They're **laughing at** her. They **made jokes about** her.

funny 1 *(a funny film)* a **comic** actor, an **amusing** story, an **entertaining** play, a **hilarious** programme, a **humorous** speech, a **witty** remark, a **real laugh**, a **hoot** **2** *(a funny feeling)* a **strange** sound, a **peculiar** laugh, a **weird** thing, an **odd** idea, an **unusual** car, a **curious** animal

future *(In future, the drinks will cost 50p.)* In the **coming** term we will put on a Christmas play. **From now on**, ask me before you get out the jigsaws. We'll get to level 4 in the **next** few minutes.

radiator grille of car

Gg

game *(a game of tiddlywinks)* a football **match**, a swimming **contest**, a **sports** hall

gang *(a gang of teenagers)* a **mob** of fans, a **band** of thieves, our own **club**

gang up *(They ganged up on Kate.)* Eddie's **teamed up** with Gary and Sean now. He's **gone over** to them. The wizard is **in league with** the evil queen.

gap *(a gap in the hedge)* a **space** for a picture, a **hole** in the fence. Fill in these **blanks**. There's a 15-minute **interval** in the play. Let's take a **break** for a drink.

garbage *(Take the garbage out.)* a **rubbish** bin, a **trash** can, **litter** in the street

gather *(gathering everyone in the hall)* Could you all **assemble** outside the gym? Have you **got** all your things **together**? I'm **collecting** photos for an album.

generous *(a generous uncle)* Jamie's **kind** – he always brings us crisps. Max is **unselfish**. He is a **charitable** person. The hospital got a **benevolent** donation from a millionaire. Jo's very **free** with her money.

gentle *(a gentle child)* Wayne is a **kind, quiet** boy. Polly is **sweet** to her baby brother. Be **careful** with the kittens. Don't worry about the dog – she's **harmless**. a **friendly** dog, a **good-tempered** pony, a **tame** otter

get 1 *(Where did you get that bike?)* Where did those sweets **come from**? How did Ray **come by** this Rangers shirt? He managed to **acquire** three shirts. He **found** them at school. You should **buy** one. The school **obtained** several new computers. **2** *(I've got a new board game.)* Marcia's Dad **owns** a riding stable. The black pony **belongs to** her. **3** *(getting the food from the oven)* Stuart **fetched** the spoons and **brought** me a mat. Then he **went and got** the plates. **4** *(Mum gets £300 a week.)* How much money does he **earn**? Paul **receives** £5 a week pocket money. **5** *(She's getting bored.)* Mrs Fisher **became** angry. I'm **starting to feel** sleepy. Tom's **growing** more sensible. **6** *(I don't get the joke.)* Mark never **catches on**. He didn't **understand** the maths question. I couldn't **make out** what Miss Coles was saying. I'll help you **get the hang of** it. Once you've **grasped** it, these questions will be easy. Didn't you **realise** she was trying to get rid of us?

get away 1 *(We should get away by four.)* I've got to **leave** after tea. The train **departs** at twelve. **2** *(I tried to catch the cat but it got away.)* The bird **got free**. The prisoner **escaped**. He **gave** the warders **the slip**. He **did a bunk**.

get going *(Let's get going soon.)* Before we **start out**, let's have a snack. We **began** making the model. He **kicked off** with an easy question. **Get a move on**! **Hurry up**!

get in *(The kids got in the car.)* Where did you **get on** the train? I **boarded** the bus. The ferry passengers **embarked** at Hull.

get into *(Rebecca's got into computer games.)* **fascinated by** spiders, not **interested in** cricket. Kirsty **became involved with** a gang. She's **mixed up in** a police case.

get off 1 *(Get off my foot!)* **Move off** the mat! **2** *(Get off at the bus station.)* I **dismounted** from the horse. The fishermen **went ashore** with their catch. Passengers may **disembark** from the ferry now. Don't forget to **get down** at our stop. They **arrived** at Glasgow Airport. **3** *(They arrested a man but he got off.)* He was **set free**. He was **found not guilty**. He was **discharged**.

get on 1 *(The kids got on the bus.)* I **boarded** the bus. Ferry passengers **embarked** at Portsmouth. **2** *(How's Luke getting on at school?)* He's **coping** OK. He's **doing fine**. The teachers say he's **made progress**. **3** *(Mum and Myra don't get on.)* Pete and Shane **made friends** on the first day of school. I **feel at home with** the Gibsons.

get over *(You'll get over it!)* Nan **recovered** from her operation. Scott **survived** the mountain-climbing course.

get rid of *(This spray gets rid of ants.)* It **kills** flies too. I hope it doesn't **destroy** bees. Here's Mrs Owen – **lose** that chewing gum!

get through *(I tried to phone her but I couldn't get through.)* I'm going to **contact** her parents. Have you **got in touch with** Derek yet?

get up *(I get up at 7.30.)* The children **jumped out of bed** when the alarm went. Jan **appeared** at twelve. Early to bed, early to **rise**!

get wrong *(He got it wrong.)* He **made a mistake**. He's **barking up the wrong tree**!

ghost *(the ghost of the queen)* a **spirit**, a **phantom**, a **spook**, a **spectre**, a **shade**, a **ghoul**, a **zombie**

gift *(a birthday gift)* wedding **presents**, a Christmas **box**

give *(I gave Mum the book.)* I **let** her **have** the felt-tips. Class 6E **presented** Miss Eddis with some flowers. The school **provides** the books. Several parents **donated** prizes for the raffle. Lady Addams is **offering** a reward for information on the stolen diamond. Auntie Joan **left** us her house in her will. The king **granted** him a wish.

give away 1 *(giving away stickers with petrol)* These tickets were **free of charge**. You can have a turn **without paying**. **2** *(Don't give away that I was here!)* He **told** you my secret. He **split** on me. One of the gang **informed** on the others.

give back *(I must give back these games.)* Have you **returned** your library books? The saint **restored** the old man's sight.

give in 1 *(I gave in my science book.)* She **handed in** a note from her mum. **2** *(Rosie didn't want to go to bed but in the end she gave in.)* You'll have to **resign yourself** to playing a small part this year. I **couldn't resist** these wonderful bargains. I **gave up** when I saw who I was playing against. I **admitted defeat**.

give out 1 *(Anna gave out the books.)* Jane **shared out** the strawberries. Let's **divide** the drinks **up** first. **2** *(The engine was giving out clouds of black smoke.)* The truck **gave off** smoky fumes. The factory **discharged** dirty water into the stream. **3** *(The batteries have given out.)* The series has **come to an end**. Your membership card's **expired**.

give up 1 *(Give up, or we'll shoot!)* We forced the soldier to **give in**. The troops **surrendered**. **2** *(I couldn't do the sums so I gave up.)* Mum **stopped** going to her evening class. It's a pity if you **don't finish** after all your work. Rachel **dropped out** of college.

give way *(The pillars in the temple gave way.)* The whole building **collapsed**. The bridge **buckled** in the earthquake.

glad *(Mum will be glad to see you.)* **pleased** to meet your teacher, **delighted** to go to the wedding, **thrilled** to meet a real film star

glue *(Sarah glued a photo into her folder.)* Jim **pasted** in a picture of his boat. She **stuck** a poster behind the door. Kate **attached** a note to the fridge.

go 1 *(The bus goes along this road.)* The traffic **moves** into the city in the morning. It **passes** over two bridges. We **travelled** by train when we went to London. Can I **walk** to the beach with you? **2** *(I should go now.)* I've got to **leave** early. The train **departed** at 4.28. The plane **takes off** in an hour. We'll **start out** before dawn. We **set out** at five in the morning. It's time to **make a move**. **3** *(The train goes from Plymouth to Exeter.)* The road **runs** beside the river. This lane **leads** to Robert's house. The path **stretches** right round the coast. My belt **reaches** round me twice! **4** *(The car goes better when it's warm.)* Planes **run** on jet fuel. The sewing machine doesn't **work**. The machine **operates** all night. **5** *(Those books go in the cupboard.)* The dictionary **belongs** in the classroom. Do large books **fit** in the shelves? That skirt doesn't **match** your top. **6** *(The daylight's going fast.)* The colour's **fading** from this rug.

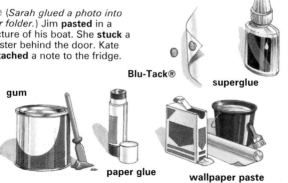

Blu-Tack®

superglue

gum

paper glue

wallpaper paste

go away 1 *(Don't go away!)* Martin **left** the room. We'd better **clear out** before Mum comes. The kids **disappeared** to watch TV. **2** *(We're going away next week.)* The Johnsons are **going on holiday**. He's **going on a** business **trip** to Germany.

go back *(He went back to say goodbye.)* Mr Dass is **returning** to India next week. Don't **go home** without me! The army **retreated** to their camp. The lorry **backed** into the yard. I **reversed** out of the garage.

go bad *(The meat has gone bad.)* These sausages have **gone off**. The vegetables are **rotting**. The cheese is **going mouldy**. The milk's **turned sour**.

go by 1 *(Did Melanie go by just now?)* She **passed** me in the corridor. **2** *(A minute went by.)* The hours **ticked by** as we waited for news. Time **elapsed** since start: 18.26 minutes.

go down 1 *(The lift went down to the basement.)* We **walked down** the stairs. Can you **climb down** the ladder? The leaves were **falling** from the trees. The plane started to **lose height** and **landed** at the airport. **2** *(The cost of petrol went down.)* CD prices have **dropped**. The temperature **plunged** to freezing. The number of accidents has **decreased**. The sun **set**. **3** *(The ship went down.)* It **sank** without trace. A boat **foundered** on the rocks and the sailors **drowned**. It **submerged** very quickly.

go for 1 *(I'm going for the Athletics Medal.)* Sharon's **aiming for** a place in the team. **2** *(Their dog always goes for me.)* It **attacked** Mum last week. It **picked a fight** with Sam's cats. Then the cats **set on** it!

go in 1 *(to go in the house)* They **entered** by the side door. **2** *(Carlton went in for the poetry competition.)* Marilyn **entered** the 100 metres. Are you going to **take part in** the contest?

go off 1 *(She's gone off with the keys!)* Tony's **gone away**, so there are four of us left. The kids **disappeared** to watch TV. Martin **left** the room. We'd better **clear off** before Dad comes. **2** *(The fireworks went off round the bonfire.)* The bomb **exploded** at half past two. They **set off** a bomb.

go on 1 *(Colin went on the big wheel.)* Dani's going to **ride** Thistle. **2** *(Ms Wills went on with the lesson.)* **Continue** reading. **Carry on** with your drawings. **Don't stop** running. **Keep going**! **Stick it out**! **Keep at it**! **3** *(Old Lizzie does go on a bit.)* The film **got boring**.

go over 1 *(Mr Evans went over the instructions.)* He **repeated** the instructions. **2** *(I asked Mum to go over my story.)* Dad **looked over** the sums I did. **Study** the section on building the pyramids. **Scan** the list for Sally's name.

go through 1 *(Ms Ash went through the Open Day arrangements.)* She **explained** what to do. She **described** it all in detail. **2** *(Nan's gone through a bad operation.)* She **experienced** a lot of pain.

go up 1 *(The lift went up to the top floor.)* The sun **rose** in a clear sky. The eagle **soared** into the sky. A plane **took off**. **2** *(The price has gone up.)* The price has **risen**. The number of people with computers is **increasing**. Prices of houses have **soared**.

go with 1 *(Tom's going to the concert with Natalie.)* Mum's gone to **keep** Grandad **company. 2** *(The pink tights go well with this skirt.)* Their shirts **matched** their shorts. The curtains **tone in with** the sofa.

go without *(If I go without breakfast I don't feel well.)* Lynne's **given up** sweets. I can't **deny myself** chocolate.

goal 1 *(a goal in the first five minutes)* In this game try to get as many **points** as possible. What's your **score? 2** *(Her goal is to go to college.)* Her **aim** is to be a doctor. Patrick's **ambition** is to play football for Ireland. Our **objective** is to raise £500.

good 1 *(good weather)* a **fine** morning, an **ideal** picnic spot, a **perfect** day, an **excellent** band, a **lovely** party, a **wonderful** movie, a **sensational** game, a **super** new jacket, **cool** friends. **2** *(having a good time)* having **fun**, a **great** time, **enjoying yourself 3** *(a good friend)* a **trustworthy** person, a **reliable** partner, a **firm** promise, a **helpful** book **4** *(a good job)* **well-paid** work, a **profitable** business, a **worthwhile** career **5** *(good behaviour)* a **well-behaved** class, an **obedient** child, a **cooperative** group **6** *(Lew is good to his old uncle.)* a **kind** boy, an **unselfish** friend, a **generous** person, a **caring** community **7** *(good at map reading)* **clever** at making up puzzles, **brilliant** at drawing, a **skilful** plumber, a **talented** dancer, a **gifted** singer **8** *(good for you)* a **healthy** meal

good-looking *(a good-looking man)* a **beautiful** woman, a **pretty** child, a **sweet** baby, a **handsome** actor, a **nice-looking** boy, an **attractive** guy

good-tempered *(a good-tempered boy)* a **calm** woman, a **happy** class, a **placid** dog, an **unflappable** teacher, a **friendly** shopkeeper, a **gentle** girl

grab *(Donna grabbed her purse and ran out.)* She **snatched** my pencil case from my desk. That man **took** my bag! I **clutched** my uncle's hand as we crossed the road. Cody **pounced on** a doughnut.

gradually *(I got gradually sleepier.)* Carl got used to school **bit by bit**. Mum pulled the plaster off **a bit at a time**. The leaves **slowly** turned brown. **Eventually** we understood.

grasp 1 *(He grasped the rope.)* She **held on tight** as we crossed the road. I **gripped** my bag in my hand. I **clutched** my books under my arm. Deirdre **kept a grip on** the money. **2** *(Once you've grasped this, the questions will be easy.)* He didn't **understand** the maths question. I couldn't **make out** what she was saying.

grave *(my great-aunt's grave)* the pharaoh's **tomb**, a family **vault**, the **crypt** of the church, a **graveyard**

war **cemetery**

greasy *(a greasy hamburger)* **oily** chips, **fatty** meat

great 1 *(a great monster)* a **large** box, a **big** house, a **huge** man, an **enormous** tree, a **gigantic** spaceship, a **colossal** mountain, a **massive** amount **2** *(a great idea)* a **brilliant** game, a **sensational** present, a **cool** shirt, an **excellent** song, a **wonderful** time, a **fantastic** player, a **super** holiday **3** *(great artists)* a **first-class** scientist, a **famous** doctor, a **well-known** writer, an **important** building, a **top** actor, a **world-class** tennis player, a **leading** athlete

greedy *(Greedy Alex has finished the ice cream!)* He **eats too much**. He's a **pig**, a **greedy-guts**.

green *(green grass)* **emerald**, **jade**, **sea green**, **bottle green**, **olive**, **pea green**

greet *(Ms Gage greeted them on their first day at school.)* Let's **welcome** our speaker, Mr Chan. The teacher **shook hands** with my father and **introduced herself**. The soldiers **saluted** the general.

¹**grin** *(grinning at me from the back of the bus)* The baby **smiled** at the teddy bear. Louisa **beamed** when she won her prize. Serena **smirked** and said, 'I told you so.'

²**grin** *(a huge grin)* a **smile**, a **beam** of delight, a **smirk**

grip *(Mrs Mott gripped her daughter's hand.)* She **held on tight** as they crossed the road. I **grasped** my bag in my left hand. I **clutched** my books under my arm. Deirdre **kept a grip on** the money. The dog **held fast** to Anna's trousers. He **clung on** even though she was running. He managed to **hang on**!

groan *(He groaned in pain.)* The boy **moaned** with cold. The door **creaked** open behind him. The class **sighed** when Ms Dixon said there was a test.

ground 1 *(on the ground)* some water on the **floor**, some **land** for building. The ball fell to **earth** somewhere by the trees. **2** *(a football ground)* the **playground**, a playing **field**, a hockey **pitch**

group *(a group of children)* a **set** of CDs, a **crowd** of fans, a **gang** of boys, an **army** of kids, a **band** of robbers, a **bunch** of flowers, a **clump** of trees, a **litter** of puppies, a **pack** of wolves, a **herd** of cows, a **flock** of birds, a **swarm** of bees, **lots** of them

shoal of fish

grow 1 *(The plants grow quickly.)* Your brother's **getting big**! He's **shot up** and now he's starting to **fill out**. He's **gained weight** this term. The roses are **thriving**. **2** *(The number of homeless people is growing.)* The number is **going up**. The price of CDs is **increasing**. Our class is **expanding** – we have three new people. Our knowledge of the universe is **advancing**. **3** *(Alice is growing tidier.)* Nicola's **getting** fat. He **became** angry. I'm **starting to feel** sleepy.

The seeds started to **sprout**.

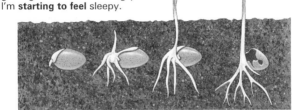

grown-up *(The grown-ups sat around drinking tea.)* It costs £2 for **adults** and £1 for children.

¹guard *(a dog guarding the house)* **Keep** your money **safe**. A fence **protects** the factory. One player **defends** the castle; the other attacks it. Each player **shields** his army from the enemy.

²guard *(a security guard)* a **jailer**, a **lookout**, a **caretaker**, a **sentry**, a **watchman**, a **bodyguard**, a **warden**, a **doorkeeper**, a **gatekeeper**, a **sentinel**

¹guess *(Guess how old he is!)* They **estimated** the length of the playground. Dad **reckons** they'll win. I've **got a hunch** he's wrong. I **daresay** Rovers'll win tonight. Yes, I **think** so.

²guess *(Have a guess at the weight of this cake.)* At a rough **estimate** – 4kg.

¹guide *(Mark guided Gran to the games shop.)* Let Zara **show** you **the way**. She **led** me to the office. I was **conducting** some visitors round the school. The teacher **shepherded** the children into the classroom.

²guide 1 *(The book was called 'A Beginner's Guide to Making Model Planes'.)* a **reference book** about war, 'The Rose-Growers' **Handbook**' **2** *(a guide to the museum)* a **guidebook** about our town with a new **street map** and bus **timetable** **3** *(Our travel guide was called Johnny.)* The **courier** took us to the hotel. The tour **leader** made sure we all got on the bus. I had an **escort** when I flew to America.

guilty *(The jury said the man was guilty.)* He **did it**. Who is **to blame** for this mess? Kirsty was **responsible** for losing the key.

55

Hh

habit *(annoying habits)* the **custom** of a bride wearing white, a **routine** check of the plane, my **usual** way home

hair 1 *(She did her hair.)* her new **hairstyle**, a short **haircut**, a curly **hairdo**, a **mop** of fair hair, the baby's **curls 2** *(black hair)* a horse's **coat**, soft **fur**, a lamb's **fleece**, sheep's **wool**, a hedgehog's **bristles**

hairy *(hairy arms)* a **shaggy** pony, **woolly** lambs, a **bushy** tail, a **bristly** beard

hall 1 *(He hung his coat in the hall.)* a narrow **passage**, the hotel **lobby**, a hospital **corridor**, the school **entrance**, the **reception** area, sheltering in the **porch 2** *(a concert hall)* the city **theatre**, an **auditorium** holding 2000 people, Sydney **Opera House**, a football **stadium**

hammer 1 *(hammering in a picture hook)* **knocking** a nail into the wall, **driving** a nail into the door, **bashing** a hole in the ice, **battering** a door down **2** *(hammer on the desk)* **banging** on the door, **thumping** the table, **pounding** the table with her fist

¹hand 1 *(He had a pen in his hand.)* a lion's **paw**, a butterfly's **feeler**, a beetle's **antenna**, an octopus's **sucker 2** *(Can you give me a hand?)* Will you **help** me make this? The deputy head **assists** the head. **3** *(the hands of a clock)* a **pointer** on a dial, a **cursor** on a screen, an **indicator** on a speedometer

²hand *(Hand her a cup.)* **pass** the potatoes, **deliver** the note, **give** her the salt

¹handle

door **handle**

hilt of sword

knob

handlebar

²handle 1 *(Mrs Sykes handles the secretarial work at school.)* Mrs Wells has 36 children to **deal with**. How are you **coping** with your pets? He can't **manage** this number work on his own. Lisa **organised** the concert. **2** *(The cat hates being handled.)* Don't let him **touch** the books. She **fondled** the dog's ears.

handsome *(handsome boys)* a **good-looking** man, a **beautiful** girl, **pretty** flowers, an **attractive** house, a **lovely** day, a **nice-looking** meal, a **gorgeous** dress

hang *(The flag hung from the pole.)* The monkey **swung** from the tree. His scarf **trailed** out of his bag. The swing **was suspended** from the tree. Your laces are **dangling** in the mud. Her hair **droops** over her eyes. His hair **flops** into his food. The skirt **sags** round the hem.

hang on 1 *(Hang on a bit!)* **Wait a moment! Hang about! Hold on! Hold it!** He **hesitated** before knocking. Let's **delay** the game. She **paused** for a moment. **2** *(Hang on to my hand.)* **clinging** to the ladder, **keeping hold** of the bag, **holding on** tight, **gripping** his hand, **hugging** her mother, **clutching** my book, **keeping a grip** on the money, **holding fast** to the railing **3** *(You can hang on to those tapes.)* **Keep** the games. The cash machine **retained** the card.

hang out *(He hangs out with Liam.)* **spending time** together, **hanging around** with Dan

hang up 1 *(Hang up your bag.)* He **hooked** his coat over the chair. The cowboy **hitched** his horse to a fence. **Fasten** this to the door. **2** *(I was phoning Jay and he hung up!)* Jay **put the phone down.** He **rang off.** We were **cut off.**

happen *(The accident happened yesterday.)* Sports Day **takes place** in June. Something important's **cropped up.** A strange incident **occurred** at Weirdwood Manor. I'll tell you how it **came about.** It all **arose** because of Lord Weirdwood. He **chanced** to marry a witch! It **turned out** for the best in the end.

happiness *(This card wishes you happiness.)* The boy jumped for **joy.** I get a lot of **pleasure** from music. Painting gave him hours of **contentment.** She smiled to show her **enjoyment.** The friends hugged each other in **delight.**

happy *(a happy smile)* **glad** to see you, **pleased** to meet your teacher, **delighted** to go to the wedding, **thrilled** to meet a rock star, **over the moon** when she won riding lessons, **contented** to be at home, **overjoyed** to see him, in a **cheerful** mood, **lighthearted** after the tests, a **jolly** old man, a **Merry** Christmas

harbour *(a fishing harbour)* a fishing **port,** sailing boats in the **marina,** a calm **lagoon**

hard 1 *(a hard biscuit)* a **firm** surface, a **solid** ball, a **stony** path, **tough** meat, a **rigid** book cover **2** *(a hard sum)* a **difficult** question, a **tough** test, **uphill** work, a **puzzling** problem, an **impossible** task. It's **easier said than done.**

hardly *(hardly breathing)* Paul can **only just** reach the door. She's **scarcely** able to write her name. It's **barely** warm enough to swim.

¹**harm** *(Fluoride in the water doesn't do any harm.)* **damage** to your lungs, an **injury** to your back

²**harm** *(Fluoride doesn't harm you.)* **damaging** your lungs, **hurting** yourself, **ill-treating** animals. Reading in poor light **impairs** your sight.

harmful *(Smoking is harmful to your health.)* a **damaging** drug, a **dangerous** criminal, a **fatal** disease, an **unhealthy** climate, a **malignant** growth, a **poisonous** plant, **toxic** waste, a **venomous** snake, an **unsafe** building

harmless *(a harmless animal)* a **safe** medicine, a **nonthreatening** illness

h

hat

hood · **beret** · **baseball cap** · **fez** · **sun hat** · **turban** · **sou'wester** · **bearskin** · **helmet** · **top hat** · **stetson**

hate *(Darren hates sport.)* She **can't stand** eggs. Lots of children **detest** cabbage. He **can't bear** cats. Darren **loathes** them too. I **dislike** beetroot. Mum **doesn't care for** shellfish.

have 1 *(Have you got a bike?)* Kate **owns** a bike. The gerbil **belongs to** Pia. Every child should **possess** a dictionary. You can **keep** this sticker. 2 *(Their car has seven seats.)* The car **comes with** a cassette player. It **includes** a radio too. 3 *(Rose had a book for her birthday.)* Mum **got** a letter from Nan. She **received** it this morning. 4 *(I had sausages for tea.)* Saul **ate** an apple. The family **gets through** a lot of rice. 5 *(We had a spelling competition.)* We **were given** some words to learn. The competition was **held** today. Dad **went through** an operation. He **experienced** a lot of pain.

have to *(Dad has to work tomorrow.)* He's **got to** be there by eight. You **must** give her the game. You **ought to** buy one of the caps. Mark **should** let me play.

¹**head** 1 *(I hit him on the head.)* a rabbit's **skull** 2 *(Use your head!)* She's got all the **brains** in the family. racking your **brain** for the answer, using your **sense**, showing a lot of **intelligence** 3 *(the head of the school)* the gang **leader**, the pirate **chief**, the **headman** of the tribe

²**head** *(head teachers)* **main** roads, the **most important** things to remember, the **principal** reasons, the **essential** ingredients, **key** facts

³**head** 1 *(Mick headed for the gate.)* He **ran towards** it. He **made a beeline for** it. He was **approaching** the school office. He **made for** cover. 2 *(Bonnie heads a company.)* She **manages** it. Dad **ran** the school raffle. I'm **in charge of** this club. Bob **organises** the football. The Prime Minister **governs** the country.

heal *(The cut healed slowly.)* The syrup **cured** my throat. A good sleep will **make** you **feel better**. Dr Taylor **looks after** these patients.

healthy *(a healthy baby)* feeling **well**, keeping **fit**, **as sound as a bell**, in **good condition**, food that's **good for you**

heap *(a heap of clothes)* a **pile** of washing, a **mass** of ironing, a **mound** of odd socks, a **stack** of leaves, a **bundle** of letters

hear 1 *(I heard a shout.)* I didn't **catch** what she said. Sheena **overheard** Dad talking about her. **2** *(I hear she's going away.)* We **were told** he'd gone. **They say** he's gone to prison. I **gather** she's ill. We **got to hear about** it yesterday.

heart 1 *(a heart problem)* Grandad's **ticker**'s fine. **2** *(the heart of the jungle)* the **middle** of the room, the **centre** of the city, the Earth's **core 3** *(She knew in her heart that she loved him.)* loving **feelings**, strong **emotions**

heat *(the heat of the sun)* the **warmth** of the radiator, the **glow** of the fire

heavy *(a heavy sack)* **as heavy as lead**, a **loaded** basket, an **overweight** dog, to **weigh a lot**

hedge *(a hedge round the garden)* a wooden **fence**, park **railings**, a stone **wall**

height 1 *(of average height)* 1.8 cm **tall**, 30 storeys **high**, an **altitude** of 30,000 feet **2** *(the height of excitement)* In **peak** condition, at the **top** of his career, **on the crest of a wave**, at the **highest** level. It's **as loud as it will go**. He's got the **maximum** number of points. **3** *(afraid of heights)* a steep **drop** from the cliff, falling over a **precipice**, a **sheer** mountainside

¹**help** *(Help Jack to do his homework.)* **assisting** the teacher, **aiding** poor countries, **rallying round** to help Nan, **supporting** our walk to raise money, **contributing** to the fund. Vijay **did** me **a favour** the other day. I should **do** him **a good turn** now.

²**help 1** *(I could use some help.)* **advice** about keeping pets, **hints** on how to spell, **suggestions** for presents, **tips** on playing the game, **assistance** to single parents **2** *(It's a help if you can swim.)* Fitness is a **plus**. One of the **benefits** of old age is that you spend time with your grandchildren. A **good thing** about this house is the view. It's an **advantage** to be tall in a crowd.

helpful 1 *(a helpful girl)* a **thoughtful** boy, a **considerate** person, a **kind** lad, a **willing** helper, a **polite** girl **2** *(a helpful book)* a **useful** tool, a **handy** shop, a **convenient** drawer

herd *(a herd of elephants)* a **flock** of birds, a **pack** of dogs, a **swarm** of bees, a **school** of dolphins

hide *(hiding in the wood)* a name **concealed** in the first clue, a ditch **screened** by a hedge, **covered** by snow, a **masked** man, **cloaked** in mystery

high 1 *(a high mountain)* a **tall** person, a **high-rise** building, a **towering** mountain, a **raised** walkway **2** *(high wages)* a **big** salary, too **expensive**, **excessive** prices **3** *(a high note)* a **shrill** scream, a **squeaky** voice

hill *(the top of the hill)* a steep **hillside**, a river **bank**, a slippery **slope**, a **mound** of earth, a sand **dune**, a high **mountain**

h

hint _(a helpful hint)_ a useful **tip**, **clues** to the crime, good **advice**, **help** with the game, a few **suggestions**, no **inkling** about the plan, a danger **warning**

hire _(hire a car)_ to **rent** a van, to **lease** a flat, a house to **let**

history _(a history book)_ the **past**, **past times**, in **olden times**, the **olden days**

¹**hit** **1** _(Tom hit Evan.)_ He **bashed** Paul, who **thumped** Greg, who **punched** Ed, who **walloped** Mark, who **whacked** Joe. Don't **smack** the dog. **2** _(They heard rain hitting the tin roof.)_ **banging** on the wall, **knocking** on the door, **thumping** the desk, **pounding** on the table **3** _(The bus hit a dog.)_ Richard **bumped into** me as he ran round the corner. We **collided**. The truck **crashed into** the gate.

²**hit** _(a hit on the head)_ a **bash**, a **thump**, a **punch**, a **wallop**, a **whack**, a **smash**, a **slap**, a **bang**, a **knock**, a **rap**, a **tap**, a **bump**

hobby _(Her hobby is taking photos.)_ an outdoor **activity**, an indoor **pastime**, the latest **craze**

hold **1** _(Sally's holding the photo.)_ Cal **had** a glass **in his hand**. He's **carrying** some biscuits. The child **gripped** his hand. **Hold on** tight! **Keep hold** of the bag. I **clutched** my books. She **kept a grip on** the money. Steve **hugged** his mother. She **cuddled** the baby. The dog **held fast** to his stick. **2** _(How much can the jug hold?)_ The jug **contains** one litre. Its **volume** is a litre. **3** _(The police held her overnight.)_ He **kept** a dog in the yard. **4** _(We're holding an Open Day.)_ Mel's **having** a party. We **organise** plays.

hole **1** _(a hole in her shoe)_ a **tear** in his jeans, a **split** in the sofa, a **slit** in the cover **2** _(a hole in the hedge)_ an **opening** in the rocks, a **cavity** in my tooth, **gaps** in the fence, a **space** for a picture, **blanks** in a crossword **3** _(a fox's hole)_ a rabbit **burrow**, coal **pit**, a gold **mine**, **potholes** in the road, a **manhole** in the pavement

holiday _(summer holidays)_ some **time off** in August, a **day off** last week, a policeman who was **off duty**, a **vacation** in Florida, a soldier's **leave**

hollow _(a hollow ball)_ The beach ball's **not solid**. My stomach's **empty**. The hamster **scooped out** a hole.

home _(a nice home)_ a lovely **house**, a big **flat**, my **place**

honest _(say_ **onest**_) (an honest person)_ a **trustworthy** shopkeeper, a **genuine** price, a **sincere** belief, a **straight** answer, a **frank** reply

honour _(say_ **onor**_) (It's an honour to meet you, sir.)_ to earn the **respect** of your friends, to deserve **admiration** for being so brave

¹**hook** _(a picture hook)_ a **peg** for a bag, a **nail** in the wall, a **catch** on the door

²**hook** **1** _(Bill hooked his coat over the chair.)_ Your jacket's **hanging up** on your peg. The cowboy **hitched** the horse to the fence. **Fasten** the picture to the wall. **2** _(He hooked a big fish.)_ Anna **caught** a tiddler. The bird **captured** a worm.

hope _(I hope he'll be all right.)_ Dad's **keeping his fingers crossed**! She **wished** he'd come back. I'm **trusting** Mum will help me. Tim's **banking on** winning the race.

hopeful *(I'm hopeful that she'll win.)* an **optimistic** person, a **positive** comment, a **confident** start, an **encouraging** mark, a **promising** report

horrible *(a horrible noise)* **terrible** weather, **dreadful** traffic, **horrid** people, **nasty** remarks, a **disgusting** taste, a **foul** smell, a **mean** woman, a **cruel** man, **unkind** treatment, a **disagreeable** person, a **wicked** ogre, an **evil** witch, a **baddie**

horrific *(a horrific murder)* a **terrible** tragedy, a **gruesome** picture, a **horrifying** story, a **nightmarish** journey, a **ghastly** dream

horror *(a horror film)* a **frightening** scream, a **scary** movie, a **creepy** house, **spooky** music, a **weird** experience, a **horrifying** story, a **nightmarish** journey, a **ghostly** voice. The sight of the knife **made** my **blood run cold**. The creaking door **made her blood turn to water**. The ghostly moaning **made** his **hair stand on end**. I've got a story to **make** your **flesh creep**.

hot **1** *(hot water)* a **warm** bath, a **heated** pool, a **scorching** day, the **burning** sun, a **baking** afternoon, a **piping hot** meal, the **blistering** sun, **scalding** water **2** *(a hot curry)* **spicy** food, a **peppery** sausage

h

hotel

motel

youth hostel

bed and breakfast

pub

house *(Come into the house for a bit.)* Go **home**. Come over to my **place**.

castle

palace

mansion

cottage

bungalow

semidetached

terraced houses

howl *(The wolf howls.)* Hounds **bay**, dogs **whine**, babies **wail**, the wind **moans**.

hug *(I hugged the puppy.)* Dad **cuddled** the baby. The twins **snuggled up** to each other. Simon **clung to** his mum. He **clasped** her in his arms. I **clutched** my books. The couple **embraced**.

huge *(a huge school)* a **large** box, a **big** man, a **hulking great** monster, a **massive** amount, an **enormous** tree, a **gigantic** ship

human *(the human race)* **man's** progress in science, polluted by **mankind**, all **people** on Earth

humorous *(a humorous show)* a **funny** film, a **comic** actor, an **amusing** story, **entertaining** jokes

humour *(Her lessons were full of humour.)* rolling about with **laughter**, giggling in **amusement**, watching a **comedy**, a **real laugh**

hungry *(We're hungry.)* a bit **peckish**, **starving**, **famished**, feeling **ravenous**

hunt 1 *(hunting foxes)* **chasing** a rabbit, **pursuing** the killer, a lion **stalking** a deer 2 *(hunting for your other sock)* **Look for** it in the bedroom, **search** the bathroom, **have a look** in the washing machine.

hurry *(Hurry up!)* **rush** to school, **dash** along the road, **run** for the bus, **sprint** down the steps, **dart** behind the door, **speed** away, **race** upstairs, **zoom** down the hill, **tear** along the path, **charge** into the room

hurt 1 *(This bruise hurts a lot.)* A burn can **be** very **painful**. My head **aches**. He has a **sore** heel. Adam's eyes **stung** from the chlorine. My head was **throbbing**. 2 *(Don't hurt Nicky.)* The rat poison **harms** pets. The falling branch **injured** one of the children. She **damaged** the book. Reading in bad light can **impair** your sight. He **bullies** his sister. They **torment** those cats. Cruel people **ill-treat** children. 3 *(You hurt Ed by saying that.)* It **upset** Mum and **distressed** the other kids.

icy *(icy water)* a **cold** day, **wintry** weather, a **freezing** night, a **chilly** morning, a bit **nippy**, **unheated** rooms, a **cool** drink

idea 1 *(a good idea)* Eleanor had a **brainwave** for a costume. Her **plan** was to cut up some old curtains. The council's got a **scheme** for a new road. **2** *(The idea of a fried breakfast makes me feel sick.)* The **thought** of the doughnuts made her walk faster. In **theory** I like sport, but not when it's raining!

ideal *(ideal weather for a picnic)* a **perfect** day, a **great** picnic spot, an **excellent** dinner. This colour's **just right**.

identical *(identical twins)* The sisters are **alike**. Jenny's **very like** her mother. The sisters **are like two peas in a pod**. All the Smiths have **similar** noses. Paint this **the same** colour.

idiot *(Don't be such an idiot!)* **fool, dummy, dope, clot, nit, nitwit, chump, twit, blockhead, fathead, thickhead, twerp, nerd, geek, dweeb, silly ass, halfwit** – words like *cretin* and *moron* are stronger and sound rude.

idle *(an idle person)* Charlie felt **lazy** all Sunday and **loafed around** all day. He **lounged about** watching TV. He was too **sluggish** to get dressed. You're **slack** about your practice.

ignorant *(an ignorant person)* **uneducated** children, **unaware of** the danger, **unfamiliar with** French, **in the dark** about her birthday surprise, a **blank** stare

ignore *(Just ignore those horrible kids.)* **Take no notice** of her teasing. Mrs Dean **turned a blind eye** to the mess. She **turned a deaf ear** to all the noise, too. The kitten was **neglected** by its owners. When I was clearing out, I **overlooked** these magazines.

ill *(Daniel Evans is ill today.)* **not feeling well**, looking **unwell**, **sick** several days this term, **not in good health**, got **something the matter with** him, **poorly**

illness *(a short illness)* heart **disease**, a chest **infection**, 15 days lost through **sickness** this term, an **allergy** to cats, **allergic** to them

illustration *(colourful illustrations in a book)* interesting **pictures**, **cartoons** in the comic, an exhibition of **artwork**, Year 3's **drawings** and **paintings**

computer graphics

63

imagine 1 *(Can you imagine being 40?)* He **dreams** of being a singer. She often **pretends** she can fly. Kim **makes up** fantastic stories. I was **daydreaming** instead of listening to Miss Howe. **2** *(I imagine he may be late.)* I **expect** he'll ring soon. I **suppose** you want some more cake. I **believe** he's still away. Yes, I **think** so. I **presume** you know Mike. He **assumes** everyone likes his jokes.

immediately *(Stop immediately!)* Go **at once!** The computer calculated the answer **instantly**. He ate it **straightaway**.

impatient *(an impatient knocking at the door)* Jim **hasn't got any patience** – he's always losing his temper. The smaller children get **restless** towards lunchtime. They get **fidgety**. We're **anxious** to start off on holiday. He's very **eager** to play.

important 1 *(an important letter)* the **main** roads, the **principal** reasons, the **essential** ingredients, **key** facts, an **urgent** phone call, **necessary** information **2** *(an important person)* a **leading** scientist, a **first-class** artist, a **famous** singer, a **well-known** writer, a **great** building, a **top** athlete, a **world-class** tennis player

impossible *(impossible to get there before dark)* We **can't** get there in time. It's **not possible**. It's **out of the question**. Your idea is **impractical**.

impressive *(an impressive player)* a **stunning** goal, a **striking** idea, a **sensational** result, an **awesome** film, an **awe-inspiring** storm, a **grand** building, an **inspiring** teacher

improve *(Her riding has improved.)* Your handwriting's **got better**. Your reading has **progressed** too. Now you need to **develop** your story writing. She needs braces to **correct** her crooked teeth. Miss gave my story a star when I'd **edited** it.

include *(The price includes a soft drink.)* The boat trip **comes with** a tour of the castle. The new disk**'s got** 50 games on it. The box **contained** lots of toys. I don't think the children's plans **involve** Mum and Dad!

increase 1 *(Prices are increasing.)* My pocket money's **going up** when I'm ten. Our class is **expanding** – we have three new people. Our knowledge of the universe is **advancing**. The number of people with computers is **growing**. It **rises** every year. **2** *(Mum increased her allowance.)* The shop **put up** its prices. She **made** the flowerbed **bigger**.

incredible 1 *(an incredible story)* an **unbelievable** price, a **farfetched** excuse, an **improbable** reason **2** *(That new song's incredible – I love it!)* a **great** band, a **fantastic** hit, **cool** boots

independent 1 *(Granny's very independent and still lives on her own.)* She's **self-sufficient** and can **stand on her own two feet**. She's always **fended for herself**. **2** *(an independent country)* India has been a **self-governing** country since 1947. It **won independence** in 1947.

industry *(the computer industry)* car **manufacturing**, the soft toys **business**, the tourist **trade**, a building **company**, a law **firm**

infection *(a chest infection)* a flu **virus**, a tummy **bug**, a cold **germ**, a sudden **fever**, a short **illness**, an **infectious disease**, a high **temperature**

information *(information on dolphins)* some **facts** about computers, **statistics** from around the world, **details** of the offer, a **record** of the amount of rainfall, the **lowdown** on the exam

innocent *(The man was innocent.)* He **didn't do it**. He was **not guilty**. The judge **cleared** him.

input *(Input the data.)* First **install** the program. Then **load** the game. **Enter** your password. **Run** the setup program.

inside **1** *(Let's play inside this afternoon.)* Let's play **in** the house. I'm going **indoors**. **2** *(I felt frightened inside.)* **Deep down**, she's still upset about Gran dying.

The Red Book contains **data** on endangered animals.

injection *(a tetanus injection)* an **inoculation** against whooping cough, **jabs** against flu

injure *(injured in a fall)* The fall **hurt** his back. The rat poison **harms** pets as well. My shoulder was **damaged** in the accident. He was **wounded** by an arrow. Reading in a bad light can **impair** your sight.

injury *(a sports injury)* a **wound** in the leg, a **cut** on the face, a **bruise**, **damage** to his knee, no **harm** done

instruction **1** *(Follow the instructions!)* a leaflet **telling you what to do**, clear **orders** to the soldiers, the **rules** of the club **2** *(a course of instruction)* He did a **teaching** diploma. Tricia has a degree in **education**.

instrument *(a musical instrument, an instrument for pulling out nails)* a **tool** for making holes, a **gadget** for opening bottles, an electronic **device** to protect computer games

insult (*He insulted me.*) She **called** me **names**. You've **offended** Mrs Sargent. I didn't mean to **upset** her.

intelligent (*an intelligent person*) a **brainy** girl, a **clever** boy, a **bright** idea, a **brilliant** answer, a **smart** move, a **quick** mind, a **sharp** brain

intend (*Cathy intends to go to Canada.*) She **plans** to fly to Toronto. She **means** to visit her relations there. She**'s determined** to go. She's **made up her mind** to go soon.

interest (*Football doesn't interest me.*) I'm just not **into** it. All sorts of sport **fascinate** Toby. He's **enthralled** by it. His sister's **keen on** horses. She's **obsessed** by them. Her friends are **crazy about** them too, but I could never **get into** them. The children are **absorbed** in the game. They **show some interest** in learning the piano.

interfere (*interfering with our private conversation*) **meddling** with our games, **fiddling** with our stuff, **poking your nose in**, **tampering** with our tapes, **messing about** with them. She **never minds her own business**!

interrupt (*Don't interrupt!*) 'Someone's coming!' **broke in** Jamie. Cheryl kept **butting in**. Max **burst in** on his brother and his girlfriend. John **intruded** when we were talking. He just **barged in**.

introduce (*Ms Holmes introduced our new art teacher.*) Mr Pitts **presented** the actors to the audience. Paul, **this is** Simon.

invent (*inventing a wasp trap*) How can we **create** a best-selling computer game? Marconi **made** the first radio. What ideas have you **thought up** for a play? Watt **discovered** that steam made an engine work.

The telephone was **invented** in 1866.

invite (*He invited Jamie to stay the night.*) Can I **ask** Josh to stay too? We **had** the Browns over. She **welcomed** us to the house.

irritate (*Those yowling cats irritate me.*) The noise from the building site **annoyed** her. The dog's **pestering** Ben. Stop **bothering** your father. Stop **aggravating** the cat. It **gets on my nerves**. Your music's **driving me up the wall**. It's **driving** Dad **crazy** too. Her questions **drive** the teacher **round the bend**. My little brother **bugs** me!

itch (*an insect bite itching all night*) That jumper **scratches** so much I can't wear it. The cat's whiskers **tickle** me. The antiseptic **tingled** on my skin.

Jj

jail _(He spent six years in jail.)_ in **prison**, in a **lockup**, the **dungeons** in the castle

¹**jam** _(raspberry jam)_

lime **marmalade**

strawberry **preserve**

²**jam** _(a traffic jam)_ a **holdup**, a **snarl-up**, **congestion** on the roads, a **blockage** on the M25, a police **roadblock**

³**jam** _(A bird's nest jammed the pipe.)_ a sock **stuck** in the drain, a **blocked** road, dead leaves **clogging** the gutter, a **bunged-up** nose, tea leaves **stopping up** the pipe

jar _(a jar of jam)_ a **pot** of honey, a **bottle** of ketchup

jealous _(jealous of her clever sister)_ **envious** of Sara's new bicycle, **green with envy**, **resentful** of Sara getting a prize

jewel _(the Crown Jewels)_ a **precious stone**, a **gem**

job 1 _(a job selling computers)_ Mum's gone to **work**. What is her **occupation**? She's in the teaching **profession**. It's her **career**. **2** _(lots of jobs to be done before we can go)_ It's a difficult **task**. One of the **chores** I don't like is cleaning the budgie's cage.

jog _(I jog two miles a day.)_ She **runs** every day. I'm **going for a jog**. He **trotted** round the track.

join 1 _(We joined the wires together.)_ We **connected** the computer to the printer. The boy **put** the parts of the truck **together**. Rosie **plugged** the lamp **into** the socket. They **link** the computer to the weapons system. **Attach** your label to the picture. **Fix** the bumper onto the car. **2** _(Join the two parts together.)_ Paxby Town and Paxby Rovers **united** and became 'Paxby United'. **Combine** yellow and blue to make green. Three companies **merged** to make one big one. **3** _(I joined the Chess Club.)_ Mikki **became a member of** the Pony Club. We **belong** to the Computer Society.

joke 1 _(Tell me a joke.)_ a **gag**, a **funny story**, a **pun**, a **play on words**, an old **chestnut**, a **crack** about my hair looking like a haystack **2** _(He dressed up like Dad for a joke.)_ He played a **trick** on me. He was just **kidding**. The report about aliens landing was just a **hoax**.

journey _(a train journey)_ a **trip** to the zoo, a school **outing**, a coach **tour**, a short **drive**, a bus **ride**, a smooth **flight**, a river **cruise**, a sea **voyage**, an **expedition** to the jungle, an **excursion** to see the seals, a **hike**, a long **trek**, a tiring **walk**

joy *(The little girl jumped for joy.)* This card is to wish you **happiness**. He gets a lot of **pleasure** playing with toy cars. It's **bliss** to sit by the fire on a cold winter's day. Get hours of **enjoyment** at the theme park! The friends hugged each other with **delight**. She was in **rapture** as the story unfolded.

judge *(a judge in a court of law)* a football **referee**, an **umpire** for the cricket team

juice 1 *(a glass of juice)* an orange **drink**, lemon **squash**, blackcurrant **cordial 2** *(the juice of a lemon)* the **sap** of a tree, the **milk** from a coconut

jumble *(a jumble of old toys)* The hall's a **mess**, the staff room's a **muddle** and the classes are in **chaos**, all because of Open Day!

a **jumble sale** stall

¹jump 1 *(Ben jumped over the wall.)* He **leapt** over the hedge, **sprang** onto the lawn and **vaulted** over the fence. The dog **bounded** through the bushes. **Hop** into bed! **2** *(You've jumped over question 5.)* You've **missed** it **out**. You can't just **omit** it!

²jump 1 *(a high jump)* a big **leap**, a single **bound**, a pole **vault 2** *(I woke with a jump.)* He **jumped a mile** when I shouted. He gave me a **start**.

jumper *(a woolly jumper)* see **sweater**

jumpy *(a bit jumpy since the accident)* having **the jitters**, an **anxious** woman, a **tense** person, being **upset**, **scared** of singing in front of the class, feeling **under stress**, **uneasy** about the test

junior *(junior school)* a **primary** school, a special race for the **younger** ones, in the **youth** team, a **juvenile** court

junk *(a load of junk)* a pile of **rubbish**, a **garbage** heap, dropping **litter** in the street, **refuse** collection, toxic **waste**

¹just 1 *(Fred's just arrived.)* He came in **this moment**. **2** *(It was just a joke!)* It's **only** a few minutes' walk from here. **3** *(It's just two o'clock.)* It's **exactly** four minutes past. The lesson had **hardly** started when she came in.

²just *(a just decision)* a **fair** hearing, a **reasonable** punishment, an **unbiased** referee, an **impartial** judge, the **right** thing to do

Kk

keen 1 *(a keen footballer)* **interested** in astronomy, **eager** to go for a walk, **enthusiastic** about this new project, **anxious** to do well **2** *(a keen mind)* a **bright** answer, a **shrewd** businessman **3** *(keen hearing)* **sharp** eyes, **quick** reactions, **acute** eyesight

keep 1 *(Can I keep this game?)* I let him **have** the tapes. I'll **hang on to** these decorations for next Christmas. Auntie's **put away** the big shirt until I grow into it. The cash machine **retained** Mum's card. We **stored** the biscuits in a jar. **2** *(Keep trying!)* **Go on** writing for a minute. Ms Jenkins **carried on** with the lesson. We managed to **stick at** the project. She **continued** reading. I hope this rain doesn't **last**. **3** *(Keep down: they'll see us!)* Are you going to **stay** away from school tomorrow? The teachers **remained** standing while the children sat down. **4** *(Don't let me keep you.)* Miss Lucas **made** me **late**. She **delayed** me for ten minutes.

key 1 *(the keys to the classroom)* a bottle **opener**, a **corkscrew** **2** *(the keys of a computer)* a **button**, a **knob**, a **bar** **3** *(the key to the map)* an **index**, an **explanation** **4** *(the key to the problem)* the **secret**, the **solution**, a **clue** **5** *(The key point is that you must save your work.)* the most **important** thing, **essential** facts, a **main** road, **necessary** information

kick 1 *(Martin kicked the ball.)* He **booted** it over the line. He **passed** it to Keith; **2 be kicked out** *(Samantha's been kicked out of the team.)* She's been **dropped**.

¹**kid** *(Bring the kids!)* They've got three **children**. The **youngsters** should go and eat now. Her **sons** and **daughters** are at my school. My sister's a **toddler** and my brother's only a **baby**.

²**kid** *(Don't listen to him, he's only kidding!)* The man **tricked** me into buying a fake watch. You must be **joking**!

kidnap *(They kidnapped the film star's son.)* The boy was **abducted** yesterday. The kidnappers **snatched** him from his home. They also **took** the maid **hostage**.

kill *(A man was killed on Friday.)* Police think he was **murdered**. The political leader **massacred** hundreds of people. Then he was **assassinated**. His killers were **put to death**. They were **executed**. Hundreds of people had been **slaughtered**. A spy was **bumped off** in Italy. They had their cat **put to sleep** because it was ill. This powder **destroys** household pests. Antiseptic **exterminates** germs in hospitals. The aliens were totally **annihilated**. They're **history**!

¹**kind** *(a kind person)* a **generous** man, a **kindly** uncle, a **gentle** boy, a **sympathetic** teacher, an **unselfish** girl, a **charitable** woman, a **warmhearted** aunt

²**kind** *(What kind of chocolate do you want?)* a **sort** of bird, a **type** of bread, a **make** of computer, Mum's favourite **brand** of soap

k

kiss (*Anne kissed him.*) They **embraced**. They were in the gym **smooching**. She and Paul were **snogging** in the car. They were **having a cuddle**. Tim **pecked** Gran on the cheek.

knob (*a doorknob*) a brass **handle** on the front door, pressing the **button** on the left, a walking stick with **bumps** on it

¹**knock** **1** (*knocking on the door*) The teacher **rapped** on the desk. I **tapped** on the window. Leah **hammered** on the table. Who's **banging** on the wall? Annie **thumped** on her desk. She **pounded** on the desk with her fists. **2** (*Justin knocked Eliot down.*) He **hit** Eliot, who fell over. The car **bumped** into the tree.

²**knock** (*She'd had a nasty knock on the head.*) a **hit**, a **bump**, a loud **tap** on the desk, a sudden **bang**, a **rap** on the door, a **thump** on the head

knock out (*A falling rock knocked him out.*) It **made** him **lose consciousness**.

¹**knot** (*Sam tied the rope in a knot.*)

²**knot** (*She knotted the rope.*) I **tied** the string round the dog's neck. I **fastened** a ribbon round my neck. Pat **did up** her laces.

know **1** (*Do you know Mrs Lowe?*) I **recognise** her. I **know** her **by sight**. Janice Steele **is a friend of** hers. **Are** you **familiar with** these words? I **remember** some of them. She didn't **realise** she had to learn them. Wayne **understands** how to do those sums. **2** (*Do you know how to swim?*) **Can** you swim? Sophie **is able to** tie her shoelaces.

knowledge **1** (*general knowledge*) a lot of **information** about computers, some **facts** about transport, a lot of **data** on giant pandas, **statistics** from around the world, **details** about the offer, the **truth** about John and Hilary, the **lowdown** about the exam **2** (*If you travel, you can increase your knowledge of the world.*) He shows a lot of **wisdom** for a young boy. He's had a good **education**. A university is a place of **learning**.

reef knot   **slip knot**   **Windsor knot**   **granny knot**

Ll

label *(The label on her suitcase says 'British Airways'.)* Put this **sticker** on your book. The dog's got a **tag** with his owner's phone number on it. Maria sewed **name tapes** on her sports kit. The **sign** on the door said, 'Please don't disturb.' The **caption** under the photo said, 'London in 1933.'

lad *(The lads are playing football.)* a **boy**, a **guy**, a **youth**

ladder *(a long ladder)* some **steps** for painting the ceiling, a **rope ladder** to the tree house, a **fire escape**

lady *(a lady in a blue jacket)* Two **women** were serving in the snack bar. I spoke to the **girl** in the shoe shop. 'Come this way, **Madam**,' said the waiter.

lake *(sailing boats on the lake)* a **pool** under a waterfall, a garden **pond**, an **inland sea**, a **reservoir** that supplies Manchester with water, a **loch** in Scotland, a tropical **lagoon**

¹land 1 *(They bought some land.)* playing on waste **ground**, a ball falling to **Earth**, a building **site** near the school **2** *(a foreign land)* Canada's a big **country**. The president addressed the American **nation**. India became an independent **state** in 1947. The **Republic** of South Africa.

²land 1 *(The spacecraft landed safely.)* The ferry **docks** over there. When do you think they'll **get here**? Vic said they'd **arrive** at three. This train **reaches** Plymouth at 12.40. **2** *(A butterfly landed on my hand.)* It **settled** for a moment. The parrot **perched** on Steve's shoulder. The ship **came to rest** on the seabed.

large *(a large dog)* a **big** box, a **huge** man, an **enormous** tree, a **gigantic** spaceship, a **hulking great** monster, a **massive** amount of work, a **colossal** tree

¹last *(the last day of term)* the **final** chapter, the **closing** scene of the film, a sad **ending**, the **end** house

²last *(Her shoes only lasted for two months.)* The rain **continued** all day. The game **went on** till dark. We **carried on** playing.

lamp

oil lamp

bedside lamp

floor lamp

Hallowe'en **lantern**

work lamp

late 1 *(You're making me late for school.)* I **won't** be **on time.** Mum's getting **behind** with sticking our photos in the albums. Karen **delayed** me for 20 minutes, so we were **not in time** for the bus. Don't let me **hold** you **up.** Mal was **slowed down** by traffic. He was **running late** that day. **2** *(We watched the late show.)* He arrived **last thing** at night. Help came **at the last minute.**

lately *(You've been at Craig's a lot lately.)* We bought a computer **recently. In the last few days** we've been buying Christmas presents.

later *(See you later.)* They went home **afterwards. After this,** we can go. **Then** we realised what had happened. I always wondered what happened **next.**

laugh *(Everybody laughed at my joke.)* Nancy **giggled** at Mrs Carey's hat. Dad **chuckled** at the story. Terri **sniggered** when I fell over. The children **tittered** when Mandy forgot her lines. The comedy had me **rolling about.** I was **in stitches.** Cody **roared** with laughter. They **burst out laughing.** John **hooted** with laughter. I **nearly died laughing.** 'You're as cheerful as a damp sponge,' she **joked.**

laugh at *(Don't laugh at her.)* They **made fun of** her. They **teased** her. It's mean to **taunt** someone who's fat. They **took the mickey** out of Sarah's hairstyle.

laughter *(He rolled about with laughter.)* **giggling** in **amusement,** getting **the giggles,** a lot of **humour** in this story

launch *(BBC1 launched a new series.)* They're **introducing** a sports quiz. It **begins** in the autumn. It will **start** in September. Ladybird **published** many books this year.

law *(laws against stealing)* school **rules,** parking **regulations,** an **act** of Parliament, the Highway **Code,** the **Ten Commandments**

lawyer *(a clever lawyer)* A **solicitor** deals with house buying. American lawyers are called **attorneys.**

A **barrister** speaks in court about a case.

lay *(Lay the cards face upwards.)* Kim **set out** plates and glasses for the family. James **spread** his collection of postcards **out** on the table. He **put** them on the table. **Stand** the flowers on the windowsill. Janine **placed** the cake on the plate. Auntie Pauline **deposited** the contents of her bag on the table. – see also **LIE**[1]

lazy *(a lazy person)* I spent the whole day being **idle**. I just **lounged about** watching TV. They **loafed around** outside the shops. You're getting **slack** about your violin practice. I felt too **sluggish** to do anything.

lead 1 *(Ben led the children to safety.)* I **guided** old Mrs Benson across the road. The tour guide **conducted** us round the castle. The teacher **shepherded** the children into the classroom. Donna **pulled** her little brother into the room. Brent's mother **showed** us **the way to** his bedroom. Joe **delivered** the child safely back to his dad. 2 *(Taran led the team to victory.)* Joel's **in charge** this week. Shirley **heads** her own company. Leo **runs** a hairdressing business. He **manages** it. Who **governs** the country? Clare **organises** the local computer club. Who **captains** the team?

leader *(Take me to your leader!)* the **captain** of the team, the pirate **chief**, the **headman** of the tribe, the **boss** of the company

leak *(The tap's leaking.)* water **escaping** from the bath, **dripping** over the edge, **trickling** across the floor, **seeping** through the floor, **oozing** down the wall

lean 1 *(the Leaning Tower of Pisa)* The Tower **tilts** at a dangerous angle. It might **tip** further in a few years. 2 *(Dave leant against the wall.)* **propping himself up** on the railing, **resting** against the cupboard, **lounging** against the door

lean forward *(I leant forward to see the small picture.)* She **stooped** to look at the insect. We **crouched** over the fire.

leap *(Sean leapt over the wall.)* He **jumped** over the hedge, **sprang** onto the lawn, and **vaulted** onto the fence. The dog **bounded** through the bushes.

learn 1 *(I've learnt a new song.)* Ravi **memorised** his lines for the play. He **knows** them **by heart**. We **learnt** a poem **off by heart**. 2 *(We learnt a few things about Gran's childhood.)* We **discovered** she was born in China. We **found out** she can speak three languages. 3 *(learning to sail)* **taking lessons in** carpentry, **studying** biology

least 1 *(I haven't the least idea where they went.)* not the **slightest** interest in music. The **smallest** amount of this poison can kill you. I ate the **fewest** sweets. The **lowest** number of people went to the match that Saturday 2 **at least** *(She's lived here for at least four years.)* **no fewer than** four people in each group, **no less than** half an hour on their designs

leave 1 *(Kate left the party early.)* I've got to **go** soon. The train **departed** at 4.28. The plane **takes off** in half an hour. We **set out** at 5 am. It's time to **make a move**. We'll be **off** soon. 2 *(I left a note for Mum.)* **Put** some food out for the cat. Helena **placed** the letter under a flowerpot. 3 *(We left the stray dog at the police station.)* It had been **abandoned** by its owner. The sailors **deserted** the sinking ship. We must **evacuate** the building during fire drill. 4 *(She left her job.)* She **resigned**. She **quit**. 5 *(Leave go of the ball!)* **Let go of** my shirt! Don't **drop** the plates! 6 *(Gran left you £500 in her will.)* She **bequeathed** her house to her nephew.

I

leave out *(You left out an 's' in 'possible'.)* You've **missed out** number 3. When Mum was clearing out, she **overlooked** these magazines. Just **ignore** pages 14, 15 and 16.

legal *(It's not legal to sell alcohol to children.)* It is forbidden **by law**. Alcohol is not **allowed**. Smoking is not **permitted**. The **legitimate** owner of a car. The council is **authorised** to decide on council tax.

lend *(Tony lent us his tent.)* He **loaned** it to us. He **let** us **borrow** it to go camping.

less *(You've got less than me.)* **fewer** people at football today, free for children **under** four

lessen *(The storm lessened towards evening.)* The price of sweets has **fallen**. It was **reduced** to 33p. They **lowered** it last week. The number of girls doing ballet has **dropped off**. It's been **declining** for some time. The rain **eased off** at five o'clock. The wind **decreased**.

lesson *(an art lesson)* a dancing **class**, a carpentry **course**

¹**let** *(Bridget let me take the dog for a walk.)* Am I **allowed** to go yet? Miss Grant **gave** me **permission** to go early. She **permitted** me to go. She **agreed** to my going.

²**let** *(to let a flat out)* **hire** bikes to tourists, **rent** out camping equipment

let off 1 *(Mr Tucker let me off the spelling test.)* I was **excused** from PE. **2** *(The terrorist let off a bomb.)* He **exploded** it in the street. He **blew up** a building. The police **fired** a shot at him. The kids **set off** some fireworks.

letter *(a letter from Dad)* He left you a **message**. Here's the **note**. Did you get any **post**?

level 1 *(a level field)* a **flat** garden, a **smooth** lawn, a **calm** sea, a **horizontal** position **2** *(The teams are level.)* the **same** score as the other team, **equal** scores, **identical** scores

lid

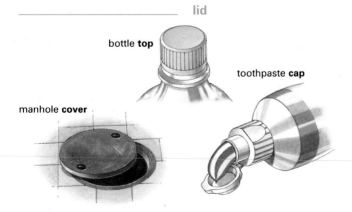

bottle **top**

toothpaste **cap**

manhole **cover**

¹**lie** (*past tense is* **lay**) *(He lay down on the bed.)* I **stretched out** under a tree. The duchess **reclined** on a silk sofa.

²**lie** (*past tense is* **lied**) *(She's lying about the money.)* She's **fibbing**. She's **telling tales**. She's **kidding**. She's **putting one over on you**. She's **pretending** that she didn't know.

³**lie** *(tell a lie)* a **fib**, a **story**, a **hoax**

life *(a happy life)* a long **lifetime**, a sad **existence**, cheerful all her **days**

¹**lift** 1 *(Can you lift this box?)* I can **pick up** two boxes that big! I can **carry** my big sister. **Raise** your arms above your head. **Put up** your hand if you know the answer. She **heaved** a case **up** the stairs. The crane **hoisted** the container into the air. He **jacked up** the car to change the wheel. 2 *(The plane lifted off the ground.)* It **took off** and **rose** into the sky. The eagle **soared** up. Warm air **ascended** from the valley.

²**lift** 1 *(The lift stopped on the third floor.)* The **elevator**'s out of order. 2 *(a lift to school)* a **ride** in Sonia's car

¹**light** 1 *(My schoolbag's quite light.)* It's **easy to carry**. It's **nearly empty**. It's a **lightweight** suitcase. He's **underweight** for his age. 2 *(a light breeze)* a **soft** tap on the door, a **flimsy** dress, a **delicate** touch, a **feathery** cloud, a **slight** chill

²**light** 1 *(a bright light)* broad **daylight**, brilliant **sunlight**, **sunshine**, the **glare** of headlights, the **dazzle** of the sun 2 *(a distant light)* the **glow** of the city lights, warm **firelight** 3 *(a flashing light)* the **flash** of his torch, the **flicker** of lights in the trees, the **twinkle** of the stars, the **glimmer** of fireflies, a **spark** of light 4 *(reflected light)* the **glint** of sunlight on water, the **sparkle** of diamonds, the **glitter** of Christmas tinsel, the **gleam** of the moon 5 *(a shaft of light)* a **ray** of sun, a **beam** of moonlight 6 *(a bedside light)* a table **lamp**, a **lantern**, a **flashlight**, a **torch**, a **spotlight**

³**light** 1 *(Let's light the fire.)* He **set fire to** the dry leaves. Can you **start** the bonfire? **Put on** the gas fire. 2 *(The torch lit up the path.)* The sunlight **showed up** the mud on the carpet. The pitch was **illuminated** by floodlights.

¹**like** 1 *(I like chips.)* Jake **enjoys** reading comics. Kylie **loves** riding. She **adores** horses. She **raves about** her riding teacher. The old couple **are fond of** their grandchildren. They **take pleasure** in their visits. The dog **revelled in** the warm sunshine. He **gets a kick out of** doing competitions. I **relish** a quiet day with a good book. She **can't resist** chocolate. She **has a weakness** for it. 2 *(Mr Wells likes us to work quietly.)* He **is in favour of** the class collecting for Oxfam. My parents **approve of** it too. Mum's **pleased with** our success. She **appreciates** what we're doing. She **admires** us for doing it. 3 *(Would you like some cake?)* Do you **want** some? Yes, I do **fancy** something sweet.

²**like** *(Jess dressed up like an old lady.)* She looks **as if** she's about 80! The sisters are **very alike**. The twins are **identical** – you can't tell them apart. They're **like two peas in a pod**. The Smiths all have **similar** noses. Choose **matching** colours.

likely *(likely to want something to eat)* He'll **probably** be hungry. He's **liable** to just turn up.

limit *(She limited herself to one slice of cake.)* Entry is **restricted** to primary children. The party's **confined** to club members.

line **1** *(a red line)* a pencil **mark**, a **crossing-out**, an **underlining**, an **outline**, a **stripe** on a shirt, a **streak** of paint, a **strip** of light, a **band** of colour, a **ribbon** of lights **2** *(a line of desks)* a long **queue**, a **row** of seats, a **chain** of people, a **column** of soldiers, a police **cordon** **3** *(lines round the eyes)* **wrinkles** on the face, **creases** in the shirt, **grooves** in a piece of wood **4** *(a fishing line)* a climbing **rope**, a parachute **cord**, electric **wires**, a computer **cable**, an extension **flex**, plastic **string**, cotton **thread** **5** *(a fax line)* a phone **connection** **6** *(a railway line)* a bus **service**, repairing the **track** where a train went off the **rails**

line up *(Line up outside.)* Please **queue** for the tickets.

¹link *(Link hands in a circle.)* The potter **joined** a handle onto the cup. They **connected** the computer to the fax machine. Ben **put** the parts of the truck **together**. **Attach** a label to the bag. Jo **tied** a label on her case. I **pinned** a badge on my coat.

²link *(a link between smoking and cancer)* the **connection** between eating good food and being healthy

list *(a list of names)* a **menu** in a café, a school **register**, a **catalogue** of books, a phone **directory**, a **table** of contents, a bank **statement**

listen *(listening to music)* Please **pay attention** to what I'm saying. If you'd **taken notice** you'd have heard it all. Are you **listening in** on the other phone? She's **eavesdropping**! I **pricked up my ears** when I heard it.

litter *(a litter bin)* a **wastepaper** basket, a **rubbish** heap, a **garbage** dump, **refuse** disposal, a load of **junk**, a **trash** can

¹little *(a little mouse)* a **small** boy, a **short** woman, a **tiny** child, a **teeny** shirt, a **weeny** bit, a **wee** baby, a **titchy** bite, a **toy** dog, a **minute** kitten, a **miniature** pony, a **pocket** dictionary, a **mini-series**

²little *(I only want a little.)* a **bit** of your sandwich, a **spoonful** of cream, a **mouthful** of cake, a **drop** of milk, a **dab** of antiseptic, a **speck** of dirt, a **small amount** of work, a **trace** of grey, a **touch** of paint, to pay **peanuts** for something

¹live *(say liv)* **1** *(Nothing lives on the moon.)* Does anything **exist** on Mars? No animal could **survive** without air. **2** *(She lives behind the school.)* Her **home is** in Hull. They **settled** in Australia. When they're in England, they **stay** with Chris. Kangaroos **inhabit** the Australian bush.

²live *(say like dive)* *(We found a live hedgehog.)* still **alive**, a **living** creature

¹load *(They loaded up the car.)* The men **filled** the van with furniture. She **packed** her cases. The box was **crammed** with presents. See that the vase is **topped up** with water. The mug was **brimming** with hot chocolate.

²**load** 1 *(loads of food)* **lots, masses, stacks, piles, heaps** 2 *(a load of bricks)* a **cargo** of bricks, a heavy **weight** to carry

local *(your local library)* a **nearby** school, in the **neighbourhood**, **not far away**, a **handy** supermarket, a **regional** office, the **surrounding** area

²**long** *(He longed to tell his friends.)* Marianne **wished** she could live in the country. Olivia **dreamt of** playing for England. I've always **wanted** a pony. I'd **love** to be a pop singer. Sometimes I **daydream** about being rich. I **fantasise** about the places I could travel to.

¹**lock**

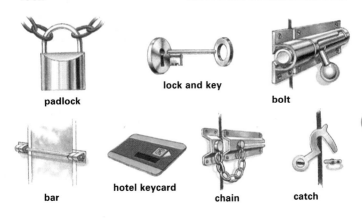

padlock

lock and key

bolt

bar

hotel keycard

chain

catch

²**lock** *(Lock the door.)* **Bolt** the front door. **Fasten** the bolt and **put the chain on**. **Seal** the box. **Secure** the chest with a lock.

lonely 1 *(a lonely man)* Grandpa has a **solitary** life with his dog. When her Mum had gone, she felt **abandoned** and **alone, friendless** in the big city. 2 *(a lonely farm)* an **isolated** cottage, a **remote** lighthouse, a **desolate** place

¹**long** *(a long queue)* a **tall** person, a **lengthy** discussion, **endless** questions, a **boring** film, lasting **ages**, an **extended** newscast

¹**look** 1 *(Michael looked at the computer.)* Warren **watched** TV all evening. Joe **regarded** the books with interest. She **examined** her fingernails. He **studied** the manual. Dr Pike **eyed** the boy curiously. Renu **gazed** at the screen. She **observed** the strange sign on it. Kerri **stared** at her brother. He **glared** at her. The baby **peeped** over the side of the cot. Nan **peered** at the paper. 2 *(They look happy.)* Her car **seems** new. Dino **appears** tired. 3 *(The house looks over the park.)* It **overlooks** the playground as well. Our flat **faces** the hospital.

²**look 1** *(He had a look at the picture.)* She gave him a hard **stare**. I had a **glance** at your report. a nice **view** of the sea **2** *(a strange look on his face)* an angry **expression**, a silly **face 3** *(I don't like the look of those clouds.)* The wild **appearance** of the tramp frightened us. Pay attention to the **presentation** of your work.

look after 1 *(looking after the baby)* Fiona **takes care of** her pets. Miss Walters **is in charge of** 1C. Give your money to me for **safekeeping**. **2** *(The head's looking after some visitors.)* Can you **see to** Mr Grey? Mr West **handles** the sports fixtures. He **attends to** all the details.

look down on *(Those London kids look down on people from the country.)* They **feel superior** to them. They **talk down** to them. It's a **snobbish** neighbourhood. The shop assistant spoke to them in a **patronising** way. She's **snooty**.

look for *(looking for her other sock)* I've **searched** everywhere. **Have a look** in the washing machine. I've **been through** all the washing already. He's **hunting for** his book.

look forward to *(looking forward to the holidays)* She **can't wait to** get the puppy.

look out *(Look out!)* **Be careful! Take care! Mind out! Watch it!**

look up *(looking up a word in the dictionary)* to **consult** an encyclopedia

look up to *(Suzanne looks up to her grandmother.)* Dad **admires** Nelson Mandela. They **idolise** pop stars. The boys **hero-worship** the football captain.

lookout *(They posted a lookout on the wall.)* a **guard**, a **sentinel**, a **sentry**, a **doorkeeper**, a **gatekeeper**

loop *(a loop of ribbon)* a **coil** of hair, a **ring** of rope, a hangman's **noose**

loose 1 *(a loose tooth)* a **wobbly** brick, an **ill-fitting** plug **2** *(a loose belt)* **baggy** trousers, a **loose-fitting** dress, a **slack** rope, **not tight enough 3** *(The dog's loose!)* setting the birds **free**, an **untethered** horse

lorry *(a delivery lorry)* a rubbish **truck**, a removal **van**

lose 1 *(losing your pen)* I **can't find** my pen. My pen's **missing**. It's just **disappeared**. Lisa's **mislaid** her purse again. These books were **misplaced** on the 'travel' shelf. **2** *(I lost at snakes and ladders.)* I **was beaten** easily. She **failed** to get a good enough score. We were **defeated** in the final. United **forfeited** the game. **3** *(The business is losing money.)* This **cost** the firm too much. It's **not making a profit**. She **wasted** money on some equipment.

lot *(a lot of time)* **many**, **much**, **plenty of**, a **load**, a **mass**, a **stack**, a **pile**, a **heap**, **lots**, **loads**, **masses**, **stacks**, **piles**, **heaps**, **dozens**, **hundreds**, **thousands**, **tons** of food

lottery *(If only we could win the lottery!)* I won a toy in the **raffle**. He won £50 in a **lucky draw**.

loud *(loud snoring)* **deafening** music, a **piercing** scream, a **thundering** crash, an **earsplitting** yell, a **shrill** voice, a **noisy** family, **rowdy** friends, a **blaring** radio, played at **full volume**, a **booming** voice, at **full blast**

¹**love** **1** *(parents' love for their children)* her **affection** for her grandchildren, a **fondness** for ice cream, a great **liking** for those biscuits, his **passion** for music **2** *(He's the love of her life.)* You're a real **darling**. Hello, my **dear**. Old Mr Park's a real **sweetie**.

²**love** *(She loves him.)* He **adores** her. She **cares about** you. He **thinks the world of** you. Bob's **crazy about** Abby. Abby is **fond of** Bob. They **like** each other **a lot**. She's **devoted to** her family **fall in love** *(He fell in love with Pauline on their first date.)* Sonia's **fancied** James for ages. Now he's **mad about** her, but she's not so **crazy about** him!

lovely *(a lovely time)* a **great** show, a **wonderful** day, **good** weather, a **fine** morning, an **ideal** picnic spot, a **perfect** day, an **excellent** CD

low **1** *(a low ceiling)* a **dumpy** figure, a **flat** landscape, a **dwarf** tree **2** *(a low voice)* a **quiet** remark, a **deep** sound **3** *(low cost)* **bargain** prices, **reduced** size

luck *(bad luck)* The third son had good **fortune**. It was **a piece of luck** finding that map. I lost it **by accident**. He leaves everything to **chance**. What a **coincidence** – so do I! That goal was a **fluke**. It was **fate** that we won the lottery. It was our **destiny** to win.

lucky *(He's often lucky.)* a **fortunate** day, a **happy** event

luggage *(luggage in the boot)* Load all our **baggage** – **suitcases** in first, small **bags** next, then the big **backpack** and small **rucksack**, and finally the **trunk** full of old clothes.

lump **1** *(a lump of sugar)* a **bit** of cheese, a **chunk** of coal, a **hunk** of bread, a **piece** of cake, a **slice** of bread **2** *(a lump on my head)* a **bump** on your forehead, a **swelling** on her knee, **bulging out**, an **abscess** on his tooth

Growing **dwarf** trees is called bonsai.

Mm

drill

machine *(a sewing machine)* a **robot** that builds cars, a **gadget** for opening bottles, computer **hardware**, a **device** for protecting computer disks

car engine

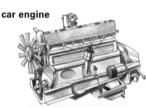

electric motor

mad 1 *(a mad woman)* **crazy**, **insane** *Slang:* **nuts**, **barmy**, **loony**, **off your rocker**, a **nutter**, a **weirdo 2** *(She's mad at you.)* **angry** with the cats next door, **cross** with her brother, **furious** with me, **wild** over the broken TV, **steamed up** about the game, all **worked up** about his stolen bike, **hot under the collar**

magic 1 *(disappearing by magic)* done by **witchcraft**, magic **spells**, Sword and **Sorcery** games, lucky **charms 2** *(a magic show)* an **illusion**, **conjuring tricks**

magician *(a street magician)* a **conjuror**, an **illusionist**, a **wizard**, a **witch**

mail *(some mail for John)* There's some **post** for him. He's got some **letters**.

main *(a main road)* the **most important** thing, the **chief** problem, the **principal** reason, **key** facts, **major** roadworks, **essential** food, a **leading** band, **Central** Park, **head** teachers, the **basic** idea

make 1 *(make a model)* **create** a picture, **form** a circle, **build** a shed, **put** a scrapbook **together**, **construct** a model, **manufacture** toys, **fashion** a bird out of clay, **assemble** a dinosaur kit **2** *(make tea)* **prepare** lunch, **whip up** a meal, **produce** a snack **3** *(Dad made me go.)* Mum **forces** us to eat greens. He **pressurised** Dad into buying the van. **4** *(making a fuss)* **causing** trouble, **provoking** a fight, **resulting** in a win **5** *(Let's make it Thursday.)* We **decided on** Spain for our holidays. **6** *(She couldn't make it.)* He couldn't **come**. We didn't **reach** the sea.

make up *(make up a story)* **imagine** what happens, **dream up** a new computer game, **invent** a character, **create** a play

man 1 *(a tall man)* a funny **guy**, a nice **chap**, an old **gentleman**, a strange **fellow 2** *(Man has polluted the Earth.)* a benefit for **mankind**, helping **people**, other **human beings**. **Humans** are the only animals to wear clothes.

manage 1 *(I can't manage this on my own.)* Anne **copes with** a young family as well as a job. Our teacher has 36 children to **deal with**. The secretary **handles** letters. They **succeeded** in getting everything in the case. Keep trying! You'll **get there** in the end! **2** *(They manage a bookshop.)* They **run** the company. Lisa **organised** the concert. Carolyn's **in charge of** the playgroup.

man-made *(man-made cloth)* **fake** fur, **artificial** roses, **processed** food, **synthetic** fibre

manners *(table manners)* good **behaviour**, showing **politeness**

many *(many people)* **a lot**, **a load**, **a mass**, **a stack**, **a pile**, **a heap**, **lots**, **loads**, **masses**, **stacks**, **piles**, **heaps**, **millions**, **thousands**, **hundreds** of miles, **tons** of food, **dozens** of presents

map *(a wall map)* an **atlas**, a London **street map**, a **plan** of the building, a **chart** of the bay

¹**mark 1** *(dirty marks on the clean wall)* a **stain** on your shirt, a **smear** of jam, a **streak** of oil, a **splodge** of paint, a **blotch** of ink, a **smudge** on your cheek, a dog with **spots**, a blue **patch**, a **point** of light, a tiny **dot**, a **speck** of dirt, a **scar** on his cheek, a **birthmark** on her arm **2** *(good marks for drama)* a high **percentage** in the exam, a low **score** in the game, winning **points** for the team **3** *(Their mark was on the box.)* Their **trademark** is written on the top. Their **logo** is a ladybird. England's **emblem** is a rose. **4** *(She made a sign to me.)* The boy made a rude **gesture**. He made a **signal** to show he was turning.

²**mark 1** *(Ms Hunt marked our folders today.)* He **corrected** my test. **2** *(Oil marked his cheek.)* It **stained** his hand, **smeared** his arm and **streaked** his face.

market *(a street market)* **stalls** selling clothes, a school **fair**, a Christmas **bazaar**, a car **boot sale**, a **jumble sale**, an **auction** of antiques

marriage *(my sister's marriage)* a **wedding** ceremony

marry *(John married Sue.)* Sue **got married** in white. They **got hitched** in June. PRINCE **WEDS** LOCAL GIRL. The girl **eloped** with a handsome stranger.

marvellous *(a marvellous day)* a **perfect** fit, an **excellent** tea, a **lovely** party, **wonderful** films, an **ideal** shape, a **sensational** game, a **fantastic** match, a **cool** band

mass *(a mass of flowers)* a **crowd** of people, a **gang** of boys, an **army** of schoolchildren, a **bunch** of roses, a **swarm** of bees, **millions** of them

master *(Master of the Black Tower)* the pirate **chief**, a gang **leader**, the school **head**, the village **headman**

mat *(a bath mat)* a fluffy **rug** in front of the fire, a patterned **carpet**, **place mats** on the table

¹**match** *(a tennis match)* a golf **game**, a music **contest**, a chess **competition**, a sports **event**

²**match** *(matching colours)* Her top **goes with** her shorts. They **tone in** well. The curtains **complement** the green of the chairs.

material *(silky material)* stripy **fabric**, woollen **cloth**, pink shiny **stuff**, **textile** design

m

matter 1 *(It doesn't matter.)* It's **not important. Never mind!** 2 *(What's the matter?)* What's the **problem**? What's **wrong**? What's the **trouble**? What's **up**?

may 1 *(He may come with us.)* Lucy **might** like this book. You **could** be the lucky winner! 2 *(May we leave?)* **Can** I come? **Could** you move your bags? **Would you mind** if I left early? Are we **allowed** to go in? Will they **let** us?

maybe *(Maybe he's here.)* **Perhaps** you'll see him. There'll **probably** be three, but **possibly** four. It's **possible** I'll be late. I **may** not. I **might** be moving.

²**mean** 1 *(What does % mean?)* BC **stands for** Before Christ. What are you **getting at**? She **got across** her real feelings. She **communicates** them well. Yawning **expresses** your boredom. The dove **symbolises** peace. The treaty **signifies** the end of war. 2 *(The dog means to be friendly.)* He **intends** to come.

¹**measure** *(Measure the room.)* **calculate** the length, **estimate** the width, **weigh** it

²**measure** *(a tape measure)* a gas **meter**, a **weighing machine**, a **cash register**

kitchen scales

ruler

speedometer

calculator

meal *(a big meal)* a huge **spread**, a quick **snack**, a real **feast**, a royal **banquet**

¹**mean** 1 *(a mean look)* a **nasty** woman, a **bad** man, a **cruel** act, **unkind** treatment, a **wicked** ogre, an **evil** witch, a **spiteful** remark, a **malicious** girl 2 *(mean with money)* a **stingy** boss, a **selfish** boy, a **miser**, **tight** with money

medicine *(stomach medicine)* a **cure** for cancer, a new **drug**, proper **treatment** for heart disease, a **prescription** for hay fever, cough **mixture**, indigestion **pills**, one **tablet** a day, two **capsules** four times a day, **antiseptic** for a cut, **antibiotics** to cure an ear infection, a **dose** of cough **linctus**, a throat **lozenge**

medium *(medium size)* **middle-sized** socks, an **average** mark, **mean** rainfall

meet 1 *(Have you met his mum?)* Ruth **introduced** us. I **got to know** her. 2 *(They meet every Monday at judo.)* They **get together** at playtime. 3 *(I met Kim in the street.)* Then I **ran into** her again. I **saw** her at school too. I **ran across** Ian. 4 *(Meet us after school.)* Please **collect** us. **Pick** us **up** soon!

meeting *(a staff meeting)* a school **assembly**, a teachers' **conference**, an international **gathering** in the **convention** centre, an **encounter** with a pop star

melt *(The snow's melting.)* **soften** the butter, **defrost** the meat, **thaw** the chips

memorise *(Memorise the numbers.)* **learn** your tables, **know** them **by heart**

mend *(Can you mend this toy?)* **repair** clocks, **fix** leaks, **restore** old pictures

mention *(Did someone mention ice cream?)* Janis **brought up** the subject of Christmas presents. He **referred to** the poster. Mum **raised** the question of the higher bus fares. Mr King **introduced** the topic of the end-of-term disco.

mess *(What a mess!)* I can't find anything in this **muddle**. Your room's a real **shambles**. The flat was in a state of **chaos**. There was a **jumble** of clothes on the floor. There was a **hotchpotch** of shoes under the chair. Your room's a **tip**.

message *(She left a message.)* a typed **letter**, a quick **note**, a warning **sign**

messy 1 *(a messy house)* an **untidy** page, a **chaotic** room 2 *(messy hands)* **dirty** feet, **filthy** socks, **grubby** face, **grimy** walls, **muddy** boots, **mucky** kids

method *(a method of learning tables)* a new **way** of making a pot, some exercise **techniques**, a **manner** of painting, a new dance **routine**, a **recipe** for chocolate cake, a **formula** for making cheap fuel

middle 1 *(the middle of the wood)* the **centre** of town, the **heart** of the jungle, the Earth's **core** 2 *(the middle shelf)* the **central** station, the **main** post office

¹**might** *(I might come.)* I **may** change my mind. You **could** be the lucky winner!

²**might** *(Do not challenge the might of the emperor!)* His **power** is greater than yours! He has the **strength** of ten men. May the **Force** be with you!

mill *(Windmills used to grind corn into flour.)* **water mill**

sawmill

coffee **grinder**

cotton mill

pepper mill

m

[1]**mind 1** *(I don't mind waiting.)* **It** doesn't **bother** me. I don't **care**. **It** doesn't **matter** if you don't finish it. I'm **easy** about it. She never **worries** what she wears. **2** *(Mind out!)* **Look out**! **Take care**! **Be careful**! **Watch it**! **3** *(Mind what you're doing!)* **Take notice** of what Mum says. **Pay attention** in class.

[2]**mind 1** *(She isn't using her mind.)* You've got more **intelligence** than that. Get your **brain** working! Use your **sense**! I can't understand the **psychology** of these people. **2** *(She knows her own mind.)* He told us his **point of view**. Let's have your **opinions**. She won't change her **attitude**. **3** *(You must make up your mind – which flavour do you want?)* I can't **decide** when to go. Have you **chosen** what to give Matt yet? Sara's **opted for** French, not German. Only you can **judge** if you've done your best.

miniature *(a miniature house)* a **little** boy, a **small** woman, a **tiny** child, a **teeny** car, a **weeny** bit, a **wee** baby, a **titchy** playing field, a **toy** dog, a **minute** kitten, a **pocket** dictionary, a **laptop** computer, a **mini**-series

minimum *(The minimum age for driving is 17.)* the **least** work possible, the **fewest** people, the **lowest** marks in the history of the school, the **bottom** score

miracle *(It's a miracle no one was killed in the crash.)* The Grand Canyon is a natural **wonder** of the world. Cycling on a tightrope across Niagara Falls is an incredible **feat**. The computer is a **marvel** of modern science.

mischievous *(say mis-chuvus)* *(a mischievous trick)* **naughty** behaviour, a **disobedient** child

miss 1 *(Fred missed the bus.)* He was **too late** for it. I **failed** to catch the ball. I **lost** the chance. **2** *(I miss my sister.)* The dog **pined for** its master. Colleen **longed for** her parents when she was away. She was **homesick**.

miss out *(I missed out an 's' in the word 'possible'.)* You've **left out** number 3. Ms Evans **overlooked** my story. You can **ignore** pages 28-30.

mist *(A sea mist covered the cliffs.)* a **haze** blurring the horizon, a thick **fog**, a cloud of brown **smog**, a few **clouds** on the mountain tops

mistake 1 *(I made a mistake.)* a **fault** in the program, an **error** message on the screen, a **slip-up** in the arrangements, a **slip** in my homework, a **blunder** in class **2 by mistake** *(I called the teacher 'Mum' by mistake.)* I trod on your foot **by accident**. It **wasn't on purpose**. That goal was a **fluke**. I **happened to** meet Sue in the street. What a **coincidence** – so did I!

mix 1 *(Mix blue and yellow.)* **Combine** red and blue to make purple. **Add** yellow **to** red to make orange. Sam **stirred** the tea. She **blended** flour and butter. **2** *(I mixed up the twins.)* I **got muddled**. It's easy to **confuse** them. **Shuffle** the cards.

mixed *(mixed sweets)* **assorted** toys, **various** colours, **miscellaneous** books

mixture *(a mixture of butter and sugar)* a **blend** of colours, an **assortment** of biscuits, a **variety** of colours, a **jumble** of clothes, a **combination** of smells

¹**moan** **1** *(The wind moaned round the chimneys.)* It **howled** over the hills and **whined** through the trees. The trees **groaned** in the wind. The baby **wailed** all night. **2** *(She moans about her work.)* He **complained** about the food. Jim's **making a fuss**. He's always **fussing** about something. The little girl **whined**. Kathy never stops **grumbling**. Don't **whinge** all the time!

²**moan** **1** *(the usual moans)* make a **complaint**, have a **grumble** **2** *(a low moan)* a wolf's **howl**, the **whine** of a plane, a loud **groan**, the baby's **wails**

model **1** *(a model of a Roman villa)* a **toy** car, a **copy** of a famous painting **2** *(This computer is last year's model.)* an old **make** of car, a popular shoe **design**, a new **version** of a computer game, her favourite **variety** of chocolate

the snowy **peaks** of the Alps

modern *(a modern house)* **new** pens, an **up-to-date** map, a **fashionable** jacket, **recent** designs, a **contemporary** building, **innovative** ideas

moment *(a moment ago)* Wait a **minute**! Can you hold on **for a bit**? This'll only take a **second**. I don't believe him for an **instant**.

money *(Have you got any money?)* plenty of **cash**, **coins** and **notes** kept in the safe, **change** for £10, foreign **currency**

mood *(in a bad mood)* in a good **temper**, in a worried **state of mind**

more or less *(It's more or less time to go.)* **around** four, **about** an hour, **almost** ready, **round about** midnight, **approximately** ten litres, **roughly** five hours

mostly *(mostly sunny)* **mainly** cloudy, **chiefly** his fault

motor *(a motor for a boat)* a car **engine**, a washing **machine**

mountain *(a high mountain)* a **range** of hills, a high **ridge**

m

move 1 *(Kim moved the bags out of the way.)* Sunil **carried** a plant to school. **Take** this box into the kitchen. I **fetched** the papers. Ian **brought** cakes with him. **Push** the chairs over and **pull** the rug back. **Shift** the chairs over here. She managed to **free** her trapped foot. **2** *(The woman moved towards us.)* She **walked** fast. She **stepped** over the dog. She **approached** the gate. The plane **flew** overhead. The boat **glided** along. **3** *(moving fast)* Bill **ran** down the steps and **jogged** down the road. We **hurried** home. The car **hurtled** by and **sped** down the road. The bus **swept** past the stop. Carol **danced** down the path. **4** *(moving slowly)* The children **dawdled** home. They **trailed** past. The snail **inched** its way up the wall. Lucy **strolled** round the mall. A tram **trundled** by. **5** *(moving quietly or secretly)* He **slipped** from the room. Anna **crept** through the window. Adam **wormed his way** to the front. Josh **wriggled** through the bushes. The cat **slid** away. A snake **slithered** into the garden. **6** *(moving awkwardly)* Julie **limped** into the room. The soldier **stumbled** in.

mud *(There's mud on your skirt.)* a pile of **earth**, good **soil**, covered in **dirt**

muddle *(These papers are in a muddle.)* Kirsty's bedroom's in a **mess**. Your room's a real **shambles**. The flat was in a state of **chaos**. There was a **jumble** of dirty clothes on the floor. I'm **confused** about what we're doing.

mug *(He was mugged.)* He was **attacked** and **robbed**. Darryl's gang **set on** us.

multiply 1 *(7 multiplied by 3 is 21.)* 8 **times** 2 is 16. **2** *(Germs multiply in dirty places.)* They **breed** quickly in warm weather.

mumble *(I mumbled an answer.)* **muttering** under his breath, **murmuring** in my ear

munch *(munch an apple)* **bite** your nails, **chew** gum, **crunch** some crisps, **nibble** a biscuit, **gnaw** a bone, **chomp away** on a hot dog

[1]**murder** *(murdered for her money)* She was **killed**. He **slaughtered** a lamb. The army was **massacred**. The leader was **assassinated**. He was **put to death**.

[2]**murder** *(a brutal murder)* a **killing**, the **assassination** of President John Kennedy, the **slaughter** of innocent people, a **massacre**, a drunken driver convicted of **manslaughter**

murderer *(a mass murderer)* a serial **killer**, a political **assassin**, a **homicidal maniac**

must 1 *(You must be home by five.)* Angie **has to** be home by six. You **should** go now. I **ought to** finish this. **2** *(You must be joking.)* You've **got to** be joking! **Surely** you're not serious? He's **probably** left. He's **bound to** be cold.

mutter *(He muttered, 'Excuse me.')* Speak up, you're **mumbling**! They **talked in low voices**. The girls were **talking in an undertone**.

mysterious *(a mysterious noise)* a **puzzling** message, a **strange** smell, a **weird** feeling, a **baffling** crime

mystery *(a mystery story)* a word **puzzle**, a hard **problem**, a clever **riddle**

Nn

nag *(nagging about doing the dishes)* He **asks** us to do it every night. He **goes on and on** about it. Evan **begged** for the games. The kids **pestered** us to play with them. They're always **going on** about getting more pocket money.

nail *(He nailed a horseshoe over the door.)* He **hung** pictures on the wall. She **pinned** a poster up. I **fastened** a light to the ceiling. Let's **screw** the mirror to the bathroom wall. Stacey **tacked** down the stair carpet.

naked *(a naked child)* **bare** arms, getting **undressed**, a painting of a **nude**

name *(His name is Joseph Wong.)* His **surname** is Wong and his **first name** is Joseph. What's your **Christian name**? He put his **signature** on the letter. He's **called** Calvin. She's **named** Sarah.

narrow *(a narrow lane)* **skinny** shoulders, a **weedy** chest, a **tapering** line

nasty **1** *(a nasty girl)* a **mean** boy, a **bad** person, a **cruel** man, a **horrible** thing to say, **unkind** treatment, **horrid** people, a **wicked** ogre, an **evil** witch, a **disagreeable** person, a **rude** comment, a **spiteful** child, a **malicious** lie **2** *(nasty weather)* **terrible** winds, **dreadful** traffic, **awful** food, **disgusting** food, a **foul** smell

natural **1** *(natural materials)* **real** butter, **genuine** fur, **pure** water, **organic** vegetables **2** *(natural fears)* **normal** reactions, **instinctive** behaviour

nature **1** *(a nature film)* **wildlife** in Africa, the **outdoor life**, the **natural environment** **2** *(a kind nature)* a lively **personality**, a stubborn **character**, a very calm **temperament**

naughty *(a naughty trick)* a **mischievous** kitten, a **disobedient** puppy, a **badly-behaved** boy, a **spoilt** child, **unruly** children

near *(near the sea)* **close to** the edge, **next to** the school, a **short distance away**, **nearby**, in the **surrounding** countryside, **around** four o'clock, **about** midnight

nearly *(nearly bedtime)* **almost** eight o'clock, **not quite** ready, **practically** finished, **about** 15 children, **around** 15 kilos

n

thin slice of melon

slender tail

fine-tipped pen

neat *(a neat bedroom)* a **tidy** classroom, an **orderly** bookcase, a **well-groomed** man

necessary *(It's necessary to make a plan first.)* what is **needed**, the **required** action, an **urgent** phone call, the **essential** ingredients, **key** points, the **most important** thing to remember, the **main** roads, the **principal** reasons, a **vital** fact

need *(I need some more pens.)* The cake's **got to have** 11 candles. I'm 3 candles **short**. The town **lacks** facilities for teenagers. The school's **in need of** a new hall. Do you **require** any help? We **could do with** a multimedia computer.

neighbour *(nice neighbours)* the **people next door**

neighbourhood *(a quiet neighbourhood)* This school is the oldest in the **area**. There is one park in this **district**. The west is the wettest **region** of Britain.

nervous *(feeling nervous)* a **worried** man, an **anxious** woman, a **frightened** child, **scared** of the dark, **under stress**, a **tense** person, being **upset**, **concerned** about the test, **uneasy** about leaving home, **jumpy**, **under pressure**

network *(a network of friends)* a communications **system**, a complicated **structure**, a **framework** of rules

new 1 *(a new jacket)* a **brand-new** computer, a **fresh** page, **clean** sheets, an **unused** pencil **2** *(a new fashion)* a **modern** house, a **recent** photo, an **up-to-date** map, a **current** phone book, a **fashionable** haircut

news *(Have you heard the news?)* a newspaper **report**, an eyewitness **account**

nibble *(nibbling a biscuit)* Julia **picked** at her food. The kids **snacked** off crisps and sweets.

nice 1 *(a nice person)* a **friendly** girl, a **kind** man, a **sympathetic** doctor, an **easygoing** boy, a **warmhearted** woman, a **sweet** old man, a **good-natured** child **2** *(a nice holiday)* **good** weather, a **fine** morning, an **ideal** picnic spot, a **perfect** day, an **excellent** band, a **lovely** party, a **wonderful** film, a **sensational** game, a **cool** new single, **fantastic** trainers

night *(a stormy night)* yesterday **evening**, when it got **dark**, in the **nighttime**, at **dead of night**

Foxes are **nocturnal** animals.

no *(No, I can't see him.)* **'Certainly not!'** **'No way!'** **'Negative**, Captain.'

noble 1 *(a noble family)* a **stately** palace, the **Royal** Family, a **regal** wave, a **majestic** ceremony, an **aristocratic** family **2** *(a noble deed)* a **brave** act, an **honourable** fight, **heroic** exploits, a **gallant** warrior, a **chivalrous** knight

noise 1 _(a scary noise)_ the **sound** of a fire crackling, an engaged **tone** on the phone, a **click** of the computer, the **chink** of coins. Speak after the **beep**. **2** _(What a noise!)_ What a **commotion**! a **din**, a **racket**, a terrible **clamour**, **uproar** in the classroom, a terrible **row**, a **rumpus** – see also BANG, CRASH, CRY, LAUGH, RUSTLE, SCREAM, SHOUT, SING, SOUND, WHINE, WHIR

noisy _(noisy neighbours)_ a **loud** snore, **deafening** music, a **piercing** scream, a **thundering** crash, an **earsplitting** yell, a **shrill** voice, **rowdy** kids

nonsense _(He's talking nonsense.)_ That's **rubbish**. The computer printed a load of **gibberish**. That's completely **untrue**. It's absolutely **wrong**.

nonstop 1 _(nonstop banging from the building site)_ working **day and night**, sleeping **round the clock**, in **constant** pain, **24-hour** service, an **endless** list of things to do. 'The **Never-Ending** Story.' **2** _(a nonstop bus)_ a **direct** train, an **express** service

normal _(a normal Sunday)_ an **ordinary** tea, an **average** family, the **usual** time, a **typical** day, our **regular** walk to school, a **routine** check

normally _(We normally have tea at six.)_ **usually**, **generally**, **mostly**

note _(Leave Ginny a note.)_ He left a **message** on the stairs. I found a **letter** from Rachel.

note down _(He noted down our names.)_ I **wrote down** the times of the buses. Just **jot down** the phone number. **Mark down** the things you want. He **entered** his name and address on the form.

nothing 1 _(There's nothing here.)_ What did you find? **Zilch!** Did you see anything? **Not a sausage!** Did you get any money? **Not a bean!** **2** _(Dad beat me two games to nothing.)_ Our team won four – **nil**. We won four – **nought**. The score's thirty – **love**.

[1]**notice** _(Did you notice that red car?)_ I **saw** the car on the way to school. Luke **spotted** it, too. I **realised** that he was talking to me. It **dawned on** me that I hadn't eaten all day. Jonathan didn't **take** any **notice** of me. Richard **was aware** that we were talking about him. I didn't **take it in**.

[2]**notice** _(Mrs Ray put a notice on the board.)_ a **sign** saying 'Silence, please', the **poster** about the pantomime, a **sticker** with the price on it, an **announcement** for a sale of books, a **leaflet** about the new shop, an **advertisement** for secondhand clothes

nought _(A million is a one followed by six noughts.)_ The winning ticket is two-**o**-seven. Her room is number one-**zero**-two.

now 1 _(The family is away just now.)_ **At the moment**, they're in Spain. **At present**, we have no car. **Currently** we don't need one. **2** _(Do it now!)_ I left **at once**. He told her **immediately**. The noise stopped **instantly**.

number 1 _(the number 7)_ Write it in **figures**, not words. XXV is 25 in Roman **numerals**. It's a **digital** clock. There are four **digits** in the number 2254. **2** _(A number of children own computers.)_ a **quantity** of papers, a small **amount** of milk, a great **deal** of work, a **total** of 11 pupils absent

Oo

obedient *(an obedient dog)* a **well-behaved** class, a **well-trained** team, a **disciplined** army, a **law-abiding** family, a **tame** pigeon

obey *(The soldiers obeyed the general.)* They **carried out** their orders. Charlotte **did what she was told**. School's OK if you **keep to** the rules. The school **conformed to** the safety instructions. We had to **comply**.

¹**object** 1 *(They examined the strange object.)* There are some **things** to put away. Ms Keane has found some **articles** belonging to this class. The box contained several strange **items**. 2 *(The object of the game is to reach the castle.)* The **aim** in bowling is to knock down all the pins. The **goal** in Monopoly is to become the richest player. At this level, the **target** is 900 points.

²**object** *(Mr Boyce objects to people bringing penknives to school.)* He **disagrees** with our plan. The students **demonstrated** against cruelty to animals. They were **protesting** against the treatment of hens.

oblong *(an oblong building)* a **rectangular** playground

observe 1 *(Try to observe the insect feeding.)* **Watch** it carefully. **Note** what it does. Let's **monitor** its behaviour. Scott **looked at** the birds' nest. She **examined** her fingernails.

He **studied** the game manual. Dr Pike **eyed** the boy curiously. Renu **gazed** fascinated at the screen. I've **noticed** you looking sleepy today. 2 *('You look sleepy,' observed Val.)* 'You're late,' he **remarked**. 'You're looking well,' she **commented**.

obtain *(The man obtained a false passport.)* How did he **get** it? How did Ray **come by** this Rangers shirt? He managed to **acquire** three shirts.

obvious 1 *(It's obvious you need help.)* It's **clear** you don't like him. It's quite **plain** she wants you to come. I don't want to see him – is that **understood**? 2 *(an obvious bloodstain)* Your black eye's not so **noticeable** today. The lights of our cities are **visible** from the moon. He has a **distinct** scar.

obviously *(Obviously I can't pay for all of you.)* No, **of course** you can't. She's **certainly** not going. I'll **definitely** have to pay. He's **clearly** too old. You've **plainly** put in a lot of work on this model.

occasion *(a memorable occasion)* two important sporting **events** on TV this Saturday, team **fixtures** every Sunday, a funny **incident**, a frightening **experience** at the fair

occur *(An accident occurred outside the bingo hall.)* What **happened**? Sports Day **takes place** in June. Something important's **cropped up**. Strange tales **arose** at Weirdwood Manor. It **turned out** for the best in the end. It all **came about** because of old Lord Weirdwood.

ocean *(the Pacific Ocean)* the North **Sea**

odd **1** *(an odd idea)* a **funny** feeling, a **strange** sound, a **peculiar** laugh, a **weird** song, an **unusual** car **2** *(17 is an odd number)* an **uneven** number, **unmatched** socks

The god Pan was a **curious** creature: half-man, half-goat.

offend *(I didn't mean to offend him.)* Sheri **insulted** me! She **called** me **names**. Now you've **upset** your mother.

offer **1** *(Suzie offered us her sweets.)* She **asked** us if we **wanted** them. She **held out** the bag. She **suggested** we should take some home with us. **2** *(He offered to help.)* Three people **came forward** to help with the raffle. Thanks for **volunteering**.

often *(I often see her.)* Tom's away **a lot**. Jamie **regularly** goes to hockey practice. Poor Sue was sick **over and over again**. Your son is **frequently** late.

oily *(oily chips)* a **greasy** hamburger, **fatty** meat

old **1** *(an old woman)* an **elderly** man, an **ancient** wizard, an **aged** relative (*say* ay-jed), my **elder** brother **2** *(dirty old jeans)* a **worn-out** coat, a **shabby** jacket, a **secondhand** chair, a **ruined** house **3** *(a valuable old chest)* an **antique** table, a **historic** castle, an **early** type of calculator

old-fashioned *(old-fashioned ideas)* an **out-of-date** timetable, an **unfashionable** coat, a **dated** frock. Big hats are **out** now. Grandpa's really **out of touch**.

once 1 *(I've been to Wales once.)* I only want to try the game **one time**. It was **the only time** I've tried it. **2** *(Once there was a magic horse.)* **At one time** Gran lived in the country. That was **long ago**. He's a TV repairman now, but he was a farmer **before**. **Previously** this was a school for boys only. **Formerly** there were only six classrooms.

only 1 *(the only school in the village)* our **one and only** grandson, a meeting of **single** parents, one **lone** tree on the hilltop, a **solitary** star in the sky **2** *(I'm only waiting for Sam.)* I was **just** asking.

¹**open 1** *(He opened a window.)* She **undid** the parcel. Cathy **unlocked** the door. Dave **unfastened** his collar. Can you **untie** your laces? Mum **uncorked** the bottle. **Push open** the window. **Unwrap** your present. **2** *(The play opens tonight.)* It **starts** at 7.30. It **begins** with a song. He **kicked off** with an easy question. Let's **launch** the festival with a word from the head teacher.

an **unwrapped** present

²**open 1** *(an open window)* The door's **ajar**. The house was **unlocked**. Your shirt's **undone**. The suitcase was **unfastened**. The window was **wide open**. **2** *(open till eight)* The factory's **working** today. It **operates** until eight o'clock. **3** *(open countryside)* **unfenced** moorland, **wild** landscape, **common** land

opening *(an opening in the hedge)* a **hole** between the rocks, a **gap** where he lost a tooth, a **space** for a picture, **blanks** in this puzzle

opinion *(She asked us all for our opinions.)* Janet's **point of view** is different from mine. She won't change her **mind**. Her **attitude** is fixed. What is your **view** about it? **To my mind**, eating meat is wrong. To other people's **way of thinking**, this may seem strange, but that is my **viewpoint**.

opponent *(an opponent in the war game)* The **opposition** don't stand a chance! We beat the **opposing team**. There are ten **competitors**. The **contestants** should arrive by ten o'clock. Phil and Steve are **rivals** for first place.

opportunity *(a good opportunity to finish your book)* a **chance** to visit the secondary school, a **risk** of missing the train if we don't hurry, a good **time** to ask for more pocket money

opposite 1 *(Big is the opposite of small.)* Joe thinks the work gets easier in secondary school but the **reverse** is true! On the **contrary**, you have much more to do. **2** *(opposite the church)* The church is **on the other side** of the road. It's **across** the road. Her house **faces** the church.

orchestra *(a large orchestra)* a jazz **group**, a new **band**

¹**order** 1 *(The general ordered the soldiers to move forward.)* The sentry **commands** you to stop. The officers **directed** the troops to retreat. Mrs Adams **told** us to put away our things. The teacher **instructed** us to sit. 2 *(ordering some drinks)* We **asked for** ice creams. Mum **sent away for** a sweatshirt. Jon **reserved** a football magazine. They've got my boots **on order**. We **booked** seats for the pantomime.

²**order** 1 *(Have they brought your order of fries?)* There have been two **requests** for this music. 2 *(Follow my orders!)* The general gave the **command**. Obey the **rules**. You will follow my **instructions**. 3 *(in alphabetical order)* numbers in **sequence**, a **system** for finding books in the library, a special **arrangement** of books, **grouped** in a new way

ordinary *(an ordinary day)* a **normal** Sunday, an **average** family, my **usual** way home, a **typical** day at school, our **regular** bus driver, a **routine** visit to the dentist, the **standard** bus fare, an **everyday** event

organisation *(a large organisation)* a big **company**, a powerful **institution**, the Chess **Association**

organise *(Dad's organised a trip to the zoo.)* Zack **planned** to go to the match with Sean. Rachel's **arranged** to meet us after school. He couldn't **manage** everything on his own. I'll **sort out** the stalls for the school fair. It's tiring **coping with** a young family.

original 1 *(an original story)* a **creative** person, a **lively** imagination, an **imaginative** drama, **innovative** software, an **inventive** comedy, an **unusual** ending 2 *(The original horses were small.)* American Indians were the **first** people in America. His **earliest** memory was feeding the ducks on the pond.

ornament *(a brass ornament)* a lace **trim** on a wedding dress, a flower **arrangement**

Christmas tree **decorations**

other *(the other side of the road)* the **opposite** side of the street, a **different** bat, an **alternative** plan

ought *(I ought to finish this letter.)* Mark **should** let me play. Dad **has to** work tomorrow. He's **got to** be there by eight. You **must** give me back my games.

outhouse

shed

log cabin

shack

lean-to

outing *(a school outing)* a **trip** to town, a day's **journey**, a coach **tour**, a short **drive**, a bus **ride**, an **excursion** to see the seals

outside *(Let's play outside this afternoon.)* going **outdoors**, playing **in the open air**

outwit *(Our gang outwitted Chris's gang.)* We **fooled** them into thinking we'd gone. We **tricked** them out of the prize. It's easy to **outsmart** them. The general **outmanoeuvred** the enemy.

over 1 *(over your heads)* **above** the door, **higher than** the trees **2** *(over ten kilos.)* **more than** two metres tall, people **above** the age of 65, marks that are **better than** average **3** *(The term's over.)* The film's **finished**. It **closes** with a wedding. Nana will be glad when the winter **ends**. **4** *(He played the CD over and over.)* He's playing it **again and again**. She **repeated** what she'd said. You're playing it too **often**.

owe *(You owe me 50p.)* You **borrowed** 50p. Mum doesn't want to get **into debt**.

¹own *(Her dad owns a sports car.)* Gary's **got** a red motorbike. The green one **belongs to** Mia. Every child should **possess** a dictionary. You can **keep** this sticker.

²own 1 *(Is that your own Discman?)* Joshua got a puppy of his **very own**. **2** *(I made this model on my own.)* I did it **by myself**. Gran lives **alone**. Please work **separately**.

own up *(Joanna owned up to the thefts.)* She **admitted** she'd done it. Kenny **confessed** to stealing.

o

Pp

pace 1 *(three paces forward)* Take another **step** back. In two **strides** I was free. **2** *(a fast pace)* I drive at a sensible **speed**. He ran off at a furious **rate**.

¹**pack** *(packing our cases)* They **filled** the bag with snacks for the journey. **Stuff** the cushion with foam. He **crammed** his mouth full of toast. I **loaded up** the car. We **squeezed** into the back seat. It was **jammed** with parcels. People **crowded** onto the bus. She **pressed** the coins into my hand.

²**pack 1** *(He had a pack on his back.)* a **schoolbag**, a **rucksack**, a **backpack**, a **haversack**, a **satchel** **2** *(a pack of cards)* a **set** of dominoes **3** *(a pack of ten cans of drink)* a **packet** of sweets, a **box** of fudge, a **bag** of crisps

packet *(a packet of sweets)* a **box** of fudge, a **bag** of crisps, a **parcel** of clothes, a **package** of books, a **bundle** of magazines

pad 1 *(a notepad)* a **block** of A4 paper, a plain **notebook**, a school **jotter** **2** *(pads to protect your knees)* Put some **padding** in your trousers for the bouncy castle!

paddle 1 *(paddling in the sea)* She **waded** across the stream. **2** *(paddling a boat)* Richard **rowed** across the lake.

pain 1 *(a pain in my chest)* I had an **ache** in my side. He felt a **twinge** of stiffness after climbing up the hill. My legs were **hurting**. **2** *(He was in pain.)* The man was in **agony**. The doctor gave him something to stop his **suffering**.

painful *(a painful bruise)* an **aching** head, a **sore** knee, a **bruised** arm, a **throbbing** tooth, a **stinging** eye, **excruciating** pain

¹**paint** *(red paint)* putting some **colour** on the flowers, colouring with **inks**, some pink hair **dye**

p

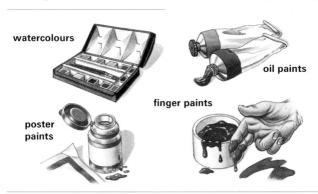

watercolours

oil paints

finger paints

poster paints

²**paint** *(painting the table yellow)*
colouring a drawing, **dyeing**
some cloth, **decorating** the room

painting 1 *(a painting of a bird)*
There's a **picture** of Joanne.
The **illustrations** in this book
are beautiful. This game's got
great **graphics**. 2 *(I enjoy
painting.)* good at **art**, an
exhibition of our **artwork**, bad
at **drawing**

pair *(a pair of shoes)* a **couple** of
minutes, **two shirts**, **twin**
towns, a piano **duet**

palace *(Buckingham Palace)*
a **mansion**, a **manor house**,
a **castle**, a **stately home**

pale 1 *(pale blue)* **light** green,
faded jeans, a **washed-out** shirt
2 *(a pale face)* a **colourless**
face. Ben went **white** and
was sick.

pan *(a cooking pan)*

pant *(panting as he ran up the
hill)* He **puffed** as he climbed to
the top. Nan **wheezes** at night.
I **gasped** with surprise.

papers 1 *(That fire's been in the
papers.)* The **newspapers** used
the story. The head teacher,
Mr Edwards, gave an interview
to the **press**. 2 *(He got some
papers from the lawyers.)* They
sent us the **forms**. She's got a
lot of **paperwork** to deal with.
Please sign all the **documents**.

parcel *(a parcel of toys)* a **packet**
of sweets, a **bundle** of papers, a
bag of clothes, a **box** of fudge,
a **package** of cereal

part *(part of an apple)* a **bit** of
potato, a **slice** of cake, a **fraction**
of the time, a **section** of the
shop, a **share** of the work, a
particle of dust, a **division** of
the company, a car **component**,
a **branch** of the Post Office

wok

saucepan

kettle

frying pan

witch's **cauldron**

panic *(I ran away in a panic.)* He
jumped in **fright**. The cat leapt
up in **alarm**. The bomb scare
caused **hysteria** in the crowd.
In his **confusion** he dropped
the papers.

particularly *(particularly cold
today)* **extremely** windy,
especially wet, **unusually** dark

party *(a birthday party)* a **get-
together**, a family **reunion**, a
housewarming, a **barbecue**

pass 1 *(We passed Ben walking to school.)* We **went past** him. They **went by** in the car. We **overtook** them. The truck **proceeded** down the street. **2** *(Six minutes passed.)* Six months had **gone** by. Time **elapsed** since start: 1.26 minutes. The time to the end of school **ticked by** slowly. **3** *(Pass the sugar.)* He **handed** me his report. Lucy **gave** the note to her father. She **delivered** it last night. **4** *(to pass an exam)* Rob **scraped through** his exam – but only just. She **qualified** as an accountant.

passage *(just across the passage)* a long **corridor**, a dark **passageway**, a small **hall**, a narrow **alleyway**, a secret **tunnel**, a light **hallway**

past *(in the past)* I haven't seen Joe **recently**. I saw him **a long time ago**. In the **olden days** there were no cars.

paste *(Sara pasted a photo into her folder.)* Jim **glued** in a picture of his boat. She **stuck** a poster behind the door. Kate **attached** a note to the fridge. We've got to **fasten** the shelf onto the wall.

¹**pat** *(patting the dog)* Kiri **stroked** the cat. She **tickled** its ears and **rubbed** its back. I **slapped** the horse on the back. I **dabbed** disinfectant on the cut.

²**pat** *(I gave him a pat.)* a **stroke**, a **tickle**, a **rub**, a **dab**, a **slap**

patch *(a bald patch)* an **area** of grass, a **smear** of jam, a **streak** of oil, a **splodge** of paint, red **spots**

path *(a narrow path)* a **footpath**, a wide **pavement**, a **track** across the field, a **bridlepath**, a long **lane**

patience *(He hasn't got a lot of patience.)* She needed all her **calmness** organising the birthday party. His **self-control** was all used up. The people in the queue showed a lot of **restraint**.

patient *(Be patient!)* Keep **calm**! **Wait quietly**! **Don't complain**!

pattern 1 *(a dress pattern)* a **guide** to cut out a paper doll, a **model** of a plane **2** *(a pattern of flowers)* a Batman **design**, pretty **decorations**, a leaf **print**

¹**pause 1** *(She paused before moving her piece.)* She **hesitated** before posting the letter. Let's **delay** the match. **Wait a moment**! **Hang on**! **Hang about**! **Hold on**! **Hold it**! **2** *(Can you pause the game?)* I **stopped** the game while I answered the phone. The receptionist put me **on hold**.

²**pause** *(After a short pause, the game loaded.)* a **break** in the game, a short **gap**, a brief **interruption**, a **delay**, an **interval** in the film, a **rest**, a short **stop**

¹**pay** *(I paid £3 for a hamburger!)* I **gave** £30 for the top but Dana **spent** twice that. Charlotte **repaid** the money she owed me. She **coughed up**. What will you **earn** from your paper round? I'll **make** enough to buy a CD player.

²**pay** *(You'll get your pay when you've finished the job.)* Her **earnings** last week were £250. His basic **wage** is £300 a week. Her **salary** is £15,000 a year.

payment *(You will receive payment in two days.)* putting off **paying the bill**, a **fee** for her work, a **contribution** to the World Wide Fund for Nature, to owe two **instalments** on the TV, getting a **refund**

p

peace 1 *(He likes a bit of peace on Sundays.)* the **quiet** of the woodlands, the **silence** of night **2** *(Peace was declared in 1945.)* In the war he was in the Navy, and in **peacetime** he was a teacher. **3** *(The peace was signed in Paris.)* a peace **treaty**, a peace **accord**, a **ceasefire**

peaceful *(peaceful countryside)* a **calm** sea, a **quiet** life, the **gentle** murmur of the stream, a **still** evening, feeling **serene**

peculiar *(a peculiar smell)* a **strange** look on his face, an **odd** idea, a **weird** story, a **funny** noise, an **unusual** car, a **curious** animal, an **abnormal** fear

¹**peel** *(apple peel)* banana **skin**, lemon **rind**, walnut **shells**, tree **bark**

²**peel** *(peeling an orange)* to **skin** potatoes, to **crack** nuts

¹**peep** *(peeping round the corner)* Joshua **peeked** at my answers. Don't **spy** on us!

²**peep** *(I had a peep at the baby.)* Take a **look** at this letter. I saw at a **glance** it was marked 'Secret'. She had a quick **squint** at the postcard before giving it to me.

peg *(a clothespeg)* a picture **hook**, a **nail** in the wall

people 1 *(A lot of people like ice cream.)* Not many **folk** live on the moors. The car was stolen by a person or **persons** unknown. **2** *(People aren't perfect.)* **Humans** are the only animals to wear clothes. **Man** has polluted large areas of the Earth. They're working to benefit **mankind**. **3** *(the American Indian people)* the Chinese **nation**, the human **race**, a South American **tribe**, a **country** at war, the **population** of Derbyshire, the village **community**

perfect 1 *(a perfect circle)* There are **no mistakes** in your spelling test. You have **full marks**. a **flawless** diamond, a **faultless** performance in ice-skating, an **exact** copy **2** *(a perfect day)* **ideal** weather for a picnic, a **fine** morning, a **great** picnic spot, an **excellent** dinner, a **lovely** party, a **wonderful** film

perform *(performing a musical)* My sister is **acting** in a play. Last term the class **put on** a concert. The Lee sisters **played** some duets on the piano. They're going to **appear** in a concert.

perfume *(the perfume of roses)* a lemon **fragrance**, the **scent** of cut grass, the **aroma** of baking bread, the **smell** of new-mown grass

period 1 *(a short period of time)* We waited for a **time** outside the office. I'll be with you in a little **while**. **2** *(Mr Gray has a free period after lunch.)* We've got a double art **lesson**.

permanent *(a permanent dye)* a **regular** job, **steady** work. The film made a **lasting** impression on the children. A good education lasts **for ever**. Can I have it **for keeps**?

permit *(Children are not permitted in the bar.)* Am I **allowed** to get in free? Tom **let** Brett have a turn on his bike. Miss Grant **gave** me **permission** to go early. **May** I leave the room? **Can** I help you?

person 1 *(a kind person)* He's a strange **character**. Suppose **somebody** sees you? Dogs have a better sense of smell than **human beings**. **2** *(They paid £1 per person.)* It cost £1 a **head**. Each **individual** must pay £1. – see also PEOPLE

98

personal *(a letter marked 'Personal')* a **private** house, a **secret** code, an **individual** prize

personality 1 *(an attractive personality)* a strong **character**, a kind **nature**, a sad **disposition** **2** *(a TV personality)* a film **star**, a sports **celebrity**, a **famous person**

persuade *(I persuaded Amy to come.)* Ms Hicks **made** her **realise** she was doing something dangerous. Paul **convinced** his father that he needed a bike. He can always **talk** him **round**. Alan **tempted** Scott to get the new game. He **encouraged** him to buy it, but his parents **coaxed** him out of getting it.

phone *(I'm phoning my friend.)* Liz **rang** last night. I know why she **called**. Please **telephone** this office. I have to **contact** Mr Lewis. I **dialled** his number. Why don't you **ring** him **up**? Don't interrupt – I'm **on the phone**.

photo *(a school photo)* a book of **photographs**, a **picture** of our dog, a **portrait** of my sister, an extra **print** for Gran, colour **slides**, an **enlargement** of the wedding photo, holiday **snaps**

pick 1 *(What names did they pick for the baby?)* They **chose** Jordan Mark. First, **select** an animal name for your team. We've **decided** to play a team game. I always **go for** ice cream if it's on the menu. We **picked out** a party dress for Morag. **2** *(I picked some peas.)* The children **gathered** daisies. Will you **cut** me some roses? I've **collected** a basket of plums. They're **harvesting** the wheat. **3** *(Don't pick the scab.)* She kept **fingering** her hair. If you **touch** that cut, it'll get dirty.

pick on *(Mr Caine always picks on Kevin.)* He **finds fault** with Kevin. Mr Harris **criticised** me for interrupting. You're always **attacking** your brother.

picture *(a picture of my father)* a **caricature** of the teacher, a **sketch** of a cat, a **cartoon** of a politician

portrait of a nobleman

piece *(a piece of cake)* a **bit** of cheese, a **slice** of bread, a **lump** of sugar, a **chunk** of meat, a **hunk** of bread, a **scrap** of paper, a **sheet** of paper, **part** of a pie, a **speck** of dust

¹**pile** *(a pile of leaves)* a **heap** of grass, a **mass** of ironing, a **mound** of odd socks, a **stack** of leaves, a **bundle** of letters

²**pile** *(He piled the books on the table.)* The grass was **heaped** up. Leaves were **stacked** by the gate.

pill *(Take two pills.)* a **tablet** for your throat, three **capsules** a day, some **medicine** for a stomachache, a throat **lozenge**

pimple *(a pimple on your nose)* a **spot** on your chin, **acne** on your face, Melanie's **zits**

pin *(pinning a card to the door)* You have to **fix** the legs onto the table. He **fastened** his pictures on the wall. I **nailed** a horseshoe over the door. Let's **screw** the mirror to the bathroom wall. Stacey **tacked** down the stair carpet.

¹**pinch** *(Don't pinch me!)* Marie **nipped** me. These shoes **squeeze** my toes. His finger got **squashed** in the car door.

²**pinch** *(Grandad gave my cheek a friendly pinch.)* a **nip**, a **squeeze**

pink *(pink cheeks)* **rose**, **rosy**, **coral**, **peach**, **salmon pink**, **flesh-coloured**

pipe *(a drainpipe)* a metal **cylinder**, a **tube** of paper, a plastic **straw**

pit *(a sandpit)* a **hole** in the ground, a gold **mine**, a **crater** on the moon, a **pothole** in the road

¹**pity** *(What a pity she didn't write.)* It's a **shame** you can't come. I'm **sorry** it happened. I'm **afraid** it's my fault.

²**pity** *(He pitied the people out in the rain.)* He **felt sorry** for them. We can **sympathise** with people without food, but is that enough? I really **felt for** the little boy when he forgot his lines in the play.

¹**place 1** *(a big place)* a hilly **area**, an old **district**, a dangerous **neighbourhood**, a wet **region**, a wizard's **territory**, a small **village**, a southern **town**, the next **county**, a foreign **country**,

a pretty **spot**, the **point** where the roads meet, a different **location 2** *(the place where the gun was hidden)* the **position** of the body, the **spot** where it was buried, the **point** we reached **3** *(a place in the team)* There's a **space** for one more. I booked a **seat** on the train.

²**place** *(placing food on the table)* Anna **put** the box on the floor. I **left** a note for Mum. I **arranged** my books in the bookcase. Mr Carter **set out** the science equipment. I **positioned** the candle carefully on the cake. Mum **set down** the tray on the table.

plain 1 *(plain to see)* a **clear** signal, a **noticeable** building, an **obvious** mistake **2** *(plain blue trousers)* a **simple** pair of jeans, an **ordinary** dress **3** *(plain speaking)* an **honest** opinion, a **blunt** answer, a **plainspoken** man, an **outspoken** politician, a **straightforward** person. Let's be **frank** – it's bad.

¹**plan 1** *(a clever plan)* a **plot** against the king, a **scheme** to make money, **ideas** about what job you want to do, a building **project**, a **strategy** to win the game, a **programme** to build schools **2** *(We haven't got any plans for Sunday.)* Mum made an **arrangement** to meet her friends. Have you got an **appointment** with Dr Taylor? **3** *(a plan of the city)* a **street map** of London, a **map** of the country, a world **atlas**

²**plan** *(Bob planned to go to the match with Sean.)* I've **arranged** to see Gill. She's **organised** a meeting of the chess club. They **decided** to hold the wedding in July. He **intended** to be home at six.

plane

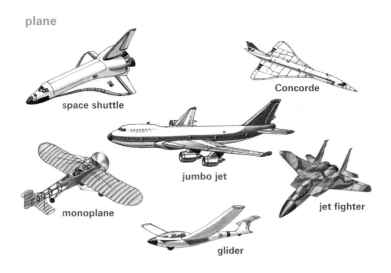

space shuttle

Concorde

jumbo jet

monoplane

jet fighter

glider

¹**plant** *(a garden plant)* Animal, **vegetable** or mineral? Grandad likes to look out on some **greenery**. There's hardly any **vegetation** in the desert.

²**plant** *(He planted some daffodil bulbs.)* I **sowed** some seeds.

plate *(a plate of biscuits)* a **dish** of vegetables, a **bowl** of fruit salad, a **platter** of cold meat

¹**play** **1** *(The children played together.)* They **enjoyed themselves** on the swings. They **had fun** on the seesaw. They **fooled about** in the paddling pool. They **messed about** in the sandpit. Joe and Ben **amused themselves** all through the Easter holidays. **2** *(Mum's playing bingo tonight.)* Would you like to **join in the game**? Our team are **taking part** in a league. **3** *(Who are they playing on Saturday?)* They're **taking on** Minsford Town.

Gunston United has **challenged** them to a friendly match. They **were against** Lobbington. Their **opponents** won. **4** *(He plays the guitar.)* I **picked out** 'Happy Birthday' on the piano. He **performed** in the school concert.

²**play** *(acting in a play)* a **drama** about the Second World War

pleasant **1** *(a pleasant neighbour)* a **friendly** teacher, a **kind** man, a **sympathetic** doctor, an **easygoing** boy, a **warmhearted** woman **2** *(a pleasant view)* **good** weather, a **fine** morning

pleasure *(It gives Gran pleasure to see us.)* The children got hours of **enjoyment** from rock pools at the beach. We wish you great **happiness**. The little boy jumped for **joy**. The friends hugged each other with **delight**. Painting gives the kids hours of **contentment**.

plenty *(plenty of chips)* **enough** to drink, **more than enough** work, **thousands** of people, **hundreds** of cars, **millions** of sweets

poetry *(Our teacher writes poetry.)* There are six **verses** in this **poem**. She likes nursery **rhymes**.

¹**point 1** *(the point of a pencil)* the **tip** of a paintbrush, the **prong** of a fork **2** *(a point of light)* a tie with red **dots**, a dog with black **spots**, a tiny **mark**, a **speck** of dirt, a **full stop 3** *(I won three points.)* winning **marks** for the team, a low **score**, a high **percentage** in the exam **4** *(There's no point in ringing again.)* It's no **use** waiting for her – she's gone home. There's no **reason** to cry about it. **5** *(At this point we'll have a break.)* At that **time**, the bell rang. That was the **moment** I fell over. **6** *(He hasn't put in all the points.)* Have you thought about these **facts**? Include the following **pieces of information** in your project.

²**point** *(She pointed to the clock.)* Paul **showed** me the way. Mrs Earp **directed** us to the office. He **aimed** the arrow at the target.

pointless *(a pointless question)* a **meaningless** answer, a **useless** journey, **unnecessary** work, a **senseless** crime, an **aimless** walk

poisonous *(a poisonous plant)* a **venomous** snake, **toxic** waste, a **lethal** dose, **dangerous** drugs, **deadly** poison

polish *(polishing shoes)* **cleaning** your boots, **shining** the brass ornaments, **scrubbing** the floor

polite *(a polite question)* a **well-mannered** boy, always **respectful**, in a **courteous** manner, a **considerate** girl. She seems **well-brought-up**.

pond *(a goldfish pond)* a paddling **pool**, a **puddle** of water, a **lake**

pool 1 *(a swimming pool)* the swimming **baths**, a **Jacuzzi 2** a **lake**, a **reservoir**, an **inland sea**, a **lagoon**

poor 1 *(a poor person)* We're not **badly off** now. You're always **broke**. I'm **hard up** too. He was only a **penniless** woodcutter. The company went **bankrupt**. A **needy** family. **2** *(poor quality)* **badly made** shoes, a **cheap** bike, an **inferior** record, **shoddy** workmanship, a **lousy** game, a **terrible** film. My drawings are just **no good**. He used **third-rate** paint. **3** *(Poor Janis!)* Janis is **unlucky**. I'm **sorry for** her.

¹**pop 1** *(Fireworks were popping all round us.)* The balloon **burst** right beside her. The bangers **exploded**. One **went off** next to our dog and he ran away. **2** *(June popped in for a cup of tea with Mum.)* Peter **came in** with her. I'm just **going out** for some crisps. Can you **run over** to Debby's with these magazines?

²**pop** *(the pop of a balloon)* the **bang** of a gun, the **crack** of a bullet

³**pop** *(pop music)* **rock** music, **rap** music, **rave** music, **house** music, **jungle**, **heavy metal**

popular *(a popular singer)* a **well-liked** boy, a **famous** brand of jeans, a **well-known** make, his **favourite** crisps

port *(a busy port)* a **harbour** for fishing boats, boats moored in the **marina**, a calm **lagoon**

¹**post** *(a lamp post)* a **pole** with a 'For Sale' sign on it, **pillars** in front of the main door, iron **columns** holding up the balcony

bollards round a car park

posh *(a posh house)* a **rich** area, an **expensive** school, a **well-educated** boy, a **snobbish** man, a **snooty** girl, **patronising**

position 1 *(in an uncomfortable position)* an **arrangement** of roses on the table, the **layout** of the hospital **2** *(The flat is in a central position.)* a convenient **place** to live, a nice **spot** **3** *(in second position)* a high **rank**, a low **level**, an average **grade** **4** *(a government position)* a good **job**, a new **post**

positive *(I'm positive I took the note home.)* Are you **sure** you had it? Yes, I'm **certain** I did.

possess *(Jean doesn't possess a winter coat.)* She does **have** a raincoat. Her dad **owns** a sports car. Gary's **got** a red bike. The green one **belongs to** Pia.

possessions *(All her possessions were in one small case.)* Have you got your **things**? Tim's **stuff**'s in the car. Collect your **belongings**, Michael.

possible *(It's possible to do it.)* It **could** snow today. Colin **might** come over. This idea's not **workable**. It's not **practical**. How **likely** is it that she'll come? There's some **possibility** she will.

²**post** *(posting a parcel)* **sending** a birthday card, **mailing** a letter

³**post** *(some post for John)* There's some **mail** for him. He's got some **letters**.

poster *(a poster of the Beatles)* a warning **sign**, a **notice** on the board, an **advertisement** for an airline, a football **sticker**

postpone *(The match was postponed till next week.)* Mum had to **put off** her trip. We **delayed** the start because of the rain. We **cancelled** the match.

pour 1 *(Water was pouring out of the taps.)* The juice **ran** out of the jug, **trickled** over the table, **dripped** off the edge and **flowed** under the door. Rain **streamed** down the windows and **splashed** into the gutter. **2** *(Pour the coffee)* **Help** yourself to a cup. She **emptied** the pot into her cup. **Tip out** the milk.

power 1 *(Electricity gives us power.)* Gas and oil are sources of **energy**. I haven't the **strength** to get out of bed this morning. She spoke with great **force** against the nuclear test. **2** *(The witch had power over the children.)* The driver **controls** the wheel. Alan had an **influence** on Scott – he got him interested in art. He had the **authority** to buy computers for the school.

p

powerful *(a powerful king)* a **strong** wind, an **influential** politician, a **mighty** emperor, a **dynamic** leader

practice *(piano practice)* sports **training**, a drama **rehearsal**

practise *(practising the piano every day)* He **trained** for the race. We **rehearsed** the play. As you **do exercises** you'll get better at it. **Work out** every day.

praise *(His teacher praised him.)* I **congratulated** her on her prize. She **admired** his drawing and **complimented** him on his story.

pray 1 *(to pray to God)* They **worshipped** in a mosque. **2** *(She prayed she'd miss the exam.)* He **hoped** the teacher wouldn't ask her to read. Kate **wished** when she cut her birthday cake.

precious *(a precious stone)* a **valuable** ring, an **expensive** necklace, a **priceless** picture, **costly** robes

prefer *(I prefer hot chocolate to tea.)* Emily **likes** horses **better** than dogs. Mrs Woodhouse **favours** the girls. She **has a preference** for green.

prepare 1 *(She's preparing a surprise for us.)* I'm **getting ready** to go out. Amanda **arranged** a visit to the zoo. She **organised** it. **2** *(Dad prepared my birthday tea.)* Mum **made** tea. I **cooked** some buns. **3** *(My brother's preparing for his GCSEs.)* His friends are **revising** too.

¹**present** (*say prez*-ent) *(a birthday present)* an anniversary **gift**, a Christmas **box**, a **reward** for good work

²**present** (*say prez*-ent) *(Everyone's present today.)* The whole class is **here**.

³**present** (*say prez*-ent) *(the present time)* **modern** cars, a **current** champion, a **recent** design, the **existing** laws

⁴**present** (*say pree*-zent) **1** *(Mr Watts presented the prizes.)* I was **awarded** the 'most improved' medal. Dad's friends at work **gave** him a set of CDs when he left. **2** *(A new broadcaster presented the news.)* The programme is **introduced** by an Asian girl.

press 1 *(Press the ENTER key.)* She **pushed** the door open. He **squeezed** the cat's tail. The spider was **squashed** flat. Jill **flattened** the papers. **2** *(She's pressing her skirt.)* Andrew **ironed** a shirt.

pretend *(I pretended to be angry.)* Kim **makes up** fantastic stories. He **fantasises** about winning the lottery. I was **daydreaming** instead of listening to Miss Howe. She often **imagines** she's able to fly. The children sometimes **tell fibs**.

¹**pretty** *(a pretty cottage)* a **lovely** day, a **beautiful** beach, a **dainty** little girl, a **good-looking** man, a **nice-looking** meal, a **gorgeous** costume, an **attractive** garden

²**pretty** *(I'm pretty sure he's taller than you.)* James is **fairly** good on his tables. That cake's **quite** nice. Phil's house is **rather** far away.

prevent *(We're learning how to prevent fires.)* We must **stop** thefts from people's schoolbags. I couldn't **help** laughing aloud. We must **discourage** smoking. Try to **avoid** burning the sugar. The robbery was **foiled** by the police. Traffic was **blocked** from coming into town.

price *(a reasonable price)* The **cost** of keeping a pet has gone up. The delivery **charge** is £10. The lawyer's **fees** are £260.

print *(We printed out our story.)* I'm **typing** a letter. She **photocopied** the letter. It was **published** in a magazine.

prison *(in prison)* in **jail**, kept in a **lockup**, the castle **dungeons**

prisoner *(a prisoner for life)* They were **captives** in the castle. A **convict** has escaped. The tourists had been taken **hostage**. Old Smith was a **jailbird**. The **inmates** of the prison staged a protest.

private *(a private garden)* Each person had an **individual** prize. Don't read letters marked 'Personal'. They may be **secret**!

prize *(a prize for the best costume)* a science **award**, a **medal** for running, a **badge** for mountain climbing, a **shield** for top swimming team, a **rosette** for Best-behaved Dog

the **FA** (Football Association) **cup**

probably *(He'll probably come after school.)* He's **likely** to bring Sean. They're **most likely** to arrive at teatime.

problem 1 *(a problem with her eyes)* There's **something wrong** with her eyesight. She's had **trouble** with it before. She has **difficulty** seeing. It's a **worry** for her family. We've run into a **snag**. We've had a **setback**. **2** *(In the puzzle book there were hard problems to solve.)* Miss Khan gave us some number **puzzles**, **riddles** and **brainteasers**. They were difficult **questions**.

proceed 1 *(The royal party proceeded along the Mall.)* They **went** slowly past. The horse-drawn coach **moved** down the road. They **advanced** towards the gates. As they **progressed**, the crowd cheered. **2** *(They proceeded to eat everything on the table.)* Bob **went on** to win.

procession *(a procession of carnival floats)* They had a **parade** of children in costumes. The protesters organised a **march** on the City Hall.

produce 1 *(He's produced some good work this term.)* She has **done** a lot. The class **made** a model of the school. We are **creating** a view of the town. **2** *(The factory produces computer games.)* **manufacturing** toys, **making** shoes, **building** a garage, **fashioning** a bird out of clay, **forming** a circle **3** *(The ref's decision produced an argument.)* The walk in the fields **brought on** her hay fever. An accident **led to** huge traffic jams. **4** *(producing a meal)* **making** tea, **preparing** a picnic, **whipping up** a snack

p

profit *(a profit of £16 on our cake sale)* The company **made money** last year. Chris's **earnings** were £30 last month. The **proceeds** from the cake sale were £16. I earn **interest** on my savings.

progress *(You've made good progress this term.)* an **improvement** in his health, great **advances** in communications. Liam's made a **step forward** in his writing. The police have made some **headway** in the case.

¹**promise** *('I'll pay you back,' he promised.)* She's **given** us her **word** that she won't tell anyone. Simon **agreed** to record the programme. I **swear** it wasn't my fault! Dad **pledged** £20 to charity. I **guarantee** I will practise every day.

²**promise** *(a promise to keep her room tidy)* Tom and his dad made an **agreement** about pocket money. I thought we had a **deal**! Keep your side of the **bargain** and I'll keep mine. The prince made a **vow** to the king. She made a **pledge** of £20 to charity. The duke swore an **oath** of loyalty to the king. He gave an **assurance** he would pay the £5.

proof *(We have proof that Doby took the money.)* The **evidence** shows that Doby was alone in the room. The police have all the **facts** they need.

proper 1 *(Her proper name is Elizabeth, but we always call her Liz.)* She wants to be called by the **right** name, but we keep forgetting. **2** *(My little sister's got a proper bike now.)* It's a **real** one, just like mine.

property *(My yo-yo was in the Lost Property box.)* Have you got all your **belongings**? Get all your **possessions** together.

protect *(The trees protected us from the rain.)* Come and **shelter** here. We'd better **keep** the money **safe**. One player has to **defend** the castle and the other attacks it. Each player must **shield** his army from the enemy.

proud 1 *(She's too proud to talk to us now she's in secondary school!)* He's very **arrogant** and rude. His sister's **conceited** because of winning the prize. That boy is always **showing off**. He's **vain** about his looks. We thought Jodie was a **snob**. She's **stuck-up**. She looks **snooty**. **2** *(You can be proud of yourself!)* I'm very **pleased** with this picture. She's quite **confident** about singing in public. William's more **self-confident** now he's enjoying school. Dad's **delighted** with his new son. Now Keith is 14, he **takes** more **pride** in his appearance.

prove *(The police can prove that Doby took the money.)* They can **show** that he was in the room alone. The fingerprints **confirm** it. We **demonstrated** that it takes two minutes to fill this tub with water.

provide *(Mrs Coles provided me with an apron.)* She **gave** her a blue one. She also **let** her **have** some paints. The school **supplies** the books. We **contributed** burgers to the school barbecue. Several parents **donated** prizes for the raffle. Lady Adams is **offering** a reward for any information on the stolen diamond. Class 6E **presented** Miss Eddis with a bunch of flowers.

public *(a public garden)* The library is **open** to everyone. It's **not private**. We walk the dogs on the **common**. Anyone can go to the **council** tennis courts.

municipal swimming pool

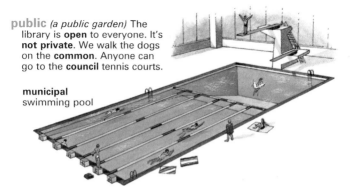

puddle *(a muddy puddle)* a **pool** of water, a **pond** in the park, **potholes** filled with water

puff *(Carla puffed as she walked up the hill.)* The dog **panted** in the heat. She **blew** on the hot soup. Grandad **wheezes** at night. Dave **breathed out** noisily. I **sighed** loudly.

puffed *(You get puffed easily.)* **out of breath**, **unfit**, **asthmatic**

pull *(pulling a scarf out of his pocket)* We **dragged** the carpet outside. He **hauled** the dripping dog into the boat. She **drew** the table towards her. He **tugged** at his mother's skirt. The truck **towed** the crashed car to the garage. Magnets **attract** iron. Grimes **pulled out** a gun.

pullover *(a blue pullover)* a **sweater**, a **jersey**, a **jumper**, a **sweatshirt**, a **top**

pump *(pumping up the tyres)* You've got to **blow up** ten balloons. I need to **put some air in** the airbed.

punch *(She punched the pillows.)* Joe **hit** Paul, who **thumped** Greg, who **bashed** Ed, who **walloped** Mark, who **whacked** Joe.

puncture *(Can you mend the puncture?)* a **flat** tyre, a **burst** tyre

punish *(Kerry was punished for lying.)* The soldiers were **disciplined** for causing a fight. The referee **sent off** two players. Dad was **fined** for speeding.

punishment *(a harsh punishment)* There's a **penalty** for not paying on time. Dale got a **detention** for not doing his homework.

pure *(pure apple juice)* It's **natural** honey. This is **real** butter. It's **not mixed** with anything else. The stream is **unpolluted**.

purple *(purple robes)* **mauve**, **violet**, **lavender**, **magenta**

purpose *(The purpose of the game is to find the treasure.)* Her **aim** is to be a lawyer. Knocking down all ten pins is the **object** of bowling. His **intention** was to smooth things over. **on purpose** *(You knocked me over on purpose!)* You got in my way **deliberately**.

purse *(I lost my purse.)* We gave Dad a **wallet** for Christmas. Mum has a pen in her **handbag**.

p

put 1 *(Denise put the cards on the table.)* Anna **placed** the box on the floor. I **left** a note for Mum in the bookcase. Mr Carter **set out** the science equipment. I've **laid** the table. I **placed** the vase carefully on the windowsill. Dad **set** the tray **down** on the coffee table. She **deposited** it on the table. **2** *(Put your age on the top.)* He **wrote** his name on the painting. **Type** the answer here. **3** *(This weather puts me in a good mood.)* It **makes** me happy. It **influences** my mood.

put away *(Jo put away her toys.)* Let's **clear** the table. It's time to **clear up** now. We need to **tidy up** the classroom.

put in 1 *(He put his foot in the water.)* I **dipped** my finger in the liquid. She **plunged** her arm in the warm bath. We had to **install** a new program. **2** *(He put in a picture of a train.)* Have you **added** Jonathan to your list for the party? I've **included** everyone from my chess club.

put off 1 *(The match was put off till Wednesday.)* Mum had to **postpone** her trip when Emma was ill. We **delayed** the start until the rain had stopped. **2** *(I was put off when someone shouted just as I was starting to sing.)* The noise **upset** me. I was **disturbed** by it. It **put** me **off my stride**.

put on 1 *(Put on your shoes.)* I'd better **get dressed**. He was **wearing** a tie. **2** *(He put on the lights.)* You can **light** the gas now. Can you **switch on** the heater? It's already **turned on**. **3** *(5F are putting on a play.)* They **staged** a concert last year, and **performed** quite well. **4** *(It's all put on – she isn't really crying.)* Rosanne **pretended** to cry. Her tears were **fake**.

put out *(to put out the lights)* Can you **switch off** the lamp? **Blow out** the candles. The firefighters **extinguished** a forest fire.

put right *(I put the clock right.)* Can you **correct** your own mistakes? Can you **edit** it? You can **improve** the spelling. You can't **make** it **better** unless you own up to lying.

put together *(They were putting a model together.)* **making** a farmyard, **fashioning** an animal out of clay, **building** a playroom, **constructing** a hospital, **manufacturing** toys, **forming** a playgroup

put up 1 *(Put up your hands.)* **Lift** your arms. Simon says, '**Raise** your heads!' **2** *(to put up a price)* The price has **increased**. It's **gone up** to a higher price. **3** *(A new building is being put up outside town.)* They're going to **build** a new library, too.

put up with *(Mum puts up with our pets.)* I can't **stand** it! How can you **bear** this noise? She can't **take** his rudeness any longer. I can't **tolerate** hot weather.

puzzle *(a crossword puzzle)* a maths **problem**, a rhyming **riddle**, a murder **mystery**, a **brainteaser**

puzzled *(You're looking puzzled.)* Annabel's **confused** about what we're doing today. I got **mixed up** about the dates. Mum's **in a muddle** – have you seen her diary? I **can't think straight** with that loud music on!

Qq

quality *(good-quality shoes)* a high **standard** of fitness. John's an **A-grade** player.

quantity *(a small quantity of sugar)* a large **amount** of white paper, a great **deal** of work, a **number** of children learning the guitar, adding another **measure** of the pancake mix

¹**quarrel** *(My sisters are quarrelling again!)* Terri and Kitty are **arguing** about whose turn it is. Stop **squabbling**, there are enough sweets for everyone. His parents are always **fighting**. They **had a row**, which everyone heard.

²**quarrel** *(a quarrel about money)* an **argument**, a **row** about homework, a **fight** about which channel to watch, a **squabble** among the children

¹**question 1** *(Can I ask a question?)* If you have any **queries**, please ask at the office. There's an **enquiry** desk on the ground floor. **2** *(Do question 8 on the next page.)* We had a hard **problem** to do today. It's a word **puzzle**. There's going to be a general knowledge **quiz** next week. What **subject** shall we talk about? This is a new **topic**.

²**question** *(The police are questioning a woman.)* They **asked** her some questions. They **interviewed** her yesterday. They **grilled** her for three hours. They tried to **pump** her for information.

¹**queue** *(a queue for the bus)* a **line** of people, a **column** of soldiers, a **chain** of children holding hands

²**queue** *(queueing for tickets)* **Line up** outside the classroom.

quick 1 *(a quick reader)* a **fast** car, a **speedy** getaway, a **rapid** exchange of fire, a **brisk** walk, a **swift** kick, an **express** letter, a **hasty** goodbye. They ran **like lightning**. She ran **at top speed**. She **went flat out**. **2** *(I need a quick answer.)* an **immediate** reply, an **instantaneous** reaction, taking an **instant** dislike to her **3** *(a quick look)* a **short** visit, a **brief** time

a **high-speed** train

quickly *(running quickly)* talking **fast**, walking **briskly**, firing **rapidly**, kicking **swiftly**, saying goodbye **hastily**, eating **hurriedly**

quiet *(a quiet place)* a **silent** house, a **peaceful** walk, the **gentle** murmur of the stream, a **still** evening, a **hushed** silence

quite 1 *(quite cold)* **rather** uncomfortable, **a bit** slow, **slightly** warmer, **fairly** good, **pretty** easy **2** *(quite unable to hear)* **all** gone, **totally** alone, **completely** finished

Rr

¹race 1 _(a swimming race)_ a **knockout**, a **competition**, a **championship**, a **tournament**, a **challenge**, a **contest 2** _(people of various races)_ Poodles and collies are different **breeds** of dog.

²race _(He raced downstairs.)_ **rushing** out of the door, **dashing** down the steps, **running** along the path, **hurrying** along, **speeding** down the road, **sprinting** past

¹racket _(a tennis racket)_

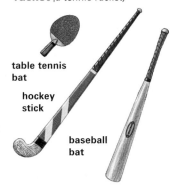

table tennis bat

hockey stick

baseball bat

²racket _(a terrible racket)_ What a **noise**! What a **commotion**! What a **din**!

rag 1 _(a floor rag)_ a **cloth** for wiping the table, a **tea towel**, a **duster 2** _(a tramp wearing nothing but rags)_ in **tatters**

¹rain _(heavy rain)_ a **downpour**, a bad **rainstorm**, a **cloudburst**, a **shower**, a thin **drizzle**

²rain _(It's raining.)_ It's **pouring, pouring with rain, raining cats and dogs, coming down in buckets**. It's **tipping down**. It's only **dripping, drizzling, spitting**.

raincoat _(a new raincoat)_ a **mac**, a **mackintosh**, **waterproof jacket, anorak, parka**, a **waterproof, oilskins**

raise 1 _(Please raise your hands.)_ Katy **put up** her hand first. Michael **lifted** the box. I can **pick up** two boxes that big! I can even **carry** my big sister. She **heaved** a case **up** the stairs. The crane **hoisted** the container into the air. He had to **jack up** the car to change the wheel. **2** _(to raise the prices of computer games)_ They **put** them **up** on Monday. All the shops have **increased** their prices. **3** _(She raised the topic of school buses.)_ Don't **mention** anything about Granny's birthday. He **brought up** the subject of pets. I **introduced** the question of higher pocket money. **4** _(raising money)_ Dad's **collecting** for Oxfam. We should **bring in** some money with our Christmas concert.

rare _(a rare stamp)_ an **unusual** car, a **unique** opportunity, fruit that is **scarce** at this time of year, **uncommon**, an **extraordinary** heatwave. People like her are **few and far between**.

rash _(a rash decision)_ a **risky** business, a **reckless** journey, a **thoughtless** act, **irresponsible** behaviour, **careless** driving, **not taking** enough **care**

rather _(rather small)_ **quite** big, a **bit** slow, **slightly** warmer, **fairly** good, **pretty** easy

raw *(raw cabbage)* **uncooked** meat, **undercooked** potatoes

ray *(the sun's rays)* a **beam** of light, a **shaft** of sunlight

reach **1** *(reaching home)* We **arrived** at the station. Your next patient's just **come**, Doctor. When do you think they'll **get** here? They didn't **appear** till midnight. James **turned up** late. **2** *(My belt reaches twice round her waist!)* The road **runs** to the river. This lane **leads to** Robert's house. **3** *(reaching for the light switch)* Can you **stretch** across for my cup? She can't **get to** to the top shelf. She's not **tall enough**.

read *(reading a comic)* I can't **make out** your writing here. He **scanned** the newspaper for interesting stories. Mark's **studying** his French books.

ready **1** *(Are you ready to go?)* A bedroom was **prepared** for the baby. When the cake's **done** we can have some. **2** *(Miss Bevan's always ready to help.)* Nobody's **willing** to lend me the money. Are we **all set**? Then let's go. The class was **all geared up** for the trip to the zoo.

real *(real leather, not plastic)* an **actual** diamond, **genuine** designer jeans, a **true** story, an **authentic** copy of a 1950s car, **not a fake**

realise *(Don't you realise how late it is?)* Lisa didn't **know** she was supposed to be in the hall. Mr Wyatt told us but she didn't **take** it **in**. I hope Wayne **understands** what he's got to do. It may **dawn on** him later, but it has not **sunk in** yet. Then he'll **wake up to** the fact that he's late. It didn't **strike me** as anything unusual.

really **1** *(I really do want to leave now.)* He's **actually** coming to our school! I **definitely** don't like carrots, but I like potatoes. **2** *(I'm really tired.)* He's **very** nice. It's **extremely** hot. It's **way** too hot.

reason *(a reason for the argument)* There's no **point** in arguing about it. What's the **cause** of those strange noises? There's no **explanation** for the noises. An oil leak was the **root** of the trouble. Aaron has no **excuse** for complaining. Even if he did call you names you have no **grounds** for hitting him.

receive *(Did you receive my note?)* Mum **got** £300 last week. How much money does he **earn**? Our stall **took** £30. The school **was given** all the money. The head teacher **accepted** it for the school.

recent *(recent news)* a **modern** house, **new** ideas, an **up-to-date** map, a **current** phone book, a **fashionable** jacket, the **latest** hit

recognise *(I don't recognise her.)* Do you **know** her? I **know** her **by sight**. Are you **familiar with** these words? I **remember** some of them. Can you **identify** the thief?

¹record (**say** re-**kord**) *(I hope you recorded the film.)* He wanted to **video** it. Can you **tape** it for me?

²record (**say** rek-**ord**) *(pop records)* a **CD**, a **compact disc**, a **tape**, a **cassette**, a **laser disc**, a **video**

recover *(Gran's recovering from her illness.)* She **got better** in hospital. She's still **convalescing** at home, but she has **got over** the flu. **Get well** soon!

red *(a red fire engine)* **red, ruby, crimson, magenta, maroon, bloodred, pillar-box red**

reduced *(The price has been reduced.)* The price has **come down.** It's the **sale** price. You can get jackets at a **bargain** price. She got a **discount** on the car.

cut-price CDs

refer *(The head teacher referred to the article in the paper.)* Road safety was **mentioned**. The head **brought up** the subject of cars parked outside the school. He **quoted** the newspaper article.

reflect 1 *(Her face was reflected in the mirror.)* The vase was **mirrored** in the polished table. Her watch **threw back** the sunlight. **2** *(The light reflected off her watch.)* The sunlight **glinted** on the water. The diamonds **sparkled** under the lights.

refuse *(He refused to give me any chocolate.)* Chris **said no** to my invitation. He had to **turn** it **down** because he's going to the doctor. He **rejected** my offer.

region *(a dry region)* the wettest **area** of Britain, a park in this **district**, islands that are the wizard's **territory**, one of the **states** of the US. Ontario is a **province** of Canada.

regret *(The headmaster regrets he cannot see you today.)* Joss is **sorry** he upset you. I'm **afraid** I wasn't very kind to him. I **wish I hadn't** said it.

regular 1 *(our regular bus driver)* my **usual** way home, a **typical** day at school, an **ordinary** tea, a **normal** Sunday, an **average** family, the **standard** bus fare **2** *(a regular beat)* **rhythmical** breathing, **steady** rain

reign *(Queen Victoria reigned for 64 years.)* In Robin Hood's time, King John **ruled** England. He didn't **govern** very well when he was **in power**.

reject *(The computer rejected the disk.)* I **turned down** the offer of a lift. Dad **refused** the free gifts.

relate *(to relate a story)* Kemal **told a story** to his sister. He **described** the match to his brother. He **reported** what had happened.

relation *(relations coming at Easter)* **members of** your **family** coming from Australia, visiting **relatives**

relax *(The boys relaxed after the game.)* Dad **enjoys** his **free time** after work. He **rests** in front of the TV. He needs to **unwind**. Ashley **feels at home** in our house.

reliable *(a reliable friend)* a person **you can count on**, a **firm** promise, a **definite** plan, a **fixed** time, a **steady** relationship, a **dependable** person, a **faithful** friend

112

relief *(It's a great relief to get home!)* It was a **help** having Gran to go to. It was a **comfort** telling her what happened. The medicine brought some **ease** from the pain.

rely *(relying on me to make up the team)* They're **counting on** me to score some goals. They **depend on** Thomas and me. They **need** us both! They **trust** us to beat the other team. I'll always **be there** for you.

remain 1 *(You must remain after school.)* Suzanne had to **stay behind**. These buns were **left**. They are **left over**. Any **spare** buns left? **2** *(Mum remained in the job even though she didn't like it.)* She **stayed** there for another year. She **carried on** but she had a new boss. They wanted her to **continue** after that. She decided **not to leave**.

¹**remark** *(a rude remark)* a funny **comment**, a serious **statement**

²**remark** *('It's getting colder,' she remarked.)* She **said** it was cold. I **mentioned** that I'd seen Kevin.

remember 1 *(I don't remember Grandad's phone number.)* You should **learn** it. It's easy to **memorise**. Does the number 585585 **ring a bell**? I've got a vague **recollection** of my aunt who died. I can **recall** her face. **2** *(Did you remember your calculator?)* Oh no, I didn't **think**! Jason **brought** his.

remind 1 *(Tod reminded me about our judo lesson.)* He **told** me it was on. He had to **jog my memory**. He **made** me **remember**. **Refresh my memory** – how old are you now? **2** *(Bert reminds me of a bird.)* He **makes** me **think** of an old crow.

remove *(Please remove your glasses.)* I **took off** my shoes. Mr Hardern **took down** the pictures from the wall. The dentist **took out** Mum's tooth. It was **extracted** without any pain. She **unfastened** the chain from her bike. I tried to **rub off** the ink. Darren **crossed out** the sum. **Delete** the file.

repair *(Judith repaired the lamp.)* Can you **mend** this plug? I can **fix** it. The man came to **service** the washing machine.

repeat *(Mr James repeated the instructions.)* He **said** them **again** to make sure we understood. Let's **go over** the dance movements. Kim **quoted** what the paper said.

replace 1 *(Replace the books where you found them.)* **Put** the bowls **back** in the cupboard. **Return** this work sheet to the folder when you've finished. **Restore** it to its proper place. **2** *(Mum showed me how to replace a light bulb.)* You need to **change** the batteries. **3** *(Mr Hunt replaced Miss Brown as head of special needs.)* He **took over from** her last term. He **substituted** for her.

reply *(to reply to a question)* I **answered** the question. The computer **responded** to the command.

¹**report** *(a report on endangered species)* The local paper had an **article** about our school. Yes, I read the **story** yesterday. There's an **account** of our science fair.

²**report** *(Louise Palmer is reporting from Paris.)* She **told the story** when she came back. John Park **described** the accident to us. He **revealed** that there had been a gas leak.

r

representative *(a representative for a software firm)* Jasmine's the local **agent** for Hula Holidays.

reputation *(a school with a good reputation)* Those computers have got a bad **name**. They want a salesman with a good **character**. The school has good **standing** in the neighbourhood.

¹**request** *(Mrs Ede requested that we come to the hall.)* She **asked** us to wait for her. The aid agencies are **appealing** for help. The children **begged** for some sweets. I **demand** to see the manager!

²**request** *(We will deal with your request as soon as possible.)* There's an **enquiry** desk on the first floor. If you have a **query**, go to the desk. Your **question** is hard to answer. an **appeal** for help, a **plea** for more money, a **demand** for better schools

rescue *(Firemen rescued two children from a blazing house.)* Ian **set** the mouse **free** from the trap.

¹**research** *(You need to research your topic first.)* You must **collect information** about transport. You need to **study** these pictures. **Look up** 'Transport' in this encyclopedia. You can **consult** a dictionary.

²**research** *(The research took three days.)* We spent the time doing our **investigations**. We did a **survey** of how we get to school.

¹**respect** *(He treated the old man with respect.)* She shows **consideration** for other people's feelings. We stared at the acrobats with **admiration**. We all **look up to** Jason. We **have a high opinion** of him.

²**respect** *(He respected the teachers.)* She **looks up to** her grandfather. I **admire** her honesty.

responsibility *(It's her responsibility to lock up.)* We all have **jobs** to do. My **task** is to put the rubbish out. He had an **assignment** to track down a drug dealer. It was his **duty**.

The mountain rescue team **saved** the climber.

responsible *(Darren is responsible for his little brother on the way to school.)* He **takes care of** Craig. He **looks after** him. She is **in charge of** 1C.

¹**rest** *(I had a rest after the swim.)* We need a **break** after this. Mum's gone upstairs for **a lie-down**. Grandpa has a **doze** after lunch. He has a **snooze**. The baby's just woken from his **nap**. I need some **relaxation** after school. I **put my feet up** and watch children's TV. At **halftime** they had a drink.

²**rest** 1 *(Grandpa rests after lunch.)* The baby **dozes off** when he's been fed. Mum's gone to **lie down** for a bit. Dad's **relaxing** with the paper. Roger was **snoozing** over his books. 2 *(Dave rested his bike against the wall.)* He **propped** himself **up** on the railing. He **leaned** against the cupboard. He **lounged** against the door. He **paused** for a moment, **leaning on** the spade.

³**rest** *(Jo drew the clown and I did the rest.)* You can eat the **remains** of the cake. She had what was **left**, but it was the **leftovers**. I ate **the last of** the cake.

restaurant *(an Italian restaurant)* a **café** with tables on the pavement, a **snack bar**, the station **buffet**, the school **canteen**

¹**result** 1 *(the football results)* What was the **score**? Here are the **marks** for your spelling tests. 2 *(the results of your actions)* They stole the money and must take the **consequences**. The weather has an **effect** on Mum's mood.

²**result** *(Gran's fall resulted in a broken leg.)* The hot weather **caused** an increase in the number of insects. The walk in the fields **brought on** her hay fever. The accident **led to** huge traffic jams.

¹**return** 1 *(Dad returned from Ireland last night.)* He **came back** at ten o'clock. When did you **get back**? What time will you **be home**? He **reappeared** at ten o'clock. 2 *(Will you return this video to the shop?)* She **gave back** her library books. She **took** them **back** on time.

²**return** *(We welcome the return of a popular series.)* Will the team make a **comeback**?

revenge *(The witch took revenge by turning the prince into a frog.)* He swore to **take vengeance** on the man who killed his brother. Laura kicked me in **retaliation** for tripping her up.

reward *(a reward for finding the money)* a science **award**, a **medal** for running, a **prize** of £20, a **badge** for mountain climbing

rich *(a rich woman)* **well-off** people, a **prosperous** country, a **wealthy** merchant, an **affluent** area *Slang:* feeling **flush**, **rolling in money**, **made of money**, **worth a packet**

rid 1 *(We got rid of our old bikes.)* Mum **gave** them **away**. Paul **sent** his sister **away** so we could play. Here's Mrs Owen – **lose** that chewing gum! 2 *(Ted's firm got rid of ten people.)* They **dismissed** Ted. He was **fired**. Gillian's been **made redundant**. He was **given the sack**. 3 *(Wonderloo gets rid of germs.)* It **kills** germs. It **destroys** insects.

ride *(We rode our bikes down the hill.)* We like **going on** the big wheel. Hayley **mounted** the pony.

right *(the right way to do it)* the **correct** answer, an **accurate** watch, the **precise** time

rind *(lemon rind)* orange **peel**, potato **skins**, walnut **shells**, tree **bark**

¹ring *(a diamond ring)* a gold **band** on her finger, a **loop** of ribbon. The animal's tail had **circles** of black and white all the way up it.

²ring 1 *(The alarm rang at seven o'clock.)* The alarm **sounded** at midnight. He **pressed** the bell twice. The old clock **chimed** in the hall. The church bells **pealed** out. The bells **jingled**. Her bracelet **jangled**. **2** *(He rang us when he got home.)* Don't forget to **phone** Bev. She didn't tell me why she'd **called**. Please **telephone** the office. I have to **contact** Phil.

³ring *(Dan gave me a ring from a callbox.)* We had a **phone call** from the police.

rinse *(I rinsed my hair.)* I **washed** the shampoo **out** of my hair.

¹rip *(I've ripped my shirt on the thorns.)* to **tear** out a page, to **split** a log in two, to **slit** an envelope with a knife

²rip *(a big rip in my best jeans)* a **tear**, a **split**, a **slit**

ripe *(a ripe plum)* Those strawberries aren't **ready to eat**. a **mature** tree, an **overripe** pear

¹rise 1 *(The sun rises.)* The balloon **went** up in the air. The eagle **soared** into the sky. The plane **took off**. Warm air **ascended** from the valley. **2** *(The price has risen by £2.50.)* The number of people with computers is **increasing**. Prices of flats have **soared** since 1960. **3** *(Early to bed and early to rise!)* **Get up**, lazybones!

²rise *(a pay rise)* an **increase** in crime, **growth** in exports

¹risk *(the risk of fire)* a **danger** of hurting yourself, the **threat** of flooding, the **hazards** of sailing

²risk 1 *(to risk your life)* to **put** yourself **at risk**, to **put** someone **in danger**. Plastic bags can **endanger** wild animals. **2** *(to risk £10 on the lottery)* to **gamble** on the horses

river

spring

estuary

stream

canal

road

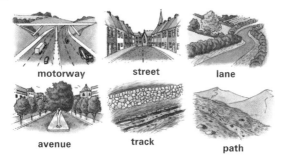

motorway   street   lane

avenue   track   path

¹**roar 1** *(I heard a lion roar.)* Wind
howled in the trees and **wailed**
in the telephone wires. The bull
bellowed. The dog **growled**.
The fighting wolves **snarled** at
each other. **2** *(Dad roared at
Fred for breaking the TV.)* 'Shut
up,' she **yelled**. 'Don't **scream** at
me, it wasn't my fault.' Grandad
bawled us **out** for waking him
up. Mum **moans** about our dirty
shoes.

²**roar** *(a loud roar of the lion)* a
howl, a **wail**, a **bellow**, a **growl**,
a **snarl**, a **yell**, a **scream**

roast *(roasting a chicken)* to
cook cakes in an oven, to **bake**
bread

rob *(They robbed me.)* He **stole
from** that girl. She was
mugged – she was **attacked** and
her purse was **taken**. The
highwaymen **held up** some
travellers. Lee **raided** the larder.
She **stole** the money. That man
took my handbag. The boy
snatched my wallet. The house
was **burgled**. During the riot,
people **looted** the stores.
Slang: The kids **pinched** his
bike. She **nicked** my pen.
They **ripped off** my camera.
Who **swiped** my bag?

Note: You use **rob** about taking
things **from someone or
somewhere**. You use **steal
about the thing that is stolen.**
You can also use **steal from a
person or place.**

robbery 1 *(There's been a
robbery in our road.)* a **burglary**
at the school, several cases of
theft, a **mugging** in the street, a
bank **raid 2** *(He's been in prison
for armed robbery.)* found guilty
of **theft**, fined for **shoplifting**

¹**rock** *(I rocked the baby to sleep.)*
trees **swaying** in the wind,
boats **bobbing** on the water

²**rock** *(a big rock jutting out of
the sea)* a **boulder**, a **stone**, a
pebble, some **gravel**

rod *(a fishing rod)* window **bars**,
a **stick** of rock, a flag**pole**, a
spoke in a bicycle wheel

roll *(The ball rolled under the
table.)* a Frisbee **spinning**
across the beach, the Big Wheel
turning

roll up *(Roll up the sails.)* She
folded up the map. **Wind up** the
window.

roof *(a tiled roof)* a **cover** over
the porch, a bus **shelter**,
cobwebs on the **ceiling**

r

room 1 *(a dining room)* an assembly **hall**, a torture **chamber**, the queen's **apartments** **2** *(No room!)* **space** for one more, two **places** on the bus, a **gap** between the words

rope *(a strong rope)* an electrical **cable**, a length of **cord**, a piece of **string**, sewing **thread**, a washing **line**

rot *(The fruit rotted.)* The melon's **gone bad**, the bacon's **spoilt** and the bread's **gone mouldy**.

rough 1 *(a rough road)* **not smooth**, a **stony** pathway, an **uneven** football pitch, a **bumpy** ride, **coarse** cloth, a **shaggy** dog **2** *(rough waters)* **not calm**, a **choppy** sea **3** *(a rough copy)* **having no details**, an **unfinished** drawing

roughly *(roughly two hours ago)* at **about** six, **around** 20 people, **more or less** time to go, **approximately** 30

¹**round** *(The Earth is round.)* a **circular** dish, a **rounded** cheek, a **curved** wall, an **oval** track

²**round** *(the winner in Round Two)* the first **stage** of the test. I reached **level** 4 of the game. I won my **heat**.

route *(the best route from London to Chester)* Can you tell me which **way** to go? Go in that **direction** for half a mile. The ship is on a northerly **course**.

¹**row** *(say like* no*)* *(a row of chairs)* a **line** of people, a bus **queue**, a **column** of figures

²**row** *(say like* no*)* *(to row a boat)* She **paddled** the canoe.

royal *(the Royal Family)* **noble** ancestors, a **regal** wave, a **majestic** ceremony

rub *(to rub your hands together)* to give your shoes a **rub**, to **polish** a table, to **scrape** the snow off your boots

rubbish 1 *(Take out the rubbish.)* a **garbage** bin, a **trash** can, **litter** in the streets **2** *(Don't talk such rubbish.)* What **nonsense**! You're talking **gibberish**. It's absolutely **wrong**.

rude *(a rude remark)* **impolite** language, **cheeky** kids, an **impertinent** question, an **insolent** child

ruin *(to ruin someone's life)* to **destroy** a city, to **spoil** a meal

ruins *(the castle ruins)* the **remains** of an old city

rule *(school rules)* the **law** of the land, parking **regulations**, the Highway **Code**

ruler *(the nation's ruler)* the country's **sovereign**, **king**, **queen**, **president**, **prime minister**

run 1 *(to run fast)* to **sprint** for a bus, to **tear** down the road, to **dash** past, to **rush** by **2** *(to run the company)* to **manage** the shop, to **carry on** the business, to **govern** the country **3** *(running water)* to **flow** down the hillside, to **fall** into a pool, to **trickle** out of a tap **4** *(a machine running smoothly)* The computer isn't **functioning** properly. It won't **work**.

run away *(to run away from school)* to **play truant** from class, to **escape** from prison, to **leave home**

rush *(to rush down the road)* to **hurry** along, to **tear** past, to **dash** by, to **charge** into the room, to **speed** away

rustle *(a rustle in the undergrowth)* the **crackle** of burning leaves, the **whisper** of the wind, the **sigh** of the breeze

Ss

sack *(a sack of flour)* a **bag** of sweets, a small **knapsack** on your back, a big **rucksack** or **backpack** for travelling a long way, a soldier's **kitbag**

sad **1** *(a sad face)* an **unhappy** boy, a **miserable** term at school, a **gloomy** look, feeling **low**, a **depressed** man, a **disappointed** player, a **pitiful** cry **2** *(a sad book)* a **heartbreaking** story, a **depressing** film, a **disappointing** game

sadness *(a feeling of sadness)* **unhappiness**, **misery**, **gloom**, **sorrow**, **grief**, **depression**

safe *(keep something safe)* to escape **unharmed**, to put something **out of harm's way**, to be **out of danger**, a **protected** hiding place, a **secure** place to keep your money

same *(to look the same)* an **identical** pen, a **similar** amount of money

save **1** *(to save someone from drowning)* to **rescue** a puppy from the fire **2** *(to save money)* to **save up** for a bike, to **store** food for the winter, to **keep** things **safe**

Pirates **hoard** their gold.

say **1** *('Yes,' she said.)* 'You're late,' she **remarked**. 'I'm hungry,' I **stated**. 'I'm Henry!' he **announced**. 'It's a fine day,' she **observed**. 'Tea's ready,' he **told** us. 'You're looking well,' she **commented**. 'I hate ice cream,' she **declared**. 'Why not?' he **asked**. 'Is my toast ready?' he **demanded**. 'Not yet,' I **answered**. 'This piece goes here,' she **explained**. 'I'm home!' she **shouted**. 'John!' I **called**. 'It's wonderful!' she **cried**. 'Oh no!' he **exclaimed**. 'I did it,' she **admitted**. 'Kate, stop it!' he **broke in**. 'Shut up,' he **whispered**. 'Don't forget to come tomorrow,' she **added**. 'Jon's already here,' he **pointed out**. 'Don't look now, but Dr Taylor's behind us!' I **muttered**. 'I love you,' she **murmured**. 'Got to go now,' he **mumbled**. **2** *(to say what you think)* to **state** your opinion, to **put** something **into words** – see also SPEAK

¹**scar** *(a scar on her face)* a **scab** on his knee, a **mark** where he'd been hit, a **wound** from a knife

²**scar** *(scarred for life)* **disfigured** in an accident, skin **marked** by spots

scare *(The noises scared them.)* to **frighten** someone, to **make** them **feel afraid**, to **terrify** them, to **horrify** them. The ghost **gave** him **a fright**. The explosion **gave** her **a shock**. She tried to **give** me **a scare**. The sight of the knife **made** my **blood run cold**. The creaking door **made** her **blood turn to water**. The ghostly moaning **made** his **hair stand on end**.

scarlet *(scarlet lips)* **red**, **crimson**, **magenta**, **maroon**, **bloodred**, **pillar-box red**

S

scary *(a scary film)* a **frightening** experience, a **weird** thing, an **eerie** noise, a **creepy** book, a **spooky** film, a **ghostly** sight

scatter 1 *(The sugar scattered all over the table.)* She **sprinkled** chocolate chips over the ice cream. We **spread** our jigsaw **out** on the table. 2 *(The children scattered.)* The gang **ran off** when the police came. The dancers **spread out** across the stage.

scene *(a colourful scene)* a funny **sight**, a beautiful **view**, an interesting **display**, a hilly **landscape**, beautiful **scenery**

scent *(the scent of roses)* a sweet **perfume**, the **smell** of bacon frying, the **odour** of burning plastic

scheme *(a clever scheme to make money)* a building **project**, a **plan** to help the elderly, a **plot** against the king

scold *(She scolded the children.)* Did he **tell** you **off**? Yes, he **ticked** us all **off**. He **gave** us a **talking-to**.

scorch *(I scorched the blouse I was ironing.)* He **burnt** the toast. The fire **blistered** the car.

¹**score** *(We scored a goal.)* to **mark up** or **chalk up** points

²**score** *(What's the score?)* The **result** was two games to one to our team. The **total** came to 15 points.

scrap *(a scrap of paper)* a **bit** of cloth, a **piece** of wood, a **shred** of cloth, a **wisp** of hair, a **particle** of dust

scrape 1 *(to scrape snow off your boots)* to **rub** paint **off** your shirt, to **remove** mud from trainers, to **scrub** dirt off potatoes 2 *(to scrape your arm)* I **grazed** my knee.

scrape through *(He scraped through his English test.)* I **just passed** the exam. She **squeezed** through the hedge.

¹**scratch** 1 *(to scratch an insect bite)* He **rubbed** the itchy spots. 2 *(The cat scratched her.)* It **clawed** the chair legs. 3 *(I scratched my new bike)* to **scrape** or **mark** paintwork

²**scratch** *(a scratch from a cat)* a **scrape** on your knee, a **graze** from falling on the gravel

¹**scream** 1 *(The baby's screaming.)* to **cry** for food, to **yell** suddenly, to **squeal** with surprise, to **shriek** with pain. Wind **wailed** in the telephone wires. The car **screeched** to a halt. The small plane **whined** overhead. 2 *(Don't scream at me! It's not my fault!)* 'Shut up!' she **yelled**. He's always getting **shouted** at. Dad **roared** at Fred for breaking the TV.

²**scream** *(a loud scream)* a **cry**, a **yell**, a **squeal**, a **shriek**, a **howl**, a **wail**, a **screech**, a **whine**, a **shout**, a **roar**, a **moan**

scribble *(He scribbled me a note.)* I **scrawled** my name at the bottom of a letter. I **doodled** while the teacher was talking.

scrounge *(The kids scrounged some sweets.)* The homeless man **cadged** a few pence off Mum. He was **begging** outside the supermarket.

scrub *(He scrubbed the frying pan.)* I **washed** my hands. She **cleaned** her boots. He **rubbed** his face with a flannel.

scruffy *(a scruffy old coat)* a **shabby** pair of jeans, a **ragged** dress, a **tatty** old bag, a **moth-eaten** jacket, a **mangy** dog

S

sea 1 *(the North Sea)* the Pacific **Ocean**, **Lake** Windermere **2** *(a sea life centre)* a **naval** ship, a **nautical** diver

Dolphins are **marine** animals.

seal *(He sealed the letter.)* **Stick down** the envelope. Pete **did up** the parcel. **Fasten** the suitcase. Hayley **tied up** the bag. The trunk's **shut** and **locked**.

¹**search** *(searching for information)* She's **looking for** her other sock. I'll just **have a look** in the washing machine. I've **been through** all the washing and it isn't there. He's **hunting for** his science book. The third son was **seeking** his fortune. The police **scoured** the area, trying to find Gemma.

²**search** *(a search of the area)* She had a **look** for the sock. The police organised a **manhunt**. They started the **hunt** for the murderer. The prince went near and far **in search of** the dragon.

seaside *(a day at the seaside)* lying on the **beach**, playing on the **sands**, close to the **shore**, a house on the **coast**, a rocky **shoreline**, a dangerous **coastline**

seat *(a wooden seat)* a plastic **chair**, a big **armchair**, a kitchen **stool**, a king's **throne**, an old **bench**, a heavy **sofa**, a low **couch**, a comfortable **settee**, a church **pew**

second *(Just a second!)* Wait a **moment**. I won't be a **minute**. Can you hold on for a **bit**? This'll only take a **jiffy**. I don't believe him for an **instant**. In a **flash** I realised who he was.

secondhand *(a secondhand washing machine)* a **used** car, a **nearly new** shop, a coat from a **charity shop**

secret *(a secret hiding place)* a **hidden** entrance, a **private** diary, a **personal** letter, **confidential** information, an **undercover** agent

see 1 *(I saw a parrot.)* I **noticed** a dove outside. Jim **observed** the birds outside his window. He could **make out** three different kinds. He **spotted** a thrush. He liked **looking at** the birds. We **glimpsed** an eagle, just for a second. Ryan **witnessed** an accident. **2** *(I see what you mean.)* Gail **understands** what I said. I don't **get** that joke. Mervin never **catches on**. I couldn't **make out** what she meant. I'll help you **get the hang of** it. Once you've **grasped** this, all the questions will be easy. Didn't you **realise** she was trying to get rid of us? I **know what you mean**. **3** *(I saw Dr Simmons in the supermarket.)* I **ran into** his daughter the other day. I **met** her outside the cinema. I always **run across** school friends there. Eliot went to **visit** his granny. **4** *(Can I go to Ken's tonight? We'll see.)* I'll **think about** it. We'll **decide later**.

S

seed *(a poppy seed)* a peach **stone**, a grape **pip**, a tulip **bulb**

seek *(seeking your fortune)* **searching** for the magic drink, **hunting** for the way into the castle, **looking** for the secret door

seem *(He seems better.)* Donna **appears** to be thinner. She **looks** very nice in that skirt. He **comes across as** very nice. It **looks as if** they aren't coming.

seize *(He seized my hand.)* She **took** my handbag. The child **grasped** the ladder. I **snatched up** my keys and ran to the door. Kyra **clutched** my arm in fear.

select *(Select disk drive C.)* He didn't know what colour to **choose**. They've **decided on** the names Catherine Anne for the baby. **Pick** a present from the pile. Alex **picked out** a puzzle. Her little brother **went for** a squeaky dinosaur.

selection *(a selection of new books)* Take your **pick** of comics. You have a **choice** – ice cream or fruit salad. There are several **options** – you can have one or two players. Make your **decision** and press ENTER. This road's blocked – is there an **alternative** we can take?

selfish *(a selfish boy)* a **mean** girl, a **stingy** person, a **miserly** old man, a **greedy** pig, a **thoughtless** woman. You're so **self-centred**; you **only think of yourself**.

sell *(She sells seashells.)* This kitten is **for sale**. They **put** their house **on the market**. Tony's **getting rid** of his secondhand bike – can I buy it? Mum's company **trades** in jewellery.

send 1 *(Yvonne sent me a postcard.)* Have you **posted** your Christmas cards? Dad **mailed** Tim his jeans. They **export** fruit. The parcel was **dispatched** yesterday. 2 *(Mrs Christie sent Donny to the Head.)* She **made** him **go** because he'd been rude. They **packed** Adam **off** to boarding school.

sensational *(sensational colours)* a **great** idea, **brilliant** work, a **wonderful** show, an **excellent** programme, a **fantastic** dancer, a **smashing** dinner, a **tremendous** performance, a **marvellous** time, **terrific** news, a **fabulous** meal, **exceptional** skill at football, a **magnificent** house, a **stunning** firework display, a **superb** cook

¹**sense** *(Use your sense!)* He can't get it into his **head**. You didn't use your **brain**.

²**sense** *(She sensed someone behind her.)* He **felt** that I was angry. They **experienced** a sudden fear.

sensible 1 *(a sensible choice)* a **practical** idea, a **reasonable** thing to do, an **intelligent** remark 2 *(a sensible child)* Sue stayed **calm** when the fire alarm went off. She is very **levelheaded**.

¹**separate** *(say sepp-*rut*)* *(The children sat at a separate table.)* They sat **apart**. The children and the adults had **different** things to eat. We had **individual** prizes.

²**separate** *(say sepp-*arayt*)* *(Her parents separated last year.)* They **parted** after ten years together. Sheena and her brother had to be **kept apart** to avoid arguments. **Split** the twig in two. We were **divided** from the rest of the group.

series 1 *(a new children's series on TV)* a **serial** in ten **parts** about a family emigrating to Australia. In last week's **episode** the children got lost. **2** *(a series of disasters)* a **chain** of events, a **string** of coincidences, in **order**, a **course** of injections, a **sequence** of numbers, a **succession** of crashes

serious 1 *(You can't be serious!)* You don't **mean it. Seriously**, did you really see a ghost? **2** *(a serious look)* a **stern** face, an **unsmiling** man **3** *(a serious illness)* a **bad** disease, a **life-threatening** accident **4** *(a serious chance of winning)* an **important** book, the **main** reason for going, a **leading** player

serve 1 *(The hotel staff serve the customers.)* Tracy **waits** on tables in the restaurant. She **looks after** the guests. She **works for** Mr Brown. Why don't you kids **make yourselves useful** and clear the table? **2** *(Mum served out the warm doughnuts.)* The maid **attended** the duchess. **Hand round** the drinks. I'll **dole** them **out. Help** yourself to biscuits. Rob **dealt out** the cards.

service 1 *(community service)* government **employment**, charity **work 2** *(a church service)* a wedding **ceremony**, a religious **meeting**, Hindu **worship 3** *(She did the old lady a service by contacting the welfare agency.)* One **good turn** deserves another! Lauren did a **favour** for Miss Palmer. **Do** Mrs Shaw **a kindness** and help her with those boxes. Jack **gave me some help** with my project.

¹**set 1** *(a set of glasses)* a **bunch** of flowers, a **group** of friends, a **pack** of cards **2** *(in the top set for maths)* in the first **year**, in seventh **grade**, in **class** 4E

a **collection** of stickers

²**set 1** *(I set the table.)* Can you **lay** another place? Kim **put** a plate for each person. James **placed** his collection of postcards on the table. **2** *(Miss Shaw set us some holiday work.)* She **gave** us a story to write. **3** *(The moon set behind the hills.)* The sun **went down** at 5.20.

set off 1 *(Kate set off early in the morning.)* It's time to **leave**. The train **departed** at 4.28. The plane **takes off** in half an hour. We **set out** at five in the morning. It's time to **make a move**. **2** *(They set off a bomb in the tunnel.)* The kids **let off** some fireworks. A terrorist **blew up** a building. **3** *(You set off the car alarm when you sat on the bonnet.)* The walk in the fields **brought on** her hay fever. An accident on the motorway **led to** huge traffic jams. This rain's **making** the pitch go soggy.

S

set out 1 *(Kate set out early in the morning.)* It's time to **leave**. I've got to **go** soon. The train **departed** at 4.28. The plane **takes off** in half an hour. We'll **start out** before dawn. We **set off** at five in the morning. It's time to **make a move**. **2** *(Set out your work in two columns.)* **Arrange** it like this. We had **put** all the chairs **in the right place**. Vivien **put** the books **in order**. **Lay** it **out** like this.

set up 1 *(The machine set up the skittles.)* They **put up** a statue to the king. They're going to **build** a new library. **2** *(Mum and Dave are going to set up a business together.)* They're **starting** a secondhand bookshop. They have to **arrange** a lot of things.

settee *(an old settee)* a big **sofa**, Grandad's **couch**

settle 1 *(Her uncle settled in Canada.)* He **went to live** in Ontario. He **moved to** a small town. He **emigrated** in 1977. Now his daughter has **made her home** in England! **2** *(This drink will settle your stomach.)* The medicine will **calm** your nerves. It's good for **treating** stomach upsets. It'll **make** you **feel better**. **3** *(The ship sank and settled on the sand.)* It **came to rest** at the bottom of the sea. A butterfly **landed** on my hand. The parrot **perched** on Steve's shoulder. **4** *(Ms Tyler settled the argument between us.)* She **sorted out** the problem. She **decided** who should have the computer first. She **arranged** for us to have equal time on the computer.

settle down 1 *(The cat settled down on my lap.)* It **made itself comfortable**. Samantha **snuggled up** on the sofa. Sam **relaxed** in front of the TV. Mum likes to **unwind** with a book. **2** *(Settle down now, and start work.)* The class **quietened down** when Miss Owen walked past. She gave us a few minutes to **calm down** after the fire drill.

several *(They saw several new computer games.)* **a few** people there, **a lot** of presents, **various** ideas

severe 1 *(a severe headache)* a **serious** illness, a **high** fever, a **heavy** cold, a **bad** winter, a **thick** frost, a **violent** storm, a **strong** wind **2** *(a severe punishment)* a **strict** teacher, a **stern** father, a **hard** woman, an **unforgiving** boss, a **stiff** penalty

sew *(Ben sewed a badge onto his schoolbag.)* I **stitched** on the button. He **threaded** the pages together. **Tack** the two sides together.

shabby *(a shabby house)* a **scruffy** carpet, a **ragged** shirt, a **moth-eaten** coat, a **mangy** dog, **tattered** wallpaper, **tatty** clothes

shack *(a tin shack)* a garden **shed**, a tiny **hut**, an old **hovel**, a **lean-to** by the garage

shade 1 *(Let's have our picnic in the shade.)* in the **shadow** of the tree, **shelter** from the sun, the winter **gloom** **2** *(There's a stripy shade on my lamp.)* We've got a **screen** to stop the sun coming in. **3** *(I don't like that shade of pink.)* a nice **colour**, red **tints** in his hair, a pink **tinge** in the sky

S

shadow 1 *(A thief lurking in the shadow.)* Let's have our picnic in the **shade**. Mum hates the **gloom** of our flat. **2** *(A shadow arose from the cave.)* a dark **figure**, the **outline** of a ship, the **shape** of a monster

His **shadow** stretched as the sun went down.

Making a **shadow** puppet

shady 1 *(a shady garden)* the **shadowy** part of the park, a **gloomy** place, a **sheltered** part of the beach **2** *(a shady deal)* **illegal** activities, an **untrustworthy** neighbour, an **untrue** statement, a **crooked** businessman

shake 1 *(She was shaking with cold.)* I **shivered** as I got out of bed. My hands are **trembling**. The leaves **quivered** in the wind. The building **shuddered** in the earthquake. **2** *(Lianne was very shaken after the accident.)* She was **upset** and **frightened**.

shame 1 *(It's a shame Gabrielle didn't win.)* It's a **pity** you couldn't be there. I'm **sorry** it happened. I'm **afraid** it's my fault. **2** *(She was crying with shame.)* She went red with **embarrassment**. She felt pangs of **guilt** and **remorse** at her mean behaviour.

¹**shape 1** *(a brooch in the shape of a bird)* a book in the **form** of a butterfly, the **outline** of a man against the light, the **figure** of a boy jumping down from the wall **2** *(Gran's in very good shape for her age.)* Keep your pets in good **condition**. The stray dog was in a bad **state**. Cycling improves your **fitness**.

²**shape** *(I shaped the clay into a ball.)* **Make** a head out of Plasticine. He **carved** the stone into a bird. The chair was **moulded** from plastic. In early spring, buds **form** on the trees.

¹**share** *(Would you like to share my crisps?)* I **divided** my biscuits with Rani. **Halve** the apple between you. Mr Day **doled out** the books. Mr Tyson **distributed** the work sheets to the class. He **dealt** them **out** so we all had one. Let's **split** the money.

²**share** *(Want a share of my apple?)* **part** of the orange, a **piece** of pie, a **bit** of cake, a **slice** of bread, two **servings** of potatoes, a **section** of the cake, a **portion** of chips, my **allowance**

S

sharp 1 *(a sharp pencil)* a **pointed** stick, a **spiked** fence, a **prickly** bush, a **spiny** hedgehog, **jagged** glass **2** *(a sharp knife)* a **cutting** edge, a **razor-like** blade **3** *(You're very sharp!)* Keep **alert** and tell me what you see. I want to see if you're **on the ball**. He's a **bright** lad. She's **clever**, too. That was an **intelligent** idea. **4** *(sharp eyes)* He's got **keen** hearing and **quick** reactions. **5** *(a sharp difference between two things)* The horizon's very **clear** today. There is a **marked** contrast between the light and shade, and a **distinct** difference between a violin and a guitar. The film's not **in focus**. A **definite** mark on the carpet. **6** *(a sharp pain)* a **shooting** pain, an **agonising** moment, a **violent** stomachache, a **fierce** headache **7** *(a sharp voice)* a **shrill** noise **8** *(a sharp remark)* a **cutting** comment

¹**shed** *(a garden shed)* a wooden **hut**, an old **shack**, a corrugated iron **lean-to**, an **outhouse**, a **log cabin**, an outdoor **storehouse**, the woodcutter's **hovel**

²**shed 1** *(The lamp shed a bright light.)* It **spread** around the room. The oil lamp **gave off** a strange smell. **2** *(The dog's shed hairs all over the furniture.)* The hairs **dropped** everywhere. Things were **scattered** round the room. The paint had **spilled** on the table. The snake **discarded** its old skin. The lorry has **lost** its load.

sheet 1 *(clean sheets on the bed)* **bed linen**, a **pillowcase**, a **blanket**, a **duvet**, a **quilt**, a **bedspread 2** *(a sheet of foil)* the **pages** of a book, a **leaf** of paper, a **layer** of pastry, an extra **thickness** of cloth, a **film** of grease

shelf *(a shelf for my videos)* a wall **unit**, a stationery **cupboard**, a **bookcase**, a kitchen **dresser**, a CD **rack**, a shop **counter**, a breakfast **bar**

shell *(a walnut shell)* the **case** of a conker, the **pod** of a pea, the **skin** of a peach, the **rind** of a lemon, potato **peel**

¹**shelter** *(The mountain sheltered us from the wind.)* The roof **protected** us from the sun. Each player must **shield** his army from attack. The trees **hid** us from the enemy. The snow **concealed** their tracks. They were **screened** by the hedge. A duvet **covered** the kids.

²**shelter** *(a bus shelter)* a sun **screen**, a wind **shield**, a tiled **roof**, a large **canopy**, a **cover** for the porch, a canvas **awning**

¹**shield 1** *(a Roman soldier's shield)* a knight's **armour**, a **mudguard**, a **buffer** for the train, **protection** from the snow **2** *(a shield against danger)* **shelter** from the cold, **protection** from crime, **safety** from the storm, a safe **haven**, a **refuge** from the rain

²**shield** *(The mountain shielded us from the sun.)* The roof **protected** us from the sun. The hedge **screened** us from the grown-ups.

shine *(The sun's shining.)* The firelight **glowed** and **flickered**. The water **gleamed**, and the fireflies **glimmered**. Tinsel **glitters**, stars **twinkle**, diamonds **sparkle** and coins **glint** in the light.

shiny *(shiny shoes)* a **polished** table, **glossy** curls, a **gleaming** car

ship

liner

pirate ship

aircraft carrier

shiver *(I shivered with cold.)*
My legs **shook**. My hands are **trembling**. The leaves **quivered** in the wind. The building **shuddered** in the earthquake.

¹**shock** *(Bob gave me a shock, bursting in like that.)* I jumped up in **alarm**. It **made** me jump! The ghost **gave** him **a fright**. They all shouted '**Surprise!**' She tried to **give** me **a scare**.

²**shock** *(Jamie tries to shock his grandparents.)* He **startled** them by swearing. They are easily **offended**. His behaviour **horrifies** them. Don't **upset** your grandparents like that. They were **appalled**. We are **dismayed** that you want to leave school. I was quite **disgusted** when the boy was so rude.

shoddy *(shoddy workmanship)* There are too many mistakes in this – it's a **slipshod** piece of work. Sam got a bad mark for her **poor** spelling and **careless** punctuation. They blamed the fire on **faulty** wiring.

shoot **1** *(The gun shoots bullets.)* Madeleine **fired** at the target. The soldiers **discharged** a volley of shots. They **bombarded** the enemy camp. They also **torpedoed** their ships. **2** *(The prisoners were shot.)* His father was **killed** in the war. A woman **was murdered** for her gold jewellery. They **executed** the murderer.

shop *(a butcher's shop)* a department **store**, a fashionable **boutique**, a market **stall**, an out-of-town **mall** and **supermarket**

shore *(a rocky shore)* the Devon **coast**, a wild **shoreline**, a sandy **beach**, golden **sands**, on the **seashore**, at the **seaside**

S

127

short 1 *(a short man)* a **small** girl, a **tiny** woman, a **little** boy, an **undersized** dog, a **skimpy** skirt **2** *(a short story)* a **brief** talk, a **concise** dictionary, a **compact** book **3** *(We're short of milk.)* We're **low** on butter, too. Strawberries are **scarce** at this time of year. **4** *(a short pause)* a **passing** moment, a **temporary** break, a **quick** thought, a **momentary** smile

shot 1 *(They heard a shot.)* the sound of **gunfire**, continuous **firing**, the **crack** of a bullet **2** *(Have another shot!)* Have another **try**. I've had a **go**. I managed it at my third **attempt**. Now you've got a **chance** to win the whole game. **3** *(Did you see that shot of the car in midair?)* a family **photo**, a school **photograph**, a **picture** in the paper, a **snap** of your pet

¹**shout** *(She shouted at the dogs.)* Neil **yelled** at me, and I **screamed** back at him. The crowd **roared** with excitement. Grandpa was **bellowing** for his tea. 'Janet!' he **called**. 'I'm coming!' she **cried**. 'We're late!' he **exclaimed**.

²**shout** *(a loud shout)* a distant **yell**, the **scream** of a child, the **roar** of the crowd, a **cry** for help, an **exclamation** of surprise, a **bellow** of laughter

¹**show 1** *(I'll show you what to do.)* She **explained** how to do it. He **demonstrated** how the new cooker works. **2** *(This test shows that Brand X washes whiter!)* The pointer **indicates** the speed. The tests **reveal** that you are very clever. **3** *(Can you show Mr Timms the way?)* She **led** him past the library to the office. Marcus **guided** his granny to the games shop.

Mr Harvey was **conducting** a party of visitors round the school. The teacher **shepherded** the children into the classroom. Zara can **accompany** you. **4** *(The picture shows a waterfall in Zimbabwe.)* It **illustrates** how beautiful water can be. The play **depicted** the life of Jesus. In the nativity play, Shaun **played** an angel.

²**show** *(We're putting on a show for the rest of our year.)* The school is doing an Easter **play**. They're also doing a **display** of dancing. There's a new **production** every year. There's a new **programme** I want to watch.

show off *(He shows off in front of my friends.)* Fiona **boasted** about her holiday. Martin **swanks** about their new car. He **gloated** about his good result. Chris **crowed** about his marks in the test.

shower *(a light shower)* a sudden **downpour**, a short **cloudburst**, a cold **drizzle**

shrink 1 *(My shorts shrank in the wash.)* They **got smaller**. They've **decreased** in size. I managed to **reduce** my waist measurement. These plums have **shrivelled** up. **2** *(Sam shrank away from the fierce dog.)* He **drew back** into his doorway. He **retreated** inside and locked the door. Lucy **winced** with pain. The dog **cringed** when it heard his voice. Mike **flinches** if you pretend you've got a snail in your hand.

shut *(shutting the window)* Please **close** the door and **lock** it. Don't **slam** it! Dan **fastened** the suitcase. Don't forget to **seal** your letters. The road's been **blocked** by the police.

shut out *(The dog was shut out.)* We **excluded** Gavin from our club.

shut up 1 *(Donald shut the dog up in the kitchen.)* Murderers are **locked up**. They **jailed** the murderer. She was **imprisoned** for life. **2** *(Why don't you shut up?)* **Be quiet**! **Stop talking**! **Silence**!

shy *(a shy girl)* a **timid** boy, a **reserved** man, an **embarrassed** smile, a **bashful** kiss, a **quiet** person

sick 1 *(He's about to be sick!)* He's going to **throw up**. Boats always make him **queasy**. He feels **nauseous**. He wants to **vomit**. **2** *(Daniel Evans is sick today.)* He **isn't feeling well**. He looks **unwell**. He's been **ill** several days this term. He's **not in good health**. He's got **something the matter with** him. He's been **poorly** all term.

side 1 *(She sat on the side of the bed.)* the **edge** of my seat, the **rim** of a cup, the **border** of the picture, the **fringe** of the crowd, dice with six **faces**, a **wing** of the hospital, the **outskirts** of a town, the **hem** of a skirt, the **margin** of a river **2** *(We've only got ten players on our side.)* a football **team**, the England **squad**, a political **party 3** *(You're always on Charlotte's side when we argue!)* You don't listen to my **point of view**. You **side with** Charlotte, but her **position** is unreasonable. **4** *(There's another side to this question.)* You have to take all the **factors** into account. Another **aspect** is: 'How much will it cost?'

¹**sigh** *(He sighed wearily.)* Paul **breathed out** noisily. Sam **groaned** with boredom. 'Isn't this boring?' she **whispered**.

²**sigh** *(a heavy sigh)* They said, with a **groan**, 'Oh, all right.'

sight 1 *(poor sight)* weak **eyes**, good **eyesight**, perfect **vision 2** *(a frightening sight)* an exciting **scene**, a marvellous **view**

¹**sign 1** *(A fever is a sign of illness.)* a **hint** of something wrong, a **clue** to the murderer's identity, an **indication** of her feelings about you, a **suggestion** of a smile **2** *(There's a sign on her door saying 'Keep Out!')* There's a **notice** about the club. I read the **poster** about the pantomime. Here's the **sticker** with the price on it. There's an **announcement** of a sale of books. I saw an **advertisement** for the new music video. **3** *(The company's sign is a ship with the company name written round it.)* Their **trademark** is Ladybird. Their **logo** is a ladybird. It's their special **mark**. The **emblem** of England is the rose. The skull is a **symbol** meaning 'Danger!'

a **placard** with a menu on it

²**sign** *(Sign the letter.)* Just **write your name** at the end. The singer **autographed** his photo. The head's **initialled** this notice about the jumble sale.

signal *(a hand signal to show he was turning left)* a **sign** for me to follow her, a rude **gesture**, a **hint** of something wrong, a **clue** to the murder

silent *(a silent house)* a **quiet** room, a **peaceful** walk, a **still** evening, a **noiseless** machine, an **inaudible** sigh

silly *(a silly joke)* a **stupid** remark, **senseless** behaviour, a **ridiculous** hat, an **idiotic** reason, a **nonsensical** book, an **absurd** idea

similar *(All the men in that family have similar noses.)* Jenny's **very like** her mother. The sisters are **alike**. They're **like two peas in a pod**. They're **identical** twins. Paint this **the same** colour.

simple 1 *(a simple sum)* an **easy** word to spell, a **beginner's** dictionary, **clear** instructions, **plain** explanations, **uncomplicated** advice **2** *(a simple jacket)* a **plain** dress, **pure** ingredients

sincere *(a sincere promise)* a **genuine** offer of help, a **trustworthy** friend, a **reliable** promise, an **honest** wish, a **real** feeling, **heartfelt** gratitude, a **truthful** statement. You could tell he **meant what he said**.

sing *(singing along with the radio)* Nicole **burst into song** as she ran out of school. She **hummed** a tune as she went home. The gang were **chanting** a rude rhyme. The canary **trilled** in its cage. Chicks were **cheeping**, sparrows were **twittering** and **tweeting**, and starlings were **chirping** and **chattering** in the park. The nightingale **called** from a nearby tree.

single 1 *(a single-parent family)* He's a **lone** parent. He's bringing up his children **alone**. Michael's his **only** son. A **solitary** tree stood in the field. One **sole** cake was left. **2** *(a single woman)* My aunt's **unmarried**. My brother wants to stay a **bachelor**. **3** *(There isn't a single thing to do.)* I've got **nothing** to eat. **Nobody** likes me.

¹**sink** *(washing saucepans in the sink)* a **tub** for soaking clothes

wash basin

washing-up bowl

²**sink** **1** *(The ship sank.)* It **went down** last night. A boat **foundered** on the reef and all the sailors **drowned**. It **submerged** very quickly. It **settled** on the seabed. They **lowered** some divers to find it. **2** *(The sun sank below the horizon.)* It **went down** at six o'clock. We saw it **set** over the sea. **3** *(Her heart sank when she saw the rain.)* Her spirits **dropped**. Hopes of saving her life **fell** during the night. Dad's hopes of a job **were dashed** when the firm closed down.

¹**sip** *(She sipped the hot tea.)* **Taste** this hot chocolate! She **drank** some of it. Josh **sampled** different fruit juices. The cat **lapped** some water.

²**sip** *(a sip of juice)* a **taste** of your drink, a little **drink** of milk, a gulp of water

sit *(We sat at the back.)* Please **sit** down. **Take** a seat. Mr Edwards **seated himself** opposite us. David **perched** on the arm of the sofa. Lara **squatted** down to stroke the puppy. Hayley **occupied** Grandad's armchair. We **relaxed** on the sofa.

site *(a building site)* waste **ground**, a **place** for the new school, the **location** of the treasure. They bought some **land** to build on. There were **plots** for three houses. The battle took place on this **spot**. The king's army started in this **position**.

situation **1** *(a funny situation)* Their marriage is in a bad **state**. In Kate's **case**, I'd run away. She died in strange **circumstances**. **2** *(the situation of the house)* a beautiful **place**, a good **position**, a nice **spot**, a central **location**

size *(What size are your shoes?)* **How big** is your TV? What's your **height** and **weight**? What's the **width** of the bed? What are your **measurements**? the **dimensions** of the computer, a man of huge **proportions**

skate *(roller-skating down the path)* You go really fast when you **roller-blade**. They **skimmed** across the lake and **glided** to a stop. Jane **slid** across the ice. He **rolled** past us.

skill *(drawing skills)* the **ability** to paint well, a **talent** for music, the **knack** of making friends easily, an **aptitude** for drawing

skinny *(a skinny girl)* a **thin** woman, a **scrawny** cat, a **bony** child, a **lanky** boy, a **lean** dog

¹**skip** **1** *(Charmaine skipped down the road.)* She **danced** into the garden, **bounded** across the lawn and **bounced** into the house. She **pranced** about in front of her bedroom mirror. **2** *(You skipped a page.)* You can **miss out** the next bit. I **left out** the 'u' in 'colour'. We **jumped** to page 34. Mrs Adams said we could **omit** the hard questions.

²**skip** *(She danced down the road, with a little skip here and there.)* The horse jumped over in one **bound**, then with a **prance**, it raced away.

¹**slap** *(He slapped her on the cheek.)* Miss, Jason **smacked** me! In the old days, naughty children might be **spanked** on the bottom.

²**slap** *(a slap on the cheek)* a **smack** on the leg, a **spank** on the bottom

S

¹**sleep** *(I slept for ten hours last night.)* Dad's **drowsing** in front of the TV. The cat's **snoozing** on his lap. He **nodded off** a few minutes ago. Marcie **dozed off** at school. Jason **went to bed** early last night. He **turned in** at nine o'clock and **dropped off** a few minutes later. 'She **hit the sack** then?'–'Yes, she **crashed out** early.'

²**sleep** *(a deep sleep)* a short **nap**, a light **doze**, a little **snooze**, some **shut-eye**

sleepy *(feeling sleepy)* **tired**, **drowsy**, **weary**, **exhausted**, **worn out** *Slang:* **bushed**, **whacked**, **knackered**

¹**slice** *(a slice of pie)* a **bit** of bread, a **sliver** of cheese, a **serving** of meat

a **piece** of cake

²**slice** *(slicing the pie)* to **cut up** an apple, to **carve** the chicken, to **chop** the onion, to **grate** the cheese, to **mince** the meat

slide 1 *(to slide down the hill)* I **slipped** on a banana skin and **slithered** across the pavement. The skaters **glided** across the ice and **skimmed** out of sight. **2** *(He slid a plate towards me.)* Then he **pushed** the butter across the table, **shoved** the jam after it and **thrust** a knife into my hands.

slight *(a slight temperature)* a **bit** of a cold, a **little** noise, a **hint** of snow, a **soft** tap on the door, a **light** breeze

slim *(a slim boy)* a **slender** girl, a **thin** woman, a **lean** body, a **slight** build

¹**slip 1** *(Mind you don't slip.)* Mrs Thatcher **tripped** on the steps. She **fell down**. He **stumbled** over the cat. The child **tottered**. **2** *(The ice cube slipped through his fingers.)* We **slid** down the sand dune. A canoe **glided** through the water. The soap **slithered** out of my hands. The car **skidded** on the icy road.

²**slip** *(You made a slip in this sum.)* a **slip-up** in the arrangements, a **mistake** in her spelling test, an **error** message on the computer, a **fault** in the game disk

slippery *(slippery hands)* a **slimy** worm, a **greasy** handle, an **oily** road, a **smooth** surface, an **icy** path

slit *(making a slit in the envelope)* a **cut** on her leg, a **crack** in the window, a **split** in the jeans, a **gash** on his head

slope *(a slippery slope)* on a **hill**, a grassy **hillside**, a river **bank**, at a **slant**

slow 1 *(a slow walk)* an **unhurried** look round the museum, a **gradual** improvement in your health, a **leisurely** stroll, a **lazy** swim, a **sluggish** river **2** *(a slow game)* a **boring** speech, **uninteresting** lessons, a **dull** afternoon **3** *(slow on the uptake)* a **stupid** man, a **dumb** kid, an **unintelligent** boy

¹**smack** *(Mum, Sheona smacked me!)* She **slapped** me on the cheek. She deserves to be **spanked** herself.

S

²**smack** *(a smack on the bottom)* a **slap** on the cheek, a **spank** on the legs

small *(a small boy)* a **little** dog, a **tiny** child, a **short** woman, a **teeny** shirt, a **weeny** bit, a **wee** baby, a **titchy** playing field, a **toy** dog, a **minute** kitten, a **miniature** pony, a **pocket** dictionary, a **compact** computer, a **mini**-series

smart 1 *(a smart coat)* a **fashionable** club, a **stylish** jacket, an **elegant** suit, a **neat** haircut **2** *(a smart move)* a **clever** boy, an **intelligent** girl, **brainy** children, a **bright** idea, a **brilliant** answer, a **sharp** reply, a **quick** reaction

¹**smash** *(I smashed the vase.)* He **broke** my radio. The car **crashed** into the tree. The windscreen **shattered**. The shells were **crushed** under his feet. I **snapped** the pencil. The plate **cracked**.

²**smash** *(a car smash)* a **crash**, a **collision** between two trucks, a bad **accident**

¹**smell** *(a funny smell)* the **scent** of roses, a flowery **perfume**, lemony **fragrance**, the **stink** of diesel fumes, the **odour** of cabbage, the **aroma** of coffee

²**smell 1** *(The food smells delicious.)* The flowers **gave off** a strong **scent**. Her notepaper was **scented** with roses. The bath oil was **perfumed** with peaches. The garage **stank** of petrol. The room **reeked** of cigarette smoke. **2** *(I smelt the soap.)* Angela **sniffed** the flower. We **breathed in** the **smell** of frying bacon.

¹**smile** *(I smiled at Neil.)* The boys **grinned** at me from the back of the bus. Louisa **beamed** when she won her prize. She **smirked** and said, 'I told you so.'

²**smile** *(a happy smile)* a broad **grin**, a **beam** of joy, a silly **smirk**

smooth 1 *(a smooth lawn)* a **flat** road, a **level** playing field, an **even** coat of paint, a **calm** sea **2** *(smooth skin)* a **polished** table, **glossy** hair, a **slippery** path

a **sleek** dog

snatch *(She snatched the sweets from Julie.)* She **grabbed** my pencil case from my desk. That man **took** my bag! Cody **pounced** on the doughnut. Police **seized** thousands of pounds' worth of drugs.

sneak *(I sneaked into the back of the room.)* Ray **crept** into the kitchen and **slipped out** of the back door. The thief **prowled** round the house, **crawled** past the windows and **skulked** outside the door.

sniff *(Angela sniffed the flower.)* I **smelt** the soap. We **breathed in** the **smell** of frying bacon. Police dogs **detected** the drugs.

soak *(The rain soaked my clothes.)* It **made** my jeans **wet.** It **drenched** my coat, **saturated** my top and even **wet** my shirt.

sofa *(a comfy sofa)* a new **settee,** an old **couch,** a big **sofabed**

soft 1 *(a soft bed)* a **comfy** sofa, a **squidgy** cushion 2 *(soft material)* **fluffy** toys, **silky** fur, **feathery** hair, **velvety** grass 3 *(soft fruit)* **mushy** peas, **squishy** mud, a **squelchy** field 4 *(soft music)* **gentle** rain, a **low** voice, a **faint** click, a **faraway** roar, a **murmuring** stream 5 *(soft parents)* **kind** teachers, a **sympathetic** uncle, a **sentimental** song, **feeble** excuses, a **weak** position

solemn *(a solemn promise)* a **serious** talk, an **important** moment

solid 1 *(a solid block)* a **three-dimensional** object, **firm** ice cream, **thick** soup. They played with a **hard** ball. 2 *(The milk's solid ice.)* It's **completely** frozen. It's frozen **through and through.** She had a **pure** gold necklace. 3 *(solid traffic all the way to the coast)* **heavy** traffic, a **dense** crowd of people

solitary 1 *(A solitary cow stood in the farmyard.)* Amy comes to school **alone.** She can cross the road **on her own.** He sang an **unaccompanied** song. It was a short **solo.** Michael's their **only** son. Kerry's a **single** parent. 2 *(a solitary house)* a **lonely** farm on an **isolated** hill, in a **remote** area. It's **desolate.**

solution *(a solution to the puzzle)* the **answer** to my question, an **explanation** of the problem, a peace **settlement,** a different **result** every time I add the figures up

solve *(solving a puzzle)* I **found the answer** to the problem. I **worked** it **out.** His writing was hard to **decipher.** We can **cure** the problem by working together. We can **rectify** things if we try.

He **decoded** the secret message.

sometimes *(Sometimes I get my own tea.)* **now and then,** **from time to time, once in a while. Occasionally** we go to Lisa's.

song *(a slow song)* my favourite **tune,** the last **number** on the Beatles album. I don't know all the **lyrics** but I can sing the **melody.** The choir sang **hymns** and **carols.**

soon *(Tracey's coming over soon.)* It's **not long** to our holiday. I'll be ready **in a short time.** The doctor will be free **presently.** He'll come **shortly.**

sooner 1 *(If you'd come round sooner you'd have seen her.)* Ashley came to see me **earlier.** You should have asked me **before.** 2 *(I'd sooner have a hamster than a goldfish.)* Would you **rather** watch television or play football? I'd **prefer** to watch television. Jake **likes** football **better** than television.

soothe *(Janie soothed the frightened guinea pig.)* She **calmed** it **down**. Mum **comforted** Craig when he cut his knee. The cream **eased** the pain of the cut. The vet **tranquillised** the injured lioness.

sorcery *(We played a Sword and Sorcery game.)* The conjuror did some **magic** tricks. The wizard put a **spell** on the queen. The door was locked by **witchcraft**. A witch used a **charm** to cure his illness.

sore *(a sore knee)* My ankle's **hurting**. Her fingers were **inflamed** and **painful**. My new shoe rubbed my ankle **raw**. His knee was still **tender** where he'd cut it.

sorrow *(The vicar came to express his sorrow when Uncle John died.)* She tried to forget her **sadness** by keeping busy. His lies caused his parents great **unhappiness**. He felt nothing but **misery** when his puppy died. He was filled with **grief**. It caused them much **heartache**.

sorry 1 *(Sorry I'm late.)* Jodie **apologised** for pushing me over. **Excuse me**. I **didn't mean to** make you jump. I **beg your pardon**, can you say that again? **2** *(We're sorry, but we won't be able to come.)* I'm **afraid** we'll be away. **Unfortunately**, we can't come. I **regret** not being able to come to your party. **3** *(I felt sorry that I'd upset her.)* I felt **bad** that I'd laughed at her. I was **unhappy** about it. I felt **sad** about the canary dying, **miserable** for days **4** *(Mrs Barnes was sorry to hear about Dad's illness.)* She was **sympathetic**. She gave me a look full of **pity**.

¹**sort** *(What sort of fish have you got?)* What **kind** of car is that? It's a Korean **make**. a new **type** of soft drink, six **varieties** of tomatoes, a **brand** of honey

a **breed** of guinea pig

²**sort** *(Gary sorted the bricks into piles.)* He **arranged** them by colour. He **separated** the long bricks from the square ones. Mr Timms **files** all our best work.

sort out *(a lot to sort out at the beginning of term)* Mum's got to **see to** the decorators today. Dad **deals with** our pocket money. We've had to **cope with** a lot of visitors. Mr Leigh **handles** all the school outings. Susan can't **manage** everything on her own. Miss Dennis **organised** an outing to a theme park. She **found the solution** to the minibus problem. She **found a way out**. Who will **clear up** the mystery? The police should be able to **iron** it **out**.

¹**sound** *(the sound of running water)* a loud **noise** in the kitchen, a special **tone** the phone makes if it's engaged, playing some high **notes** on the guitar, the **echo** from the castle walls – see also NOISE

S

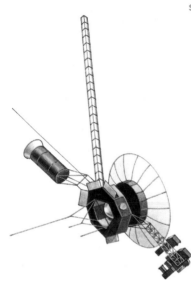

space 1 *(a grassy space in front of the school)* a **stretch** of woodland, a large **expanse** of sand, an **area** to play in. You can make **room** if you move up. There's a **place** behind the driver. **2** *(a space under the gate)* a **hole** in the hedge, an **opening** in the fence, a **gap** between two teeth, a **break** in the game, an **interval** in the play, a **crack** in the wall, a **tear** in your jeans, a **blank** in the sentence **3** *(The rock came from outer space.)* The light from distant stars comes across the **cosmos**.

Space probes cross the **universe**.

²**sound 1** *(safe and sound)* a **healthy** dog, a **fit** athlete, a **vigorous** old lady **2** *(a sound reason for leaving)* a **sensible** idea, a **reasonable** guess, a **fair** excuse, a **rational** argument **3** *(a sound player)* a friend **you can count on**, a **reliable** builder, a **trustworthy** person, a **steady** relationship

sour 1 *(sour apples)* **sharp-tasting** plums, **acid** lemonade, **unripe** grapes, strawberries that are still **green 2** *(a sour look)* a **bad-tempered** remark, a **cross** child, a **grumpy** woman, an **irritable** answer, a **peevish** girl, a **grouchy** man

sow *(They sowed pansies in the window box.)* Dad **planted** a row of beans and **put in** some shrubs.

¹**spare** *(a spare tyre)* **another** key, **some more** disks, an **extra** pair of socks, a **backup** disk, a can of petrol **in reserve**, an **additional** phone number

²**spare** *(Can you spare some money for a snack?)* I can only **let** you **have** enough for a drink. Can you **give** me a moment of your time? I can only **manage** a minute. We can't **afford** a new car.

spark *(sparks from the fireworks)* a **flash** of light, a glowing **ember**, **fire** spreading through the forest

sparkle *(sunlight sparkling on the water)* **twinkling** fairy lights, **glittering** diamonds, **shimmering** sunlight, **gleaming** raindrops, **glinting** coins

speak 1 *(Mum spoke to Tina on the phone.)* They **talked** about me. Tina was **chatting** about her new job. Tina always **gossips** for ages. You two were **chattering** all through the film. Stop **nattering**, I'm reading! I **had a conversation** with Mohan. Babies can't **communicate** properly. **2** *(Speak clearly.)* **Talk** more plainly. You **pronounce** 'rhyme' like 'time'.

special *(a special occasion)* a **particular** friend, an **important** day, a **remarkable** holiday, a **rare** opportunity, an **extraordinary** house, making your folder **different**, **out of the ordinary**, an **unusual** design, an **exceptional** book, a **unique** car

speech *(a long speech about police work)* a short **talk**, an **address** to the school, a college **lecture**, a **sermon** in church

¹**speed** *(at top speed)* a fast **pace**, a steady **rate**

²**speed** *(speeding past the school)* **hurtling** by, **sweeping** past the bus stop, **hurrying** along, **rushing** to school, **dashing** over the hill, **racing** up the mountain, **zooming** down the street, **tearing** along the road, **running** for the bus, **sprinting** down the steps, **darting** behind the door, **charging** into the room

speed up *(The train will speed up as it leaves the station.)* We asked the taxi driver to **go faster**. Mum **accelerated** when she got on the motorway. Nan **quickened** her steps when the rain started.

spell *(a magic spell)* a witch's **charm**, a wizard's **incantation**, the **magic words**, Abracadabra!

spend 1 *(He spent £3.69 on chocolates.)* I don't want to **pay** that much. Gran **gave** £5 for all these books. Ellie **pays out** pounds on the lottery but she never wins. She **uses up** all she earns. Dad thinks she **wastes** her money. All the money for repairing school buildings has been **consumed** already. **2** *(I spent an hour at the doctor's.)* **passing** a few days in Clacton, **whiling away** the time until the bus came

spike *(an iron spike)* a **nail** to hang the picture on, **studs** on his football boots, a **skewer** through the meat, a **stake** through the vampire's heart

spill *(spilling the lemonade)* milk **slopping** all over the table, cornflakes **pouring** onto the floor, tea **dripping** onto the computer keyboard, coffee **splashing** onto the books, orange juice **spraying** everywhere, water **overflowing** from the basin

spin *(The Earth is spinning in space.)* The wheels **turn round** and the train moves. The skaters **whirled** round on the ice. Tim **twirled** the Frisbee. The Big Wheel **revolved**.

spirit 1 *(full of spirit)* Kitty put a lot of **energy** into her dancing. playing with **enthusiasm**, speaking with great **force** against the nuclear test **2** *(the spirit of the dead king)* a **ghost**, a **phantom**, a **spectre**, a **spook**, a **shade**, a **ghoul**, a **zombie 3** *(the spirit of life inside us)* the human **soul**

spit 1 *(He spat when he talked.)* That dog's **slobbering** all over you. The smell of frying sausages made him **drool**. *Slang:* **gob 2** *(Take an umbrella, it's starting to spit.)* It's **drizzling** now. It's only a light **shower**.

S

spite *(She tore my book out of spite.)* She has a **grudge** against her brother. She stole his boots out of **maliciousness**. She looked at him with **malice**. She was being **vindictive**. She doesn't hide her **hatred** of me. **In spite of** *(He went swimming in spite of the red flag.)* He decided to swim **despite** the warning. He went swimming, **although** we warned him. He went **even though** we told him not to.

splash 1 *(Water splashed out of the glass.)* Her drink **spilt** on the table and **slopped** into her lap. Rain **spattered** the windscreen and **sprinkled** the pavement. Ross **showered** Tom with cola so Tom **sprayed** him with lemonade. **2** *(kids splashing about in the pool)* They **had a dip** in the river and **plunged** under the waterfall. They were **bathing** in the sea.

splinter *(a splinter in your finger)* a **sliver** of plastic, a **bit** of wood, a potato **chip**, **flakes** of chocolate, a metal **shaving**

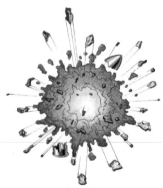

shrapnel from an exploding shell

split 1 *(He split his new jeans.)* He **tore** them on a nail. The box **broke** when I sat on it. Mum **slit** the envelope with a knife. Lightning **cracked** the old tree. The wood **splintered** into thousands of pieces. The tree trunk **fractured**. **2** *(They split the money between them.)* They **shared** the sweets and **divided** the drinks between them. The friends **separated** and went to their homes.

spoil 1 *(The slug in the salad spoilt my meal.)* His bad temper **ruined** our day out. Some kids **wrecked** the phone box. Smoking **damages** your health. The sun can **harm** your skin. Boiling the soup will **impair** its flavour. Her face was **marred** by spots. **2** *(Her parents spoil her.)* They **pamper** her. My nan **coddles** me if I don't feel well. Mr Shaw **cossets** his little dogs.

sport *(good at sport)* She likes all ball **games**. They've got **PE** after break.

¹spot 1 *(a white dog with black spots)* a skirt with black **dots**, a **point** of light, a tiny **mark**, a **speck** of dirt, a **full stop 2** *(a spot on your chin)* a **pimple** on your nose, a **zit** on your cheek, a **rash** on your chest, **acne** on your face **3** *(a pretty spot for a picnic)* a hilly **place**, the **site** of a new school, a central **position**

²spot *(Jon spotted me crawling through the bushes.)* He **caught sight of** my white T-shirt. It's easy to **see**. I didn't **notice** Jon. Can you **catch a glimpse** of him? If you **glimpse** him, tell me.

sprawl *(Fran sprawled on the grass.)* **lounging** on a sofa, **slouching** in an armchair, **lolling** around in the garden

¹**spray** *(He sprayed the pot blue.)* Paint **splashed** on the fence and **spattered** the path. Water **showered** down on us.

²**spray** *(Mum bought a glitter spray for the Christmas tree.)* The boy had a **spray can**. She has a **vaporiser** for her asthma.

¹**spread** 1 *(Lee spread butter on her toast.)* She **covered** the toast with butter and **smeared** honey on top. Soon the toast was **coated** with butter and honey. 2 *(Diseases are spread by dirty water.)* Many seeds are **distributed** by insects. Others are **scattered** by the wind. 3 *(The ocean spread in front of them.)* It **stretched out** for miles in all directions. It **extended** further than they could see.

²**spread** 1 *(a blue and yellow bedspread)* a red **cover** on the sofa, a white **cloth** on the table, a patchwork **throw** 2 *(chocolate spread)* raspberry **jam**, lime **marmalade**, blackcurrant **jelly**, peanut **butter** 3 *(They sat down to a huge spread.)* They prepared a **feast** for the wedding guests. The mayor gave a **banquet**.

spring 1 *(I sprang out of bed.)* Ross **jumped up**, **leapt** downstairs and **bounded** out of the house. **Hop** into bed! The athlete **vaulted** over the bar. 2 *(new shopping centres springing up in towns)* The town's **growing** quickly. A new shopping mall suddenly **appeared**.

sprinkle *(I sprinkled water over the flowers.)* Paddy **scattered** chocolate chips over the cake. Sarah **threw** crumbs **out** for the birds. I **dusted** the pie with sugar.

spy *(She had been a spy in the war.)* a **secret agent** for a foreign power, an **informer** for the secret police. Being an **undercover agent** is a dangerous job.

squash *(He squashed the wasp.)* Louise **crushed** the hat when she sat on it. Mick **squeezed** some oranges. I helped **mash** the potatoes. She **smashed** an egg on the side of the bowl. The sea **pounded** the rocks to sand.

¹**squeak** *(The rat squeaked.)* A bird **chirped** in the tree. The chicks **cheeped** all the time. The pig **squealed** for food. A bat **screeched** outside.

²**squeak** *(a squeak of delight)* a bird's **chirps**, **cheeps** from the chicks, the pigs' **squeals**

¹**squeal** *(The rat squealed.)* The baby **cried**. The little boy **shrieked**. The woman **screamed**. A bat **screeched**. The wolf **howled**. The dog **whined**.

²**squeal** *(the rat's squeals)* a baby's **cry**, a loud **shriek**, a **scream**, loud **screaming**, the **screech** of a bat, the **howl** of a wolf, a dog's **whine**

squeeze *(He squeezed his eyes shut.)* Moira **pinched** me. He **grasped** my arm. I **gripped** his hand. The dog **nipped** my leg.

stage 1 *(Rebecca went up on stage.)* The teachers sat on a **platform**. The winners climbed onto a **stand**. 2 *(The first stage is the easiest.)* I'm on **level** 12 already. He's doing a **Grade** III music exam. Can you read me **step** one in the instructions?

¹**stain** *(a stain on my shirt)* a **mark** on the tablecloth, a **smudge** on your cheek, a **smear** on your shirt, a **streak** of oil

²**stain** *(The juice stained my shirt.)* to **mark**, to **smudge**, to **blot**, to **smear**, to **streak**

stairs *(stairs to the second floor)* **steps** into the garden, a **flight** of steps, an outside **fire escape**

spiral
staircase

stale *(stale bread)* **old** food, **mouldy** biscuits, **dried-up** rolls, **soggy** crisps, **mildewed** potatoes

¹**stalk** *(a cabbage stalk)* a flower **stem**, a tree **trunk**

²**stalk** *(The tiger stalked a deer.)* Tigers **hunt** smaller animals. They **track** them through the jungle.

stamp 1 *(She stamped her foot.)* to **stomp** out the fire **2** *(He stamped the address on the parcel.)* She **printed** some address labels. **Mark** your paper with an 'X'.

stand 1 *(I stood and waited for Jane.)* He **stayed** outside the door. He **waited** there. The bus **stopped** in the depot all day. **2** *(Don't forget to stand when the head teacher does.)* **Stand up** while I clean under your chair. I **got up** from my chair. She **rose** and walked out of the door. **3** *(Helen stood the flowers on the table.)* She **put** them on a mat and **placed** the mat beside the lamp. I **set** the skittles **up** again. **4** *(I couldn't stand Simon laughing at me.)* How can you **bear** that noise? She won't **put up with** the neighbours being nosy. She can't **take** his rudeness any longer. Some people can't **tolerate** hot weather. He **endured** the pain bravely. Gran can't **abide** queues. Mum can't **stick** that man.

stand up for *(Vic stands up for his son.)* Will you **back** me **up** if I tell Mrs Avery what happened? She didn't **defend** me when I was in trouble. My cousin **supports** Leeds but I've always **been for** Liverpool. You **side with** whoever's winning.

stand up to *(They are afraid to stand up to Jason and his gang.)* There are government plans to **combat** crime. The teachers **took a stand against** the cuts in education. We **oppose** racism wherever we find it. The terrorists **defied** police warnings. The soldiers **resisted** the attack and managed to **ward off** the enemy. They **withstood** the attacks for days.

stare *(We stared at the weird animal.)* Lois **looked hard** at her sister. Her sister **glared** back. They **gazed** at each other. I **gaped** at her in amazement.

S

start **1** *(The race will start at 2 p.m.)* It **began** a bit late. Let's **get going.** We should **get things moving. 2** *(We started early so we would arrive in time.)* We **started out** at dawn. The train **departed** at 4.15. The plane **takes off** soon. **3** *(When did the School Council start?)* The Council **came into existence** last year. It was **sparked off** by a TV programme about a school in Bristol. **4** *(He started a decorating business.)* Later, he **set up** a company. When he **launched it** he only had two employees. **5** *(She started when the cat jumped into her lap.)* He **flinched** with pain. She **recoiled** from his touch as if she'd been slapped. It **gave** me **a fright.** It made me **jump.** The explosion **gave** us all **a shock.**

starvation *(Children were dying of starvation.)* Over half the population are suffering from **hunger.** The water shortage has caused a bad **famine.**

¹**state** *('I hate beans,' he stated.)* 'It's cold,' I **said.** She **declared** that she'd have nothing more to do with us. He **asserted** that he was captain of the team.

²**state** **1** *(Pensions are paid by the state.)* The **government** is in charge of schools. We live in a **council** house. The town library is a **public** building. **2** *(India became an independent state in 1947.)* Sudan is a big **country.** The president addressed the Italian **nation.** She comes from the **Republic** of South Africa. **3** *(Alaska is the biggest state in the US.)* My Canadian cousins live in the **province** of Ontario. The Northern **Territory** in Australia is very hot.

³**state** *(The house was in an untidy state.)* in bad **condition,** in good **shape,** in a difficult **situation,** in sad **circumstances**

state of mind *(a worried state of mind)* a nasty **mood,** a good **temper; in a state** *(in a state because he'd lost his keys)* You're getting **in a flap.** Helen was **panicking** before the exam. Don't **work yourself up** about it.

station **1** *(a railway station)* the bus **terminal,** the train **terminus,** the coach **depot,** a **stop** on the underground **2** *(He tuned the radio to a French station.)* Which **channel** is the quiz show on?

stationary *(a stationary bus)* a **parked** car. It was **standing still.** It had **come to a stop.** The bus was **at a standstill.**

stay **1** *(Terry stayed outside.)* Let's **stop** here for a moment. The kids **hung around** to see what would happen. We **waited** at the bus stop. **Hold on** till I come. He **paused** so I could catch up. Phil **lingered** in the video shop until Karen came in. **2** *(The prize goes to Ben, who stayed still longest.)* The shop **remained** closed all morning. It **kept** closing in the mornings. **3** *(My cousins came to stay with us.)* I'm **sleeping over** at Liam's tonight. We're **having** Abby **for the night.** Mum's **spending a few days** with Cathy.

steady **1** *(Hold the ladder steady.)* Are you sure the ladder's **safe?** Yes, it's completely **secure.** The computer table isn't **stable.** **2** *(a steady beat)* a **regular** pulse, a **rhythmical** drumming **3** *(a steady girlfriend)* a **regular** job, a **reliable** friend, a **constant** noise

S

steep 1 *(a steep hill)* a **sheer** drop, a **slanting** line, a **vertical** climb **2** *(a steep price)* a **high** cost, an **excessive** rise

high cliff

steal 1 *(They stole the video.)* That woman **took** my purse. The boy **snatched** her purse. The kids **pinched** my bike. *Slang:* She **nicked** my radio. Who **swiped** my snack? Someone **filched** my drink too. *Note:* You use **rob** about taking things **from someone** or **somewhere**. You use steal **about the thing that** is stolen. You can also use steal **from a person or place**. **2** *(A gang stole from that factory.)* They **burgled** the house. Then they **robbed** a bank. They **held up** the bank. Jon **raided** the fridge. He was **mugged** in the town centre. The workmen **pilfered** from the building site. Thieves **looted** a jewellery shop. **3** *(The cat stole out of the window.)* She **crept** into the garden and **crawled** through the bushes. The puppy **sneaked** into the bedroom and **wormed its way** into the bed. He **slipped away**. I **skulked** outside the classroom but Mr Benson was **prowling** through the corridors and caught me.

steam *(Clouds of steam filled the kitchen.)* A green **vapour** was coming from the cauldron. walls wet with **condensation**, a **mist** rising from the wet grass

steer *(steering a ship)* **driving** a car, **piloting** a plane, **guiding** a missile

stem *(a flower stem)* nettle **stalks**, the **trunk** of a tree

¹**step 1** *(He ran up the steps.)* There was another **flight** of steps to go. The **stairs** led to an attic. Mum put a **ladder** against the wall. I climbed the **stepladder**. I stood on the second **rung** of the ladder. We walked down the **fire escape**. **2** *(a step forward)* He took three **paces** to the right. I took another **stride** backwards. **3** *(I heard a step on the path.)* a **footstep** on the stairs, a heavy **tread** outside the door **4** *(You can make a paper dart in four easy steps.)* I'm still on the second **stage**. Have you reached the tenth **level** of the game? He's reached an important **point** in building the castle.

²**step** *(Gary stepped on a nail.)* I **trod** on Gyp's tail. Lizzie **walked** all over my puzzle!

¹**stew** *(She stewed the meat and vegetables.)* Mark **boiled** the cabbage and **simmered** the potatoes in boiling water. They **casseroled** the beef.

²**stew** *(a hearty stew)* a beef **casserole**, lamb **hotpot**, corned beef **hash**, chicken **curry**

¹**stick** *(a pointed stick)* a crooked **branch**, a **pole** sticking out of the canal, a long **pointer**, small **twigs**, a riding **whip**

²**stick** **1** *(Stick the label on the parcel.)* He **glued** the photo into the album. Rod **fixed** the stickers onto his bag. She **attached** a note to the fridge. Kate **fastened** the poster to the wall. The glue doesn't **adhere** to the shiny paper. It doesn't **grip** properly. **2** *(Just stick the bag in the cupboard.)* He **put** the saucepan on the shelf. Vanessa **put away** her painting things. **Chuck** your things in the car. **3** *(I can't stick those girls.)* Ben couldn't **stand** beans. How can you **bear** to eat meat? She won't **put up with** the neighbours being nosy. I can't **take** his rudeness any longer. Some people can't **tolerate** hot weather. **4** *(She stuck a pin in the map.)* The dentist's needle **pricked** my gum. He **jabbed** me in the arm. The knife **stabbed** him. The needle **pierced** my finger. A nail **punctured** the tyre. **5** *(Choose a topic and stick to it.)* Can you **stay** in that position? Brian **remained** loyal to his club. **Keep with** the first idea.

stick out **1** *(The nail stuck out of the wall.)* His bushy eyebrows **jutted** out. A branch **protruded** above my head. **2** *(Your brother really sticks out in a crowd.)* Carla **stands out** as the best. She zipped up her jacket so the dirty mark wouldn't **show**.

sticky *(sticky toffee)* a **gluey** mess, a **gooey** cake, paint that is still **tacky**, **gummy** sweets

stiff **1** *(stiff card)* a **hard** book cover, a **rigid** file, **inflexible** leather boots **2** *(a stiff leg)* **painful** joints, a **paralysed** arm **3** *(a stiff cake mixture)* a **thick** paste, a **solid** lump **4** *(a stiff test)* a **hard** question, a **difficult** exam, a **tough** problem, **uphill** work

still *(Keep still.)* a **calm** sea, a **stationary** bus, traffic at a **standstill**, a **windless** day, a **quiet** scene, a **peaceful** landscape, a **motionless** bird

¹**sting** **1** *(That antiseptic stings.)* My blister's **sore**. My eyes **smarted** because of the smoke. **2** *(A wasp stung me.)* The nettle **pricked** her. A mosquito **bit** him.

²**sting** *(a bee sting)* a flea **bite**, a nettle **rash**

stir *(Dylan stirred the pudding.)* Reshma **mixed** the red paint. Lisa **shook up** the orange juice. The breeze **disturbed** the leaves.

¹**stock** *(The shop stocks all kinds of sweets.)* They **had** gobstoppers **in stock**. Do they **keep** anything else? They don't **carry** biscuits. The farmer **stored** apples for the winter. The milkman also **supplies** orange juice.

²**stock** *(He's got a stock of old photos.)* a good **supply** of food, a **store** of jokes, his life **savings**, a **hoard** of gold coins, a **wealth** of stories, a hospital **fund**, a **stockpile** of weapons, a **mountain** of spare food

stone *(a round stone)* a **pebble** on the beach, a **rock** beside the sea, pieces of **gravel** on the drive, a **boulder** rolling down the mountain

stool *(a stool at the breakfast bar)* a wooden **seat**, an old **bench** – see also SEAT

S

stoop *(I stooped down to tie my laces.)* Mrs Baxter **bent** down to talk to the dog. I **leant** forward and picked up the stick. Mr Nichols **ducked** under the low doorway.

stop **1** *(The music stopped and we sat down.)* Her ballet lesson usually **ends** at three o'clock. Today it **finished** early. Fighting has **ceased** in the city. The course was **discontinued**. **Quit** the program now. **2** *(She stopped the music.)* She **broke off** the lesson. It was **cut short**. Kate **interrupted** the lesson. Dad has **given up** smoking. **3** *(The school bus stops here.)* It **pulled up** by that tree. A car **drew up**. It **halted** outside the house and **waited**. **4** *(Mum stopped Will teasing me.)* Will tried to **prevent** me from telling Mum. He **hindered** my progress on the hike. **5** *(The policeman stopped the cars.)* He **blocked** the way. The carnival floats **obstructed** the traffic. They **delayed** us for half an hour.

¹**store** *(Dad stores his garden tools in the shed.)* He **keeps** the wire on this shelf. She **saves** wrapping paper for next year. The thieves **stashed** the goods in the van. The rebels had **stockpiled** weapons. Dad **banks** most of our money.

²**store** **1** *(a department store)* a music **shop**, a **supermarket**, a DIY **centre**, a clothes **boutique**, a vegetable **market**, a market **stall** **2** *(a store of apples)* a good **supply** of drinks, a **stock** of food, life **savings**, a **hoard** of coins, a **wealth** of jokes, a charity **fund**, a **stockpile** of weapons, a **mountain** of spare food

storm *(a snow storm)* a fierce **gale**, a raging **tempest**, a terrible **hurricane**, a severe **typhoon**

story **1** *(the story of Pocahontas)* a fairy **tale**, the **legend** about the old castle, a **fable** about a greedy dog, a **parable** from the Bible **2** *(a news story)* an **article** about pollution, a **report** from Bosnia, a live **broadcast**

straight **1** *(a straight line between two points)* It's only three kilometres by the **direct** road. The picture's **not crooked** now. **2** *(Come straight home.)* Come here **at once**! You've got to phone her **immediately**. She saw me **straightaway**. **3** *(getting the house straight after Christmas)* a **tidy** room, a **neat** cupboard, a **well-organised** desk **4** *(Be straight with me.)* an **honest** statement, a **sincere** belief, a **frank** answer, **genuine** sadness, a **trustworthy** friend, a **fair** deal

straightforward *(Give me a straightforward answer.)* **clear** instructions, in **plain** English, the **obvious** way to do it, an **uncomplicated** toy, **unmistakable** orders

strain **1** *(He strained his calf muscle.)* to **twist** your ankle, to **sprain** your wrist, to **wrench** your knee, to **tear** a muscle in your hand, to **injure** yourself **2** *(straining the orange juice)* This machine **filters** coffee. I **sieved** flour and **sifted** the sugar.

stranded *(stranded on the island)* **cut off** by the tide, a **castaway** on a desert island, **deserted** miles from anywhere, an **abandoned** truck, **forsaken** by his friends, **left** to manage by yourself, **stuck** with no money

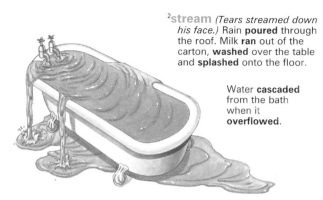

²stream *(Tears streamed down his face.)* Rain **poured** through the roof. Milk **ran** out of the carton, **washed** over the table and **splashed** onto the floor.

Water **cascaded** from the bath when it **overflowed**.

strange *(a strange man)* a **peculiar** colour, a **weird** woman, an **odd** noise, an **unusual** boat, a **baffling** question, a **curious** animal, an **abnormal** increase in pollution, a **mysterious** stranger, an **eerie** sound, an **unreal** experience, an **extraordinary** car

strap *(the strap of her handbag)* a leather **band**, a **strip** of cotton, a plastic **belt**, the horse's **reins**, a **thong** on my sandal

strategy *(the strategy of war)* a **plan** to steal the car, a **scheme** to raise money, a good **system** of working, fighting **tactics**

stray *(a stray cat)* a **lost** puppy, a **homeless** child

streak *(a streak of lightning)* a **smear** of blood, a dirty **mark**, a **line** of green paint, a blue **stripe**, a yellow **band**, a **strip** of cotton

¹stream 1 *(a cool stream)* a little **brook**, a wide **river**, a **tributary** of the Thames **2** *(a stream of water from the tap)* a strong **current**, a steady **flow**, factory **effluent**

strength *(the strength of ten men)* He hadn't got enough **energy** to run up the hill. The **force** of the water knocked him over. He tried to fight the **power** of the current. The horse kicked out **vigorously**.

stress *(Dad's suffering from stress.)* a **stressful** job, under **pressure** to do well at school, feeling the **tension**, the **strain** of working too hard, always **harassed** and **worried**, too much **responsibility**

stretch 1 *(She stretched her arms wide.)* Nancy **reached out** to hug him. He **strained** to reach the shelf. **2** *(The sweatshirt stretched when I washed it.)* It **got looser**, so I can't wear it. The nights **get longer** in the autumn. The elastic **lengthened** as she pulled it. The balloon **expanded** as I pumped more air in.

strict *(strict rules)* a **stern** teacher, a **severe** punishment, **inflexible** school rules, a **rigid** system of taking turns, **demanding** parents

S

strike 1 *(The hammer struck the nail.)* Dion **hit** his knee. He **knocked** against the chair. I **whacked** my leg on the table. How did you **bash** your chin? I **smacked** into the wall. Tamlin **kicked** the ball hard. **2** *(The clock struck two.)* The alarm **went off.** The bell **sounded** midnight. **3** *(It struck me that she was still there.)* I **realised** she hadn't left. I didn't **notice** her at first. As I looked around, I **took in** their embarrassed faces. **4** *(How did the news strike you?)* I wasn't **affected** by it. **5** *(The factory workers were striking for shorter hours.)* They **go on strike** tomorrow. They decided to **take industrial action.**

string 1 *(a ball of string)* a length of **cord,** a climbing **rope,** cotton **thread,** garden **twine,** knitting **yarn,** a fishing **line 2** *(a string of foreign words)* a **chain** of events, a **series** of crashes, **in order,** a **course** of medicine, a **sequence** of numbers, a **succession** of coincidences

¹**strip 1** *(a strip of silk)* a blue **line,** a **band** of light, a pink **ribbon,** white **stripes,** a narrow **bandage 2** *(City's new strip)* the school **colours,** wearing a **uniform**

²**strip 1** *(Steve stripped the paint off the door.)* He **removed** the top layer of varnish. I **cleaned off** several layers of dirt. **2** *(We stripped and dived into the sea.)* I **undressed** and went to bed. Jack **changed** in the changing room. He **removed** his shoes and **peeled off** his socks.

stripe *(a purple stripe)* a yellow **band,** a wiggly **line,** a **strip** of light, a **streak** of shadow

stroke *(He stroked the cat.)* He **smoothed** its fur. Mum **rubbed** my back and **massaged** my shoulders. **patting** the pony, **fondling** the baby, **petting** the guinea pig, **caressing** her cheek

strong 1 *(strong arms)* a **muscular** chest, a **powerful** machine, a **tough** guy, **brawny** arms, a **beefy** man, a **forceful** character, a **mighty** warrior **2** *(a strong colour)* a **bright** orange, a **loud** voice

¹**struggle** *(struggling to get free)* **fighting** with the enemy, **battling** against cancer, **grappling** with a problem, **striving** to win

²**struggle** *(a long struggle)* a **fight,** a famous **battle,** years of **conflict**

stubborn *(a stubborn boy)* an **obstinate** girl, a **pigheaded** person, a **persistent** fever, a **determined** person, a **tenacious** interviewer on TV, **persevering** with the sums

stuck 1 *(I was stuck on the first question.)* The second question **stumped** Dad. The third question **foiled** Alex. Mum was **defeated** by question four. **2** *(The drawer's stuck.)* The door's **jammed.** The coin was **wedged** in the corner. **3** *(We were stuck on the island all night.)* The sailors were **stranded.** The dog had been **abandoned.**

student *(a college student)* a **pupil,** a **learner** driver, a language **scholar,** a **disciple** of Jesus

study *(He's studying Chinese.)* Mum's **learning** Indian cooking. Jeremy's **doing** engineering at university. I **picked up** some Spanish on holiday.

S

¹**stuff 1** *(What's that green stuff – toothpaste?)* a sticky **substance** on the leaves, curtains made of shiny **material 2** *(Put your stuff in the cupboard.)* Where are all your **things**? Her **belongings** are here. Don't leave your **property** around.

²**stuff** *(He was stuffing himself with chips.)* I **filled** my mouth with sausage roll. She **crammed** her clothes into the bag. We **packed** our school clothes away for the summer. People **crowded** onto the train. He **jammed** his cases under the seat.

stupid *(a stupid idea)* a **silly** remark, an **idiotic** thing to say, a **dumb** suggestion, a **thick** person, **senseless** behaviour, **pointless** questions, a **daft** book, a **ridiculous** hat, a **nonsensical** rhyme, a **foolish** woman, an **absurd** story

style *(a sixties-style haircut)* the latest **fashion**, a new **way** of doing your hair, a different **version** of the game, a **trend** in computer games

substance *(a strange blue substance)* sticky **stuff**, thick **material**

subtract *(I subtracted 3 from 7.)* 3 **take away** 2 is 1. **Take** 1 **from** 9. My parents **deducted** £4 from my pocket money for the broken window.

succeed *(Linda succeeded in building the highest card house.)* She **managed** to build it six storeys high. Heather **did well** in her music test. The business is **prospering**. Richard **triumphed** on sports day. The flowers **flourished** in the pot. Kelsey **achieved** her ambition.

successful 1 *(a successful player)* the **winning** numbers, the **victorious** pair, the **triumphant** team, the **conquering** army **2** *(a successful company)* a **prosperous** family, a **flourishing** trade, a **thriving** business

suck *(The boy sucked lemonade through a straw.)* They **pumped** away the dirty water. The pipe **drained** all the water out of the aquarium.

The vacuum cleaner **drew in** all the dropped pins.

suddenly *(The door suddenly opened.)* **All of a sudden** we heard a scream. He left **in a hurry**. He came home **unexpectedly**. She closed the book **abruptly**.

suffer *(He's suffering from heart disease.)* He's **in pain**. I was **in agony** with a broken finger. Carrie's **sickening** for something. Her head's **aching**.

suggest *(Jess suggested we went go-karting.)* He **proposed** selling snacks at school. 'Try the red one,' she **hinted**.

s

suggestion 1 *(a helpful suggestion)* I've had a great **idea**. Have you got any **thoughts** about what we should give her? Mrs King had **a proposal** to make. **2** *(Here are some suggestions to help you.)* I need some **hints** on how to play. I'm not going to give you any **clues**. Take my **advice**. You need some **help**.

suit *(Pink really suits you.)* That jacket **looks good** on Sarah. The painting **fits** with the rest of the room. The colours **match** the wallpaper.

sulk *(He's sulking in his room.)* Debby **pouted** when she didn't get the strawberry on the cake. She's always **brooding** about our 'unfair treatment' of her. It's pointless to **dwell on** what's happened.

sum *(a hard sum)* Colin's good at **number work**. Miss Hill teaches **maths**. I can't work out this **problem**.

sunrise *(a red sunrise)* at **dawn**, at **daybreak**. The ship left at **first light**.

Farm animals wake at **cockcrow**.

sunset *(a red sunset)* **dusk**, **sundown**, **nightfall**, dark shapes in the **twilight**

super *(a super bike)* a **great** day out, a **wonderful** view, a **fantastic** present, a **cool** new song

supernatural *(He's interested in the supernatural.)* Things we can't explain are often called **paranormal**. **Extraterrestrials** come from other planets.

supervise *(Mr Ames supervised our football today.)* He was **in charge**. He had to **oversee** two games. He **directed** them both.

¹supply *(Viney's supplies us with software.)* They also **sell** CDs. The farm **provides** eggs for the village shop. The divers are **equipped** with special suits. The Taj Mahal Restaurant **serves** Indian food.

²supply *(a supply of sweets)* the squirrel's **store** of nuts, a **hoard** of gold, a **stock** of ammunition, all Gran's **savings**, a pension **fund**

support 1 *(Gavin supports the town team.)* They went along to **cheer for** their team. Mrs Wells **is in favour of** the new timetable. He **believes in** taking exercise every day. Mum **encouraged** me to try the curry. I **approve of** people learning to swim when they're young. **2** *(The bridge is supported by two pillars.)* Are they strong enough to **bear** the **weight**? A tree was used to **prop up** the boulder. The bridge over the stream was **held up** by a pile of rocks. The weight was **carried** by a big pole.

suppose *(I suppose you're going home now.)* I **expect** you'll win. I **imagine** I'll be here for the holidays. I **believe** she's still in Bristol. Yes, I **think** so. I **presume** you already know Dr Livingstone. He **assumes** everyone likes his stories. She **suspects** they're lying.

sure *(Are you sure it's safe?)* He's **certain** of it. Are you **positive** it won't fall down? She seems very **confident** she's right. The ladder's **definitely** as steady as a rock.

surface *(a smooth surface)* The **outside** of the computer was covered with stickers. The **top** of the sea was covered with oil. The fleecy jacket has a plastic **coating**. The books have washable **covers**. I like the **skin** on top of the custard.

Each **face** of the dice has a different number.

surprise 1 *(We wanted to give Mum a surprise on her birthday.)* Dad got a **shock** when he saw the phone bill. It was a real **bombshell** when Maria called the wedding off. 2 *(Her eyes opened wide with surprise.)* I gasped in **amazement**. The children were openmouthed with **wonder**. She cried out in **astonishment**.

surprised *(She looked very surprised when the class gave her a big bunch of flowers.)* The children were **amazed** by the circus. They were **stunned** by the trapeze artists. I was **astonished** when he left. She had a **startled** expression on her face. The audience was **dazzled** by his magic.

surprising *(surprising news)* an **unexpected** visitor, an **amazing** success story, an **unbelievable** result for City, an **incredible** piece of news, an **astonishing** story

surround *(The house is surrounded by trees.)* This sash **goes round** the waist. The police **ringed** the building. A silver chain **encircled** her neck. Her face was **framed** by curly blonde hair. The boys **crowded round** to get a better look.

suspect *(I suspect Elizabeth of taking my stickers.)* Kay **thinks** she did it. We **guessed** she'd taken something when we saw her. The police **believe** he stole the car. I **suppose** he's hidden the jewels somewhere. I **have a sneaking suspicion** that they're in the garage. I **smell a rat** – they're trying to trick us.

suspense *(The suspense kept us on the edge of our seats.)* The **tension** mounted as they reached the end of the game. The crowd buzzed with **excitement**. We were **holding our breath** waiting for the result of the competition.

suspicious 1 *(We were suspicious of him.)* We **had** our **suspicions** about him from the start. 2 *(a death in suspicious circumstances)* a **shady** character, a **shaky** excuse, something **fishy** going on, an **untrustworthy** salesman

S

swallow *(Megan swallowed her chewing gum.)* Mia **ate** a mouthful of potato and **drank** some water. Kylie **gulped down** her milkshake. The children **devoured** all the crisps while the grown-ups **nibbled** biscuits. The baby **sucked** her orange juice.

swap *(Will you swap pens for a moment?)* Can I **change** this balloon **for** a blue one? Will you **exchange** cards with me? I **traded** my stickers for this calculator.

swarm *(a swarm of bees)* a **crowd** of people, a **flock** of birds

sway *(The tree swayed in the wind.)* It **moved** from side to side. The grass **bent** under the rain. Boats **rocked** on the sea. The child **tottered** and fell over.

swear **1** *(Luke was told off for swearing in front of the teacher.)* He **used bad language** when he dropped the brick on his toe. She **cursed** the dog when it bit her. **2** *(He swore to tell the truth.)* Joe **promised** to clean out the fish tank. He's **given** us his **word**. He **testified** he had seen the man at the scene of the crime. The school has **pledged** to raise £1000 for charity.

sweat *(He was sweating after the run.)* She **perspired** in the hot sun.

sweater *(a thick sweater)* a **pullover**, a **sweatshirt**, a **jumper**, my best **top**

sweep *(John swept the path.)* He **brushed** the drive, **cleaned** the garage and **raked** the leaves into a pile. I **wiped** the table.

sweet *(a sweet drink)* a **sugary** cake, **sweetened** tea, **sickly** sweets, **sweet-tasting** milkshakes

swell *(The balloon swelled up and burst.)* The tadpoles **grew fatter** every day. The sails **ballooned** out in the wind. My hamster's cheeks **bulged** with food. The airbed **inflates** when you pump it up. Popcorn **enlarges** when it is heated. It **gets** all **puffed up**.

swerve *(I swerved out of the way.)* He **turned** quickly to get past me. Sam **dodged** the flying stone. The cat **twisted** away from him. A car **veered** round and hit a tree.

swim *(The dog swam across the stream.)* We **bathed** in the pool. They **had a dip** in the sea. He **floated** down the river and then **paddled** to the side. We **struck out** for the shore.

swing *(The gate swung open.)* An acrobat **hung** from the wire. The spider **dangled** a few inches from my nose. The clothes on the line **flapped** in the wind. Trees **swayed** in the storm. The cradle **rocked** gently.

switch **1** *(Ed switched on the lamp.)* **Turn** off the computer. **2** *(The children switched places.)* They **changed** jackets as well. Kevin **swapped** his with Tom. The magician **exchanged** the red ball and the yellow ball without lifting the cups. He **changed** them **round**.

sympathetic *(a sympathetic teacher)* a **friendly** class, an **understanding** friend, **supportive** parents, **considerate** neighbours

system *(a system of roads)* a **network** of friends, a complicated **structure**, a **framework** of rules, the correct **procedure**

S

Tt

table 1 *(a coffee table)* a teacher's **desk**, a shop **counter** **2** *(a football league table)* a **list** of contents, a **catalogue** of all the clubs, an **index** of a book, a **box** with three **columns** of figures, a file **directory**

hall **stand**

computer **console**

breakfast **bar**

tactful *(a tactful answer)* Sheila's always so **diplomatic** – she never says anything nasty. She's **polite**, and **considerate** about other people's feelings.

tactless *(a tactless thing to say)* Paul is the opposite – **insensitive** and **inconsiderate**. He says very **rash** things to people, and can sound **impolite**. **thoughtless** comments, **frank** opinions

¹**tail** *(the tail of the procession)* the **end** of the line, the **back** of the queue, the **rear** of the train, the **bottom** of the league

²**tail** *(The car seemed to be tailing us.)* You're sure you weren't **followed**? The police **tracked** the criminals to their hideout. They **trailed** them for four hours. The car was **on my tail**. Someone was **shadowing** me. The cat **stalked** the bird.

151

take 1 *(He took the game to school.)* We **got** the book from the library. I **carried** the pizza home. **2** *(He took a cake from the plate.)* I **picked up** a toy train. **Choose** a present from the tree. **3** *(Mum takes me to school.)* She **goes with** me to the gate. She **drove** me to the doctor's. The teacher **escorted** the children home. He **guided** them to the hall. Mrs Craig **shepherded** the children into the classroom. **4** *(He took Mum's hand.)* **holding** the railing, **clasping** my arm, **gripping** the rope **5** *(My money's been taken!)* **stealing** a purse, **snatching** a handbag, **pinching** a car, **removing** the jewellery **6** *(taking a train)* **catching** a bus, **getting** a taxi **7** *(It takes four hours to get there.)* The journey **used up** ten litres of petrol. We **spent** an hour at the doctor's. You **need** two days to drive to Italy. **8** *(They take credit cards.)* The shop won't **accept** a cheque. This cinema doesn't **admit** children. **9** *(Take 14 from 28.)* **Take away** 34p and you're left with 5p. I **subtracted** 24 and then **deducted** another 4. **10** *(Take two tablets with meals.)* Have you **had** your medicine? **Swallow** them with water. **11** *(The army took the town.)* **seizing** a prisoner, **capturing** a base **12** *(I take it you're staying to tea.)* I **suppose** you're eating with us. I **expect** so.

take back *(Have you taken your books back?)* She **returned** the saucepan and I **replaced** it in the kitchen.

take care of *(I take care of the gerbils.)* Miss Noakes **looks after** his dog during the week. My mum has to **care for** my grandmother now that she is ill.

take charge of *(Mrs Mitchell took charge of the class.)* Dean **manages** the factory. He **organises** everything. Val **directs** the school meals service. Who **governs** the country?

take in *(I told him my name but he didn't take it in.)* She **realised** they were waiting for her. Darrell didn't **understand** the instructions. It **dawned on** me that I was wrong.

take part in *(Are you taking part in the game?)* Tony can't **play** today. He's **competing** in the athletics trials. Each student should **participate** in some sport. My dad **is active in** the parent-teacher association. He **is involved** in organising the fête.

take place *(The carnival takes place in June.)* What **happened**? Something unusual **cropped up**. A strange event **occurred** at Weirdwood Manor.

talent *(a talent for acting)* the **ability** to make friends easily, a **gift** for music, a **genius** for getting into trouble

¹talk 1 *(You talk too much.)* You **spoke** for an hour on the phone. I **had a conversation** with Sanjay. Steve was **chatting** to his friend on the phone. You two were **chattering** all through the film. They were **gossiping** for ages. Babies learn to **communicate** by copying their parents. **2** *(talking about going for a bike ride)* **discussing** our design project, **talking over** the problem, **debating** whether to go **3** *(talking to the whole school)* The head teacher **addressed** the class. – see also SAY

t

²**talk** *(The headmaster gave us a short talk.)* a long **speech**, an **address** to the school, a university **lecture**, a **sermon** in church

talk about/over *(They talked about their families.)* Helen **discussed** the holiday with Tom. They **debated** how much pocket money to give the children. The children **shared** their feelings about bullying.

tall *(a tall boy)* a **high** tower, a **towering** peak, a **raised** walkway, a **lofty** mountain

high-rise office block

tame *(a tame pigeon)* a **trained** seal, a **housetrained** cat, a **domesticated** goat. Your hamster's very **docile**, isn't it? Yes, it's very **gentle**.

tap *(a tap on the door)* a **knock** on the window, a **bang** on the knee, a **rap** on the table

¹**tape** *(They taped the programme.)* Will you **record** the next episode? We **videoed** the wedding. The TV station **filmed** the fire. The band **made a tape** of their latest songs.

²**tape 1** *(a roll of sticky tape)* a **band** of gold paper, tied with a **ribbon 2** *(a tape of our holiday)* a **recording** of the concert, a new **video**, a broken **cassette**

target *(Her target weight is nine stone.)* Their **goal** is to raise £1000 this year. His **aim** is to become a musician. The team's **ambition** is to win the League Cup. The school's **objective** is to win the chess tournament.

task *(a boring task)* an interesting **job**, everyday **chores**, a difficult **assignment**, one of the doctor's **duties**

¹**taste 1** *(a taste of ginger)* chocolate **flavour**, a **hint** of peppermint, a lemony **tang 2** *(I had a taste of the curry.)* a **sip** of the juice, a **bite** of apple, a **morsel** of cake, a **titbit** of cheese

²**taste** *(Tarika tasted the curry.)* to **sip** the fruit juice, to **nibble** a piece of bread, **try** our golden cookies, to **sample** every cake

teach *(My aunt teaches aerobics.)* Ms South is **telling** 3C about dinosaurs. She also **coaches** the football team. She **trains** us to believe we'll win. Mr Park **instructs** them in tae kwon do. The film **informed** us about solar power. The school's job is to **educate** children.

team *(a netball team)* seven-a-**side** football, the chess **club**, the United **squad**, a political **party**, the **crew** of a ship

¹**tear** *(say like* here*)* **1** *(tears in his eyes)* **drops** still on her cheeks, a diamond shaped like a **teardrop 2 burst into tears** *(Olwen burst into tears when her Dad told her off.)* He left her in **tears** out in the car. Then she really started to **cry**. She **wept** as if her heart would break.

²**tear** (*say like* hair) **1** *(Carl tore the letter in half.)* He **ripped** it across the middle. How did you **split** your shorts? The cat **shredded** the cushions with her claws. She **laddered** her tights. **2** *(He tore after his brother.)* **tearing off** down the road, **rushing** home, **hurrying** to school, **dashing** for the bus, **running** along the road, **sprinting** up the stairs, **darting** behind the door, **speeding** away

tease *(Liam's teasing the dog.)* Now Liam's **pestering** the cats. Stop **tormenting** your sister! Malcolm **tantalises** his brothers. As a small boy, he was **persecuted** at school. They **taunted** him because he was so small. Annabel's **bothering** us.

telephone *(Gran telephoned this morning.)* She **phoned** Mum. She **rang** to say Grandad was ill. She **called** at half past seven.

tell 1 *(He told me it was three o'clock.)* I **said** I was going. He **spoke** to Mrs Walters. Dad **informed** the school that I was ill. He **explained** that I couldn't come for three days. Parents have to **notify** the school. They have to **let** the school **know**. **2** *(Miss Daykin told us to line up.)* The general **ordered** his troops to attack. The sentry **commanded** him to stop. He **directed** them to wait in the office. **3** *(Tell me a story!)* She **described** what had happened. Mum **related** it to Judy. Miss Jones **narrated** the story. **4** *(Tell me the secret!)* She **revealed** that she knew the new neighbour. He didn't want to **disclose** his secret but his sister **let** it **out**. They **leaked** the story to the newspapers.

tell off *(Mum told us off for fighting.)* Nana **scolds** us if we bring mud into the house. She **ticked** us **off**. The boss **gave** Sandra **a lecture** for being late. The head **gave** us **a talking-to** for being too noisy.

temper 1 *(He's in a temper.)* red with **anger**, in a **rage**, **having a tantrum**, in a **fury** *(Wait till I'm in a better temper.)* a bad **mood**, a good **humour**, a quiet **nature**, a fiery **temperament**

temperature 1 *(He's got a temperature.)* He's got a **fever**. He's **burning up**. a flu **virus**, a cold **germ**, a bad **infection** **2** *(What's the temperature today?)* **How hot** is it?

temporary *(a temporary building)* a **short-term** plan to give extra classrooms, a **provisional** booking for a holiday, a **substitute** teacher

tempt *(They tempted me to take a day off.)* The sales **lured** Auntie Maureen into the shops. He tried to **entice** a robin to perch on his hand.

tempting *(a tempting cake)* an **attractive** plan, a **tantalising** thought, **irresistible** prices

tend 1 *(She tends to lose things.)* Janet is **inclined to** get carsick. She **has a tendency** to put on weight. **2** *(The shepherds were tending their flocks.)* They **looked after** the sheep and **took care of** the newborn lambs.

tender 1 *(tender feelings)* a **loving** kiss, an **affectionate** gesture, a **sympathetic** listener **2** *(a tender spot on his ankle)* **sensitive** skin, **painful** joints

tense *(a tense moment)* looking **worried**, getting **uptight**, an **anxious** time, an **uneasy** silence, working **under stress**

t

terrible *(a terrible headache)* a **bad** cold, an **awful** job, **dreadful** weather, a **horrible** dream, a **hopeless** mess, an **unpleasant** smell, **disgusting** pies, **revolting** fish, a **horrendous** day, **horrifying** news, a **frightful** accident *Slang:* **lousy** food, be **the pits**

terrific *(a terrific idea)* a **great** shop, a **sensational** player, a **brilliant** teacher, a **wonderful** party, a **marvellous** time, an **outstanding** game, a **first-rate** goalkeeper, **brilliant** work, **exceptional** talent, a **magnificent** performance, a **stunning** video, a **superb** record, a **smashing** dinner

terrify *(The parrot was terrified of Joey.)* They were **frightened** of Dean, who was the school bully. I'm **afraid** of that dog. He was **scared out of his wits**. Children often **fear** the dark. Wayne **dreaded** the thought of the maths test.

terror *(He screamed in terror.)* I have a **fear** of heights. They had a **dread** of the maths teacher. She looked at the blood in **horror**. The boys ran away in **fright**. A feeling of **panic** came over him.

test **1** *(a spelling test)* **trials** for the team, a general knowledge **quiz**, a music **exam**. The **examination** lasted an hour. I came first in our **heat** in the swimming gala. Luke's got a karate **qualification**. **2** *(a test on animals)* an **experiment** with a new medicine, taking part in a **pilot** scheme, a **trial** drive of the new car

thank *(I thanked Margie for the chocolates.)* She's **grateful** to us for looking after the budgies. She sent us a basket of fruit to **show** her **appreciation**. The headmistress **acknowledged** Dad's letter.

thaw *(The snow thawed in the sun.)* The ice cream's **melting**. **Defrost** the chicken before cooking it. The chocolate started to **soften** as I heated it.

theft *(imprisoned for car theft)* convicted of **stealing** a radio, armed **robbery**, **pilfering** from the school library

thick **1** *(a thick blanket)* a **bulky** parcel, a **solid** pudding, a **sturdy** branch **2** *(thick smoke)* **dense** crowds, **heavy** mud, **lush** jungle **3** *(Don't be so thick!)* a **stupid** idea, a **silly** remark, an **idiotic** thing to say, a **dumb** suggestion

t

a **fat** book   a **large** sandwich   a **chunky** necklace

thief *(a car thief)* a bank **robber**, a **pickpocket** at the market, a house **burglar**, an experienced **housebreaker**, a **pirate** in the South Seas, a **con man**

an armed **highwayman**

thin *(a thin face)* a **slim** girl, a **slender** boy, a **lean** dog, **skinny** kids, **scrawny** legs, an **anorexic** woman, a **slight** build, **lank** hair

thing 1 *(What's that thing?)* He was holding a small black **object**. There are several **items** on sale. **Articles** bought in the sale cannot be exchanged. **2** *(Vicky said a silly thing today.)* I've done **something** wrong. Is there **anything** else you're worried about? **3** *(Mrs Thing said we didn't have to do it.)* Can you pass the **whatsit**? Do you mean that **gadget** over there? No, the **thingummy** beside it.

things *(I forgot my games things.)* Have you got your football **stuff**? No, I left my **gear** in the changing rooms. So much **clobber** to carry to school today! She picked up all her **bits and bobs**.

think 1 *(I think it's going to rain.)* I **feel** it's going to be a good day. I just **know** everything's going to go wrong! I **expect** you're hungry. I **believe** Dale's coming round. I **gather** your mother's away. We **estimated** that the classroom was 11 metres long. I **presume** you like hamburger and chips. She **assumes** Dale will come. He's a great player, in **my opinion**. **2** *(Next time, think before you speak!)* She never **uses her head**. Try and **be sensible**. **3** *(He thought about the problem.)* He **gave** it some **thought**. He **wondered** what to do. He **considered** what would happen if Dad got another job. He was **contemplating** applying for a job in Germany. Then he **worked out** what he should do.

thirsty *(He was thirsty after the game.)* We were **parched** after the long walk. My throat gets **dry** in hot weather. We were **dying of thirst** after the race. The explorers in the desert became **dehydrated**.

thorough *(a thorough search)* a **complete** checkup, a **total** transformation, a **thoughtful** description, a **careful** piece of work, a **comprehensive** description

thought 1 *(a brilliant thought)* a bright **idea**, a sudden **brain wave**, a good **suggestion**, a detailed **plan**, a silly **scheme**, a weird **theory** **2** *(I gave the problem some thought.)* After a few minutes' **thinking** Darren solved the puzzle. Use your powers of **reasoning** for these brainteasers. Give the idea some **consideration**. Give some **attention** to the problem.

thoughtful *(a thoughtful present)* a **kind** boy, a **considerate** girl, an **attentive** family, a **tactful** reminder

thoughtless *(a thoughtless remark)* **unthinking** cruelty, **unaware** of our feelings, a **tactless** thing to say, **inconsiderate** behaviour, a **careless** girl, **reckless** action, **oblivious** to what people were thinking

thread *(a thread of red silk)* sewing **cotton**, thin **string**, a **strand** of hair, a **filament** of a spider's web

threat *(the threat of war)* the **danger** of fire, the **risk** of being homeless, the **hazards** of earthquakes, the **possibility** of accidents, the **chance** of dying, the **menace** of AIDS

threaten *(The terrorist threatened to blow up the building.)* Dr York **intimidated** the children and they wouldn't answer his questions. Drunken driving **puts** lives **at risk**. A difficult test was **looming**.

thrill *(It was a thrill to meet the band after the concert.)* There is a lot of **excitement** around Christmastime. We got a feeling of **exhilaration** on the water ride. Geoff gets his **kicks** from driving fast cars. They got a **buzz** out of appearing on the stage.

throw *(throwing a Frisbee to your friend)* **chucking** a ball to each other, **flinging** his jacket onto the bed, **hurling** pebbles into the river, **tossing** the bag over the stream, **slinging** a shoe into the cupboard, **heaving** his bag over the wall, **launching** a missile, **lobbing** stones over the wall

throw away *(Throw away the broken clock.)* Mum **chucked out** Hayley's favourite game. **Get rid of** all that rubbish. Ben had to **dump** his old car. Please **dispose of** this wrapping paper tidily. Andrew **discarded** the instructions when he'd learnt the game. The factory was **discharging** black liquid into the river.

thug *(a gang of thugs)* a **hooligan**, a **lout**, a **tough**, a **gangster**, a **vandal**, a **mugger**, a **street fighter**, a **criminal**, a **ruffian**, a **hoodlum**, a **hood**, a **heavy**

ticket *(a lottery ticket)* a library **card**, a travel **permit**, a record **voucher**, a cut-out **coupon**, the price of **admission**

bus pass

tickle *(Sam's tickling the baby.)* The nettle sting was **itching** all night. That woollen sweater **scratches** so much I can't wear it. Her hands **tingled** with cold.

tidy *(a tidy cupboard)* a **neat** bedroom, an **orderly** bookcase, a **well-organised** kitchen

tie *(He tied a ribbon round the teddy bear's neck.)* Then he **fastened** a label onto it with string. Claire **tied up** the parcel. He **knotted** a scarf round his neck. He **lashed** the rope to the post. We **attached** decorations to the tree. The queen **bound** up her hair with a golden ribbon.

The boat was **moored** to the bank.

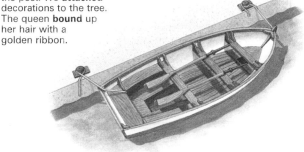

tight 1 *(tight jeans)* too **small**, a **close-fitting** top, **narrow** shoes, **stretched** to fit, **straining** across the shoulders, a **cramped** kitchen **2** *(Shut your eyes tight.)* The biscuit jar is **airtight** and **waterproof**. Put the cork **firmly** back in the bottle. The kitchen window's shut **fast**.

time 1 *(in a short time)* a **moment** of peace, a **while** ago, a **spell** on the computer, an interesting **period** of history, a **session** on the Internet, an **age** of exploration and discovery, a bad **phase** of history, a **stretch** in prison **2** *(I've asked you lots of times.)* several **instances** of rudeness, on a previous **occasion**

timetable *(I pinned the timetable to the board.)* a **programme** of events, a busy **schedule**, on the **calendar**

timid *(a timid smile)* a **shy** giggle, a **reserved** child, a **cowardly** thing to do, a **feeble** protest, a **fainthearted** attack

tiny *(tiny shoes)* a **minute** amount, a **little** girl, a **small** kitten, a **miniature** poodle, a **teeny** bear, a **weeny** book, a **wee** cottage, a **titchy** cake, a **short** ruler, a **pocket** dictionary, a **compact** computer, a **mini**-series, **microscopic** specks of dust, a **toy** dog

¹**tip 1** *(the tip of your nose)* the **end** of his ponytail, the **point** of a paintbrush, the **top** of your finger, the **peak** of a mountain **2** *(She gave us some tips on playing the game.)* a useful **hint**, **clues** about the mystery, **advice** on making your own jewellery, making a **suggestion**, offering some **help**, no **inkling** of what to do

²**tip** *(Ben tipped the chair back.)* It **tilted** back dangerously. The chair **leaned** at an angle. It **slanted** away from the table. Megan **inclined** her head to show she agreed. The ship **listed** badly to one side.

tip over *(Ben tipped the chair over.)* The kittens **upset** the milk. They **overturned** the jug and it **toppled** to the floor.

tired *(She was tired after school.)* a **sleepy** voice, an **exhausted** team, feeling **worn out**, feeling **weary**, getting **drowsy** *Slang:* **bushed, whacked, knackered**

tired of *(I'm tired of this game.)* I've **had enough** and I'm **fed up**. She got **bored with** waiting so she went home.

title *(The title of the CD is 'Music Mania'.)* Her **name** is Hayley Foster. The book's **called** *Runaway Robot*.

tool *(household tools)* a **gadget** for opening bottles, music **equipment**, a **device** for clearing the drains, scientific **instruments**, farming **implements**, cleaning **apparatus**, kitchen **utensils**

gardening **things**

¹**top 1** *(the top of the hill)* snowy **peaks**, the **summit** of a mountain, the **crest** of a wave, the highest **pinnacle**, the **apex** of a triangle **2** *(top of the list)* the **head** of the queue, **first** in the line, the **upper** branches

²**top** *(top quality)* the **best** meat, the **most important** scientists, the **most famous** bands, a **leading** sportsman, the **foremost** company, the **principal** reasons

total *(total darkness)* a **complete** change, **absolute** zero, **utter** confusion

totally *(totally full)* **all** gone, **completely** finished, **absolutely** dark, **utterly** hopeless, **way** too big

¹**touch** *(Someone touched my hand.)* Sian **felt** the key in her pocket. She **fingered** it as she walked along. Don't **handle** the glasses! The cat **brushed against** our legs. She **stroked** the horse's nose and **patted** its neck. Andrew **fondled** the guinea pig.

²**touch** *(Brendan kept in touch by phone.)* **writing to** our friends abroad, **phoning** Alison, **visiting** Grandad, **faxing** a friend, **contacting** the school secretary

tough 1 *(a tough kid)* a **rough** boy, a **strong** girl, a **sturdy** child, **streetwise 2** *(a tough problem)* a **difficult** choice, a **painful** decision, **hard** sums **3** *(a tough teacher)* **strict** parents, a **stern** headmaster, **harsh** punishment, a **relentless** criminal, a **determined** attitude, a **stubborn** person **4** *(tough meat)* a **chewy** steak **5** *(tough leather)* **strong** boots, **hardy** plants, a **durable** material

tour *(a guided tour)* a **trip** to the zoo, a **visit** to the museum, a **holiday** in Greece, a train **journey**, a sea **voyage**, a school **outing**, a **drive** into the country, a cross-country **hike**, a long **trek**, a river **cruise**, an **expedition** to the jungle, an **excursion** to see the seals

tourist *(Japanese tourists)* overseas **visitors**, day **trippers**, foreign **travellers**, hotel **guests**

tow *(towing the car)* **pulling** someone along, **dragging** his bag, **hauling** a sack of rubbish, **tugging** along a wooden toy, **dragging** his mum into the shop

tower *(a high tower)* a **high-rise** block of flats

town *(a market town)* a capital **city**, a pretty **village**, the **urban area**, a small **community**

toy *(a soft toy)* the baby's **playthings**, my sister's **games**

¹**trace** *(There was no trace of food in the fridge.)* **signs** of the robbery, no **record** of anything missing, a **vestige** of a smile, **footprints** in the snow, **fingerprints** on the gun, **evidence** of a fight, **marks** where the body had been

²**trace** *(Police traced the criminals.)* They're trying to **find** their base. I **tracked** him **down** to an old house. I **discovered** him hiding there. The police have **recovered** the stolen videos.

¹**track** *(Dogs tracked the injured deer through the forest.)* I **followed** the man down the road. The police cars **chased** the bank robbers. The boys were **hunting** rabbits. They **trailed** the stolen car. The police **tailed** the suspect.

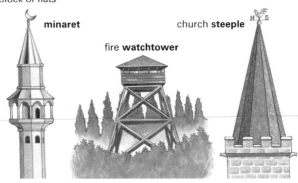

minaret

church **steeple**

fire **watchtower**

²**track 1** *(a dusty track)* a **path** across the moors, an overgrown **footpath** **2** *(We left tracks in the snow.)* muddy **footprints** across the floor, a **trail** of toys into Simon's bedroom, the **groove** of wheels in the mud

railway line

bridle path

¹**trade 1** *(Britain trades with other countries.)* He **buys and sells** cars. Mum **does business** with a company in Sweden. **2** *(I traded my sticker book for a football.)* He **swapped** his United shirt for a City one.

²**trade** *(the motor trade)* the hotel **business**, the computer **industry**, publishing **companies**, building **firms**

tradition *(a family tradition)* the **custom** of brides wearing white, the **habit** of wearing black to a funeral, the **practice** of exchanging Christmas gifts

¹**train** *(a fast train)* a railway **engine**, a diesel **locomotive**, an **express** to London

²**train** *(Mr Fielding trains our athletes.)* He **coaches** the football team. Mrs Holt **taught** us to operate the computer. Megan **exercised** for two hours. She **practised** her swimming.

transport *(We transported the washing machine ourselves.)* We **moved** the chairs to the playground. Damien **fetched** the table. The van **carried** all our furniture. They've **delivered** the Christmas tree. The ship **conveyed** the containers to the port. The bananas were **transferred** onto lorries. They had been **shipped** from Jamaica.

¹**trap** *(a trap for animals)* Don't answer – it's a **trick**! The soldiers planned an **ambush**. The rabbit was caught in a **snare**.

²**trap** *(She trapped me into telling who had hidden her pen.)* You can't **catch** me **out**. Hazel **tricked** me into giving her some sweets. Dominic **fooled** me into lending him the game. He **deceived** me into doing it.

t

¹travel 1 *(They travelled all morning.)* We **went** to see my uncle and aunt. Wanda **came** to see us. He **drove** 40 miles. She **walked** to the shops. Natasha **flew** to France. **2** *(I want to travel when I'm older.)* **touring** Scotland, people **on the move**, **taking a trip** across America, **holidaying** in Wales, **rambling** in the mountains, **cruising** on the canals, **trekking** across Africa, **journeying** to a distant land, **on a jaunt** to the seaside

²travel *(We spend all our spare money on travel.)* a **trip** to Calais, **touring** in a caravan, **going on holiday** to Florida, a **voyage** to the New World

tread *(Jon trod on the cat.)* Val **stepped** on my foot.

treasure *(buried treasure)* They found **gold and jewels** in the old trunk. He's got a **fortune** hidden away. The old king shared his **riches** with the prince. Pirates stole the **wealth** of the merchants. He keeps his **valuables** in the bank.

treat 1 *(He treats the dog badly.)* He doesn't know how to **handle** animals. I don't like the way you **behave towards** your brother. **2** *(David treated us to a drink.)* He offered to **buy** them a snack. Lara **entertained** her friends to tea. **3** *(She treated the cut with antiseptic.)* A day in bed **cured** my cold. The lemon drink **healed** my sore throat. **4** *(treated milk)* **processed** peas

tremble *(The bird trembled with fear.)* After the accident my hands were **shaking**. I **shivered** in the cold wind. The leaves were **quivering** in the breeze. He **shuddered** with fear. The plane **vibrated** as it took off. The flame **flickered** in the wind.

¹trick *(a naughty trick)* a **practical joke**, a **cheat** to get to game level 3, a **dodge** to get out of PE, a **swindle** by car dealers, a **hoax** by a clever artist, **illusions** done by a conjuror, a **scheme** to get money, the **pretence** of being a policeman, a **ruse** to get into the film, a **bluff** to fool Dad

²trick *(Daisy tricked the boys into letting her in.)* Micky **cheated** him out of £10. He **fooled** me into thinking he was a policeman. The girl **deceived** her parents. The estate agent **swindled** several people. The company **defrauded** the government of a lot of tax. They **bluffed** their way into the film.

trickle *(Tears trickled down her face.)* The milk **ran** out of the jug, **poured** into his plate, **dribbled** over the table, **dripped** off the edge and **flowed** under the door.

trim *(Gran trimmed her hedge.)* She **cut** my hair. I **clipped** the poodles. He **pruned** the tree. Brian **shaped** his beard.

¹trip *(a trip to the cinema)* an **outing** to the zoo, a **tour** of Ireland, a **journey** to Israel, an **excursion** to town, a sea **voyage**, a luxury **cruise**, a **jaunt** to Blackpool

²trip *(He tripped over the cat.)* She **stumbled** down the steps and **slipped over** on the path. I **fell down** on the bank.

triumph *(Our team triumphed again last night!)* They **won** easily. They **succeeded** in getting three goals before halftime. They were **victorious**. They **beat** Rovers 7-1. We **thrashed** King's School 5-0. I **defeated** Gran at chess.

trot *(The dog trotted away.)*
George **jogged** up the road, **ran** down the hill, **loped** across the field and **scuttled** into school as the bell rang.

¹**trouble** **1** *(The trouble is, I can't understand the instructions.)* a **problem** with the disk drive, **something wrong** with Alice, some **difficulties** at home, a **worry** for the family **2** *(That girl's nothing but trouble.)* She's a **nuisance**. Her friend's a **pest**, too. **3 in trouble** *(Joe's in trouble.)* He's become **involved** with the police. You'll be **for it**. You'll **cop it**. **4** *(Sara's taken a lot of trouble with her costume.)* She's gone to a lot of **bother** to get the colours right. She's put a great deal of **work** into it. She gets a special prize for **effort**. She took **pains** to get it right.

²**trouble** *(Sorry to trouble you!)* Don't **disturb** them, Elizabeth. It doesn't **worry** me. Don't **bother** to see us out. The delivery man apologised for **inconveniencing** us.

truck *(a goods truck)*

true *(It was a true story.)* an **honest** statement, **accurate** details, the **real** owner, the **actual** crown, the **correct** answer, **precise** timing, an **exact** copy, a **factual** account of the accident, a **reliable** witness, a **loyal** follower, a **trustworthy** salesman, an **authentic** copy, the **rightful** king, a **valid** passport, a **truthful** story

trunk *(a big trunk in the attic)* a treasure **chest**, a leather **suitcase**, a **strongbox** full of papers, a **safe** for jewellery, **coffers** full of gold

trust *(I'll trust you with the money.)* We **rely** on the team to play well. The blind lady **depends** on her dog to lead her through the town. You shouldn't **believe** everything Candice says. I **expect** you to clean your teeth every night. I **assume** you'll do your best. Nan says she **has faith** in her doctor. He **has confidence** in the teachers. You can **bank on** what he tells you.

builder's **lorry**

oil **tanker**

removal **van**

truth *(What is the truth about the ghost?)* Do you know the **facts** of the case? The **reality** is that no one saw the ghost except her. **To be honest**, she can't see very well.

¹**try 1** *(She tried to push me over.)* He **attempted** to jump the wall. They **endeavoured** to climb Everest. They **strove** to reach the peak. **2** *(I'm going to try this shirt on.)* He's **testing** the new computer program. Just **check** that your joystick's working again. She's **experimenting** with a new pancake mix.

²**try 1** *(a good try)* her first **attempt** at windsurfing, the latest **bid** to end the war **2** *(Give Timmy a try.)* Can I have a **go**?

tub *(a tub of hot water)* a pink **bath**, a washing-up **bowl**, a rainwater **barrel**, a **vat** of dye, a **cask** of wine, a water **butt**

tube *(plastic tubes)* a drainage **pipe**, a **hose** to wash the car

tug *(He tugged the rope three times.)* **pulling** along a sack of rubbish, **towing** a broken-down truck, **dragging** a blanket, **hauling** on the line, **lugging** a heavy sack

tumble *(Mitch tumbled over in the playground.)* He **fell** on his side. The vase **dropped** off the windowsill. It **went down** with a crash. The building **collapsed** in the earthquake.

tummy *(a big tummy)* a full **stomach**, a pain in the **belly**, a punch in the **guts**

tune *(a well-known tune)* pretty **music**, a famous **song**, a **number** from the new band, whistling the **melody**, an advertising **jingle**

tunnel *(the Channel Tunnel)* an underground **passage**, a **subway** to the station, an **underpass** to cross the road, a rabbit **hole**, a long **burrow**

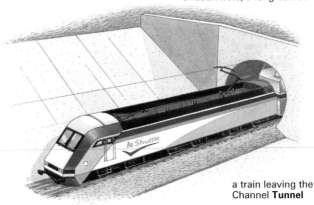

a train leaving the Channel **Tunnel**

¹**turn 1** *(I turned round to look at her.)* He **spun** around and walked away. The birds **circled** overhead. The bicycle wheel **rotated** faster. The CD **revolves** at great speed. I **flipped** the pancake over. The bus began to **swing** to the right. He **rolled** the ball into the goal. She **wheeled** round to face him. The box's lid **swivels** round on this big hinge. Sandra **pivoted** round to face in the other direction. **2** *(The bus turned left.)* I **went round** the corner. The ball **swerved** away from me and **curved** into the goal. The road **bends** to the left. The wind **veered** round during the night. The snake **twisted** in my hand. **3** *(She turned into a statue.)* The wizard **changed** her to stone. She **became** as still as a rock. Only a prince could **transform** her into a girl again. **4** *(She turned the dial to zero.)* I **switched** the radio alarm to AUTO. She **set** the oven at Mark 7. He **adjusted** the radio to get a French channel.

²**turn** *(It's my turn now.)* Can I have a **go**? Give Dominic a **try**.

twinkle *(The stars twinkled brightly.)* Lights **shone** in the distance. The firelight **glowed** and **flickered**. The sea **gleamed** in the moonlight. Fireflies **glimmered** in the trees. On the Christmas tree, tinsel **glittered**, frost **sparkled** and gold ornaments **glinted**.

twist 1 *(Jack twisted the balloon into a funny shape.)* Tanya **turned** her hair round her fingers. Smoke **curled** up from the fire. The ringlets **coiled** down to her shoulders. She **looped** the string round the posts. **2** *(The snakes were twisted together.)* One of them was **twined** round Pauline's neck. Her hair was **entwined** with ribbons and beads. **3** *(The road twisted away up the hill.)* It **turned** and **bent** so often it made them sick. It **zigzagged** up for about a kilometre. The kite **corkscrewed** up into the air. **4** *(Twist the lid off.)* I **unscrewed** the top of the bottle. **5** *(The cat twisted out of her grasp.)* The rabbit **wriggled** in my arms. The little boy **squirmed** under the table. The snake **writhed** round Vijay's arm.

two *(He's got two brothers.)* a **pair** of budgies, a married **couple**, a piano **duet**, a **couple** of minutes

type *(a new type of car)* a new **brand** of peanut butter, an unusual **breed** of dog. What **sorts** of cakes have you got? What **kind** of computer is that? It's a Japanese **make**. She dislikes any **form** of exercise.

several **varieties** of yogurt

typical *(a typical day in my life)* a **normal** meal, an **ordinary** day, the **usual** bus, his **regular** journey

Uu

ugly *(an ugly face)* an **unattractive** man, a **plain** girl, a **hideous** building, a **repulsive** mask, **revolting** make-up

unable *(Old Mr Kinnear is almost unable to walk.)* My baby sister **can't** talk yet. She **cannot** sit up either. He's **incapable** of standing for very long. Princess Reya was **powerless** against the evil lord.

uncertain *(uncertain which door to use)* Kit's **not sure** what time he'll be back. If you're **unsure** of the answer, leave a blank. He was **doubtful** that he'd be able to come. Meg's **in doubt** about it. The kids are always **vague** about mealtimes.

uncomfortable **1** *(These shoes are uncomfortable.)* They **hurt**. We were sitting on **hard** chairs all day. some **ill-fitting** shoes, a **tight** collar, an **itchy** sweater, a **rough** ride, a **bumpy** journey **2** *(He feels uncomfortable with all those clever people.)* **embarrassed** about his clothes, **unhappy** with the new teacher, **uneasy** in front of everyone

unconscious **1** *(Mr Lyons was unconscious after the accident.)* He **fainted** from loss of blood. He **lost consciousness**. The old lady **collapsed** during the hot weather. Nicky **felt dizzy** and had to sit down. The boxer was **knocked out** in the third round. He had **passed out**. **2** *(I was*

unconscious of the amusement I had caused.) He **didn't notice** them calling him. He was **unaware** they'd called his name. She did **not realise** what was wrong. She did **not know** anything was wrong. She was **oblivious** to the danger.

under **1** *(under the umbrella)* **underneath** the bridge, **beneath** the trees, below the stairs **2** *(under six stone)* **less than** ten years old, **below** 30 miles an hour, a number **lower than** 50, **not yet** ten

understand *(Do you understand the rules of the game?)* I don't **get** what he means. Do you **see** how to do it? Micki never **catches on**. I couldn't **make out** what Miss Chan meant. I'll help you **get the hang of** it. It's hard to **grasp** all at once. Did he **take in** what I said? I **realised** I had to divide by two. It finally **dawned on** her how to do it. 'These kids just don't **appreciate** how hard my job is,' complained Miss Edwards. 'Try to **comprehend**: it isn't that difficult,' said the head.

undo **1** *(Peter undid the parcel.)* He **untied** the string and **opened** the paper. Jane **unlocked** the door and **unfastened** the dog's chain. I **unbuttoned** my collar and **unzipped** my jacket. **2** *(You've undone all my good work.)* You've **spoilt** everything. Our plans are **wrecked** now. All our work has been **wiped out**. Suraj **deleted** his name from the list and **cancelled** the program. Then he **erased** the disk.

unexpected *(an unexpected storm)* a **sudden** idea, a **surprise** party, an **accidental** meeting, an **abrupt** end. It happened **out of the blue**.

unfair *(It's unfair – she didn't give me a turn on the swing.)* **mean** to her brother, **unkind** to her sister, an **unjust** punishment, a **prejudiced** person

unfortunately *(Unfortunately, he can't be with us today.)* **It's a pity** he's gone. **It's a shame** you didn't find it. **Bad luck** missing the game!

unfriendly *(an unfriendly boy)* a **hostile** crowd, **unsympathetic** relatives, an **antagonistic** group of people, a **fierce** dog, **suspicious** looks, a **stuck-up** school, a **snobbish** person

unhappiness *(causing unhappiness)* **sadness**, **misery**, **gloom**, **sorrow**, **grief**, **depression**, **disappointment**, **dejection**

unhappy *(unhappy children)* a **sad** face, a **depressed** woman, feeling **downhearted** because you've lost, a **miserable** term at school, a **pitiful** cry, a **gloomy** look, feeling **low**, **melancholy** music, a **heartbroken** girl, a **disappointed** player, a **dejected** boy

unimportant *(unimportant details)* **useless** presents, **trivial** conversations, a **worthless** report, **insignificant** people, a **waste of time**

uninteresting *(an uninteresting lesson)* a **boring** programme, a **dull** person, a real **drag**

unite *(Teachers and students are united against the school closure.)* Two small schools **combined** to make a big one. Years 3 and 4 **joined up** for drama lessons. She **blended** the sugar and butter together. The two machines are **linked** by this cable.

The telephone's **connected** to the fax machine.

unkind *(an unkind thing to say)* **bad** treatment, a **cruel** punishment, being **hard** on someone, a **mean** woman, a **nasty** man, an **inconsiderate** remark, a **horrible** thing to do, a **thoughtless** thing to say, a **wicked** monster, a **harsh** judgment, a **stern** father, a **vicious** attack, a **hardhearted** stepmother, an **unsympathetic** teacher

unlucky *(an unlucky number)* an **unfortunate** day, a **disastrous** game, **accidental** death

The **ill-fated** airliner crashed.

unpleasant *(an unpleasant person)* a **nasty** man, a **mean** woman, an **unkind** boy, a **horrible** girl, **awful** people, **terrible** traffic, **dreadful** weather, **lousy** marks, a **foul** smell, **disgusting** meat, **revolting** food

untidy *(an untidy room)* a **messy** table, a **scruffy** boy, a real **mess**, a complete **tip**, a **chaotic** class, a **jumbled** heap of socks, a **disorganised** bedroom, **careless** work, **sloppy** writing, a **slipshod** piece of work

untrue *(an untrue statement)* **wrong** information, a **false** name, **incorrect** facts, **unreliable** data, an **untrustworthy** statement

unusual *(an unusual taste)* a **strange** smell, a **peculiar** colour, an **odd** feeling, a **funny** noise, a **weird** film, an **extraordinary** laugh, **exceptional** circumstances, **unheard-of** to pass so many exams

¹**upset** **1** *(upset about her fish dying)* **sad** about the fish, **unhappy** about the exam results, **crying** because of the horrible story. Granny's **worried** because Sharon's not back yet. She feels **uneasy** if someone comes back late. She's **in a state** about her. Don't talk to her when she's **in a flap**. She easily gets **flustered** and **alarmed**. The old lady looked quite **distressed**. She was **distraught**. **2** *(upset with the children for making so much noise)* The noise **irritated** Grandad. He felt **annoyed**.

²**upset** **1** *(Belinda upset her mum by being rude.)* **annoy**, **distress**, **provoke**, **disturb**, **irritate** **2** *(Gerry upset the cornflakes.)* He **tipped up** the packet and then he **knocked over** the milk jug. He **spilt** the tea.

up-to-date *(an up-to-date dictionary)* a **modern** town, **contemporary** styles, the **current** edition of a magazine, the **latest** fashions, **fashionable** ideas, **present** trends, **topical** issues, **recent** changes

urgent *(an urgent message)* an **important** letter, a **vital** piece of information, an **immediate** answer

u

useful *(a useful penknife)* **helpful** instructions, a **good** cookery book, an **effective** medicine, a **convenient** shop near our house, a **practical** instruction book, **necessary** information

an **invaluable** knife

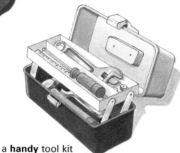

a **handy** tool kit

¹**use** (*say* **yuze**) **1** *(He's using the calculator.)* They are **operating** the computer. They're **running** a game program at the moment. The school **makes use of** the farmer's field. The machine **utilises** solar power. You will need to **employ** a ruler for this piece of work. You'll also have to **exercise** your brains a lot! **2** *(At home we use about four kilos of potatoes a week.)* The school **uses up** 20 times that. Heaters **consume** a lot of electricity. Their big washing machine **wastes** electricity. It **expends** a lot of power. It just **eats** it up.

²**use** (*say* **yuze**) *(It's no use asking me; I haven't seen your kitten.)* There's no **point** in waiting here. It's no **good** complaining about the weather. It's a **waste of time** and **effort**.

useless 1 *(a useless ornament)* a **pointless** story, a **fruitless** search, a **futile** waste of time **2** *(useless at maths)* **bad** at English, **hopeless** at sport, no **good** at cooking, a **rotten** goalie *Slang:* **the pits** when it comes to computers

usual *(my usual desk)* my **normal** voice, a **typical** Sunday, an **ordinary** day, the **average** class, our **regular** trip to the town, in his **customary** seat, **traditional** Christmas food, **everyday** life, a **routine** checkup

usually *(I usually drink orange juice.)* Mum **normally** fetches us from school. It's **generally** crowded on Saturdays. We **mostly** watch TV after school. Mum buys ice cream sometimes – **chiefly** in the summer. He has tea at six **as a rule**.

u

Vv

vain *(vain about her hair)* **proud** of her appearance, very **pleased with herself**, **full of himself**, **bigheaded**. Her success has **gone to her head**.

valley *(a deep river valley)* a **chasm**, a **ravine**, a **gorge**, a **pass**

the Grand **Canyon**

valuable 1 *(a valuable necklace)* an **expensive** car, **precious** stones, **priceless** antiques, **costly** jewels **2** *(valuable help)* a **useful** lesson, something **positive** that has come out of this, an **advantageous** experience, a **good** thing to know, a **worthwhile** point, an **invaluable** piece of advice

value 1 *(The value of the necklace is £150.)* I paid £15 for this sweater but it's **worth** £30. The **cost** of all the CDs is £13.99. The **price** is the same as it was last year. **2** *(the value of learning to ride a bike)* The **good thing** about our flat is that it's close to the school. It's a great **help** if you can swim. Knowing how to use a computer is a **plus**. The **advantage** of being tall is that you can see from the back of the hall. One of the **benefits** of old age is that you have time for your grandchildren.

vanish 1 *(My watch vanished as the magician waved his wand.)* It **vanished into thin air**! My calculator's **gone**! It's completely **disappeared**! The ship **disappeared from sight** over the horizon. I was about to speak to Jordan but he'd **left**. The crowd began to **melt away**. We waved until the bus **faded** from sight. **2** *(a vanishing species of Brazilian frog)* This type of frog may **die out** soon. It would be a shame if it **became extinct**. Unless we do something to protect it, the frog could **face extinction** and **disappear** from the face of the Earth. It may **cease to exist**.

variety 1 *(A budgie is a variety of parakeet.)* different **sorts** of dinosaur, a new **kind** of vegetable, a good **make** of bicycle, an odd **type** of fish, a strange **breed** of cat, a **brand** of chocolate spread **2** *(This book gives you a variety of words to choose from.)* a **mixture** of sweets, an **assortment** of fruit, a **medley** of songs, a **combination** of different sorts of songs, the **diversity** of the rainforest

various _(We saw various games but we like this one the best.)_ He tried on **different** football tops, and in the end bought the Scotland one. England has **varied** scenery. She bought the **assorted** biscuits. The family came with their **miscellaneous** pets.

very 1 _(very nice)_ _Informal words:_ **really** horrible, **terribly** sorry, **awfully** slow, **incredibly** boring **2** _(very hot for the time of year)_ **extremely** cold, **unusually** wet, **extraordinarily** windy, **especially** nice. It's **so** hot. **3** _(very sick)_ **badly** injured

vicious _(a vicious attack)_ a **mean** trick, a **spiteful** look, a **malicious** thing to say, a **cruel** joke, a **brutal** attack, a **ruthless** killer

a **ferocious** tiger

victory _(a great victory for Jones)_ an unexpected **win**, a tremendous **triumph**, a **success** for the team

view 1 _(a view of the river)_ a wonderful **sight**, a peaceful **scene**, an **outlook** over the park, a **panorama** of sea and sky, pretty **scenery 2** _(In his view, pets are a nuisance.)_ She has a different **opinion**. She won't change her **mind** about it. She has a lot of strange **ideas** about diet.

violent 1 _(a violent criminal)_ a **brutal** murder, a **savage** attack, a **fierce** opponent, a **vicious** animal, **aggressive** behaviour **2** _(a violent dislike of cats)_ a **strong** smell, a **powerful** earthquake, **intense** love, **fierce** hatred

visible _(The ship was visible on the horizon.)_ It was already in **sight**. It was **easy to see**. a **clear** signal, a **noticeable** stain, some **glaring** mistakes in the school magazine

¹**visit** _(They visited us.)_ Granny **came to stay** with us last Christmas and we'll **go to see** her next Christmas. Russell's **coming round** for the day. Let's **drop** in at Lucy's. Dad went to **call on** the new neighbours. Nan's gone to **consult** the doctor.

²**visit** _(a school visit to the toy factory)_ Nan enjoyed her **stay** in the country. Dr Forbes had to make three house **calls** in the night. Michaela's got an **appointment** at the hairdresser's.

visitor _(having visitors to stay)_ a **guest** at the hotel, having **company** over Easter, an American **tourist**, **travellers** from far away, an early **caller**

vomit _(The medicine made him vomit.)_ He **was sick** twice. It made him **throw up**. The fatty meat made him **gag**. She **retched** when she saw the blood. _Slang:_ **puke**

¹**vote** _(Vote for Christy Barker!)_ **Choose** Christy Barker as your Class Representative! Our class **elected** Tara King as Class Representative.

²**vote** _(We took a vote and Tara won.)_ In the **election**, we had a secret **ballot** so I don't know who voted for Tara.

v

Ww

wag *(Spot wagged his tail.)* His tail **waggled** from side to side. Johnny **waved** a flag. The leaves **fluttered** in the wind.

wages *(Dad's wages are paid into the bank.)* Mum's getting more **pay** this month. He spends a lot of his **earnings** on his car. a **salary** of £22,000, **income** from money his Gran left him

wail *(The baby was wailing.)* She **cried** for her mummy. Wind **howled** in the trees, **roared** in the telephone wires and **moaned** round the house. Police cars **whined** round the corner. Sam **bellowed** with pain. She **shrieked** in fear.

wait *(Wait a moment.)* **Hang on**, I'm coming. **Hold on**, I've got to get my things. I can't **stay** – my bus is going. Hilary **paused** the video. I **hesitated** before posting the letter. Let's **delay** the match. It cannot be **postponed**. We had to **stand by**.

wake *(I woke early today.)* Don't **wake** the others **up**. Mum **calls** us at seven. Lenny **gets up** late – he doesn't **stir** till midday on Saturdays.

walk *(I walked out of the house.)* Bianca **stepped** into the room. I **trod** on a drawing pin. Ben **strode** in and turned the TV off. We **strolled** down the road and **sauntered** into town. He **trudged** up the hill to school. Rogan **tiptoed** to the bathroom. The dog **pattered** across the floor. Jo **hiked** through the mountains. She **trekked** for ten kilometres.

wall *(a wall round the garden)* a **partition** between two rooms, a **barrier** across the road, high **battlements**

The castle's **ramparts** were strong.

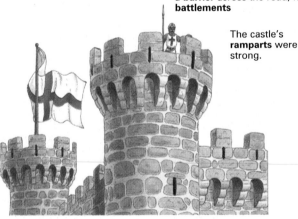

W

wander *(We wandered round the shops.)* They **strolled** through the shopping centre and **sauntered** down to the park. They **drifted** round the park for a while before **ambling** home.

want *(I want something to eat.)* I'd **like** a hot dog. I **fancy** some chips. I **wish** I had a nicer room. Mrs Sampson **needs** you to help. She **requires** two people to move the chairs. The king **desired** more gold. When Tracy's on a diet, she **craves** chocolate.

war *(The First World War started in 1914.)* The **fighting** lasted four years. The **Battle** of Hastings took place in 1066. He studied the techniques of **warfare**. No further **exchanges** were reported. more casualties in the **conflict**, a hero during the **struggle** for freedom, fighting in the Burma **Campaign**, people killed in the **crossfire**

warm *(a warm bath)* a **hot** meal, a **mild** day, **lukewarm** water, **tepid** lemonade, **cosy** boots, **thick** blankets

warn *(She warned me not to drink it.)* She **advised against** it. She **told** me not to buy it. The policeman **cautioned** her to drive carefully. The flashing light **lets you know** you're running out of time. The alarm **alerted** us to the fire.

warning *(The head gave out a warning about drugs.)* At the first **sign** of trouble, they run off. There was a bomb **scare** and the police were put on **alert**. There's a smoke **alarm** in this classroom. The policeman let her off with a **caution**.

wash *(Derek washed the dishes.)* I **cleaned** the frying pan. **Bathe** the cut in clean water. Laura **soaked** the big pans. We had to **scrub** the table. Ross **showered** after his game. Mrs White **laundered** the shirts. I **shampooed** my hair. He **mopped** the kitchen floor.

¹**waste** *(Don't waste time.)* Rosie **spends too much** on magazines. It's a pity to **throw away** good food. They **squander** their money on computer games. He **blew** his bonus on a holiday.

²**waste** *(toxic waste)* a **rubbish** heap, a **wastepaper** basket, a **litter** bin, **refuse** disposal, a pile of **junk**, a **garbage** pail

watch 1 *(Katy watched me paint the table.)* She **looked at** the painting with interest. We **observed** the foxes. Mrs Fuller showed us how to change a plug; Gavin **attended** carefully. He **took notice of** what she was doing. **2** *(Mum asked Teresa to watch the baby.)* She's **looking after** him till one. She likes **taking care of** babies. I'm too busy to **keep an eye on** him. She often **babysits** for us.

watchman *(a night watchman)* a **caretaker**, a **guard**, a **sentry**, a **warden**, a **doorkeeper**, a **gatekeeper**, a **sentinel**

¹**wave** 1 *(I waved to her.)* The driver **gestured** wildly at the boy in the road. She **motioned** to him to keep quiet. **2** *(The flag waved in the wind.)* Her scarf **billowed** out behind her.

²**wave** *(She was afraid of the big waves.)* A **breaker** crashed into the rocks. There was a strong **swell** and the boat tossed up and down. The **surf** broke on the shore.

w

way 1 *(Can you show me the way to open this box?)* a new **method** of division, a **means** of transport, a special **technique** to fasten the door, the right **procedure** to start the game **2** *(He asked the way to the station.)* Andy gave him the **directions**. We took a roundabout **route** to school. We went by the new **road**. **3** *(He's doing his hair in a new way.)* That's an old **style** of dancing. She was dressed in punk **fashion**.

weak *(weak arms)* a **feeble** kick, **powerless** to move, feeling **ill**, a **sickly** baby, a **spindly** stalk, **wobbly** legs, **dim** light

wealthy *(a wealthy lawyer)* a **rich** businessman, a **well-off** family, **moneyed** people, an **affluent** neighbourhood, a **prosperous** New Year *Slang:* feeling **flush**, **rolling in money**, **made of money**, **worth a packet**

wear 1 *(wearing a new shirt)* Gemma's **dressed** in ballet clothes. She **put on** her red skirt. Dana's **modelling** the latest earrings. Mr Bird was **sporting** a bright yellow tie. **2** *(The sea wore the cliffs into amazing shapes.)* The soles of my shoes are **worn down** and the heels are **worn away**.

wear out 1 *(Walking up that hill wears you out.)* She gets **tired** walking, and running completely **exhausts** her. **2** *(You can't have worn out those shoes already!)* They're **broken** and have **got** big **holes** in them!

wedding *(my cousin's wedding)* The **marriage** is on Saturday.

weigh *(I weigh 36kg.)* My brother **tips the scales at** 45kg. Mum **measured** out the flour.

weight *(a heavy weight)* a **mass** of concrete, the **density** of this metal, **ballast** in the bottom of a ship

welcome *(He welcomed us to the school.)* He **greeted** all the new children and **ushered** us **into** the hall.

well 1 *(I'm very well, thank you!)* Mum's **fine**, too. Joe looks very **healthy**. Yes, he's **fit** again now. He's **in good health**. **2** *(She draws well.)* Suzanne spells **correctly** and forms the letters **properly**. Mark plays football **skilfully**. To cook **successfully**, always use the correct amounts. They get on together **excellently**.

wet *(a wet morning)* a **rainy** day, a **damp** towel, **drenched** to the skin, **soaked** to the skin, **dripping** hair, **moist** air, **saturated** with sweat, a **waterlogged** field

¹**wheel** *(a steering wheel)* They pushed the logs on **rollers**.

The UFO was shaped like a **disc**.

²**wheel** *(wheeling his trike)* She **rolled** the car to the roadside. I **pushed** my bike up the hill.

while 1 *(He cleaned his shoes while she made tea.)* We drew pictures **at the same time as** Mrs Phipps read to us. 2 *(in a short while)* after a **time**, a **period** of eight years, an **interval** of five minutes, a short **stretch** as goalie, a **spell** on duty

whine 1 *(The dog whined to go out.)* Then she **cried** to come in. The baby **whimpered** softly. 2 *(The children whined about having to go to bed.)* Dad **moaned** about the traffic. They **grumbled** about the weather. Lucy **whinged** about having an ice cream. You're always **fussing**. People **complain** a lot!

whip 1 *(Ben whipped his horse to make it go faster.)* Parents used to **beat** their children if they were naughty. Dad'll **thrash** you! He **hit** the robber. Lazy students used to be **caned** at school. The jockey **lashed** his horse. Slaves were cruelly **flogged**. 2 *(whipped cream)* He **whisked** the eggs and **stirred** the cake mixture.

whir *(the whir of a lawn mower)* the **buzz** of machinery, the **rumble** of cars, the **hum** of the hair dryer, the **whizz** of an insect

whirl *(whirling round to the music)* **turning** to look, **wheeling** round to face her, the wheel **spinning** out of control, dancers **twirling** on the stage, a sign **revolving** on top of a building, clothes **rotating** in the washing machine, a ballet dancer **pirouetting**

¹**whisper** *('Don't make any noise!' she whispered.)* 'Don't wake Timmy,' he **said softly**. 'I'm so tired,' she **sighed**. 'Darling,' he **murmured**. 'I love you,' she **breathed**. 'Get down!' he **hissed**. 'Mr Bell's coming,' he **gasped**. The audience were **talking in low voices**. They **spoke** to each other **in an undertone**.

²**whisper** *(speaking in a whisper)* a **sigh**, a **hiss**, a **murmur**, a **breath**, a **wheeze**, a **gasp**, an **undertone**

whole *(a whole day)* **all** his money, the **entire** world, a **complete** set, the **total** number of books, a **full** hour's work, **everything** clean and tidy, **everyone** in the class, eating **the lot**, hating **every** minute

wicked *(a wicked giant)* a **bad** queen, a **mean** witch, an **evil** wizard, a **foul** deed

wide *(a wide river)* a **broad** avenue, a **large** size, a **spacious** room, a **roomy** car

wild 1 *(a wild rat)* a **savage** beast, an **untamed** cat, a **ferocious** wolf, an **unbroken** pony 2 *(a wild landscape)* **rough** hills, **uncultivated** moorland, **natural** woodland, **unspoilt** countryside, a **jungle** 3 *(a wild party)* an **unruly** child, **uncontrolled** behaviour, **boisterous** games 4 *(a wild night)* **stormy** weather, a **windy** day

willing *(willing to change places)* **ready** to help, **glad** to come round, **happy** to lend you the money, **content** to take a small part, **pleased** to sell tickets, **delighted** to cook dinner, a **cooperative** child, an **obliging** person, being **helpful**

w

¹**win 1** *(Dion won the 800 metres race.)* Our school **came first** in the quiz. We **beat** St Paul's. We **triumphed** easily over St Paul's. We **succeeded** in getting 13 questions right. We **came out on top**. We **were victorious**. We were **in the lead**. We **thrashed** King's School 5-0. I **defeated** Gran at chess.
2 *(They won a silver cup.)* Annie **got** the first prize, Ben **achieved** second, Chris **gained** the third, David **obtained** the fourth and Emma **secured** the fifth.

²**win** *(It's a win for Dabbington!)* a **victory**, a **triumph**, a **success**, the **conquest** of Britain by the Romans

¹**wind** *(say wind) (a strong wind)* a **puff** of wind, a sudden **gust**, a **draught** down my neck, cool **air** coming in, a soft **breeze**, an icy **blast**, blowing a **gale**, a terrible **hurricane**

²**wind** *(say wynd) (winding the window up)* **turning** the key, **twisting** the string into a ball, **curling** her hair round the tongs, **looping** the thread onto the machine

coiling the rope

wipe *(wiping the dishes)* **cleaning** the worktop, **mopping** the floor, **drying** the plates, **polishing** the table, **clearing** the windscreen, **rubbing** the silver candlestick

wise *(a wise old woman)* a **thoughtful** answer, a **sensible** thing to do, an **intelligent** reply, a **shrewd** salesman

¹**wish** *(Lindy wished she could have a pony.)* He **hoped** he would see her again. I'm **longing** to see him. The lonely child **yearned** for a friend. I **would like** to have a baby brother. I **would love** it. The prisoner **craved** freedom. The witch **desired** a casket of jewels. I **hope** she gets what she wants.

²**wish** *(It was her dearest wish to see her daughter married.)* My **dream** is to become famous. It's his **aim** to play for the first team. Her **goal** is to make a lot of money. He's got no special **ambition**. Mum's **objective** is to speak Spanish. Julie's **target** in the spelling test is 90%.

witchcraft *(powerful witchcraft)* using **magic** tricks, putting a **spell** on the frog, **charms** to cure illness, ancient **sorcery**

wizard *(a powerful wizard)* a wicked **sorcerer**, a famous **magician**, a clever **conjuror**

wobble *(The chair wobbles when you sit on it.)* The ladder **tottered** and fell. The cradle **rocked** from side to side. The boat **bobbed** on the water. The machine **vibrated**. The bus **shuddered** to a stop. It **shook** violently. The bird **quivered** with fear. The baby **jiggled** about in her chair.

W

wood *(a small wood)* an area of **woodland**, an apple **orchard**, a dark **forest**, animals in the **jungle**, an **olive** grove

a tropical **rainforest**

woman *(an important woman)* a **lady** on a bike, a **girl** eating fish and chips, a fierce **female**

wonder *(I wondered what to do.)* I **thought about** whether to phone home. I **gave** the problem **some thought**. She **considered** which flavour ice cream to have. Jonathan **contemplated** his future.

wonderful *(a wonderful party)* a **great** idea, an **excellent** dinner, a **lovely** day, an **awesome** film, a **sensational** game, a **terrific** singer, a **marvellous** story, an **outstanding** player, an **ideal** solution, a **perfect** place to eat, an **exceptional** talent, an **enjoyable** film, a **super** drawing

¹**work 1** *(Where does she work?)* What does your dad **do**? Where is he **employed**? He's **engaged** in social work. He was **hired** by a Japanese company. What's her **job**? **2** *(My sister works hard.)* He's been **performing** badly at school. Dino **laboured** to produce a good picture. They're **slaving away** in the kitchen. The elves **toiled** all night. **3** *(I learnt how to work the video camera.)* It doesn't **go** if the red button's down. Can you **operate** this computer? The truck **runs** on diesel. Brad **drives** a crane. He's **using** the new food processor. **4** *(Our Christmas appeal worked well; we raised £500.)* His scheme didn't **succeed**. Advertising on television is very **effective**.

w

²**work 1** *(She has to travel for her work.)* What's her **job**? He's started a teaching **career**. Nursing is a caring **profession**. His last **occupation** was night watchman. Her **business** is doing well. He's looking for **employment** at the moment. She applied for a **position** in a large company. There are no **posts** vacant at the moment. The Prime Minister will announce new **appointments** to the Cabinet. **2** *(Have you finished the work on the Egyptians?)* I handed in my **project** today. Here's my **homework**. He had an **assignment** to do at the weekend. She's finished the **task**. **3** *(Repairing the car took a lot of work.)* He puts a lot of **effort** into his carpentry. Mum finds it a **strain** juggling a job and looking after a family. Dad says it's worth the hours of **drudgery** to have the car working again. The prisoners were sentenced to hard **labour**. After a night of **toil**, the elves were tired.

work out 1 *(He worked out the answer.)* Ziya **solved** the problem. He **thought about** it for a long time. I **found the answer** easily. He **decoded** the secret message. Her handwriting was hard to **decipher**. **2** *(Louise works out in the gym every morning.)* She **exercises** for 40 minutes. Her brother's **training** for the marathon.

world *(the tallest mountain in the world)* the longest river on **Earth**, the fattest man on the **planet**, finding Australia on the **globe**

worried *(Rick's worried about the exam.)* a **nervous** mother, **anxious** parents, a **concerned** teacher, a **troubled** sleep, **uneasy** about her safety, **jittery** about coming home alone, a **frightened** child, **scared** of singing in front of the class, **under stress**, a **tense** person, being **upset**, feeling **jumpy**, having **the jitters**, being **under pressure**

¹**worry** *(Does the radio worry you?)* No, but it might **disturb** Dad. Sorry to **trouble** you. Don't **bother** to apologise. You didn't **inconvenience** us.

²**worry** *(She was ill with worry.)* **anxiety**, **fear**, **concern**, **upset**, **distress**, **care**, **stress**, **pressure**, **apprehension**

worth *(How much is this VCR worth?)* It **cost** £120 secondhand. The **price** has changed. It hasn't much **value** now, it's old.

This ring's **valued at** £250.

¹**wound** *(say* **woond***)* *(a deep wound on his leg)* She had a **cut** over her eye. The footballer had an **injury**. Has the fall done him any **harm**? There's some **damage** to his spine.

w

²**wound** *(say* **woond)** *(wounded in battle)* **injured** during the race, **hurt** in three places, **disabled** in the war

wrap *(Wrap the book in Christmas paper.)* He **covered** the baby with a blanket. She **rolled** the necklace **up** in a silk cloth. The book was **bound** in red leather. Mum **bundled** us **up** in warm clothes. The Russians were **muffled up** in padded coats and thick scarves. a parcel **enclosed** in shiny paper, **enfolded** in a blanket, a castle **shrouded** in mystery, **enveloped** in a cold mist, sweets **coated** in sugar, wire **insulated** with tape

wreck 1 *(A ship was wrecked on the reef.)* Many ships have **gone down** there. The little yacht **capsized** and **sank**. A smuggler's ship **foundered** on those rocks. **2** *(The gang wrecked the snack bar.)* They **smashed** the tables. They **destroyed** the lights and **ruined** the coffee machine. They **spoilt** the newly painted walls and **damaged** the fridge. Then they **vandalised** a bus shelter. The owners were horrified at what had been **demolished**. Everything was **devastated**. **3** *(All our plans have been wrecked.)* Everything's **ruined**.

wriggle *(The worm wriggled away.)* The child **squirmed** in my arms. She could **wiggle** her ears. Jamie **squirmed** free. A snake **writhed** across the path. She **curled** her hair round her ears. Her hair **coiled** down to her shoulders. The road **twists** and **turns** as it climbs the hills. It **curves** upwards and then **bends** to the left. It **wound** up above the town. The path **spiralled** up the mountain. The wires **snaked** across the floor.

wrinkle *(wrinkles on his face)* Mum's getting some **lines** round her eyes. There were **creases** in his shirt. The puppy had soft **folds** of skin on its face. Dad has a **furrow** between his eyebrows from frowning. Don't **crinkle** the paper. My skirt's all **crumpled** from sitting in the car.

write *(I wrote my name on the picture.)* Please **print** your name and **sign** the form. Harry **scribbled** a note to Mum. Jan **scrawled** her address on a piece of paper. She **jotted down** her phone number. 'Do you know the answer? Oh, **put down** 28, then.' She **put** 27 instead. The locket was **inscribed** with the initials JWR.

writer *(a writer for a magazine)* a best-selling **author**, a **journalist** on a paper, a sports **reporter**, a famous **novelist**

writing 1 *(messy writing)* careful **handwriting**, big **lettering 2** *(creative writing)* the world of **books**, studying **journalism**, English **literature**, modern **poetry**, the **works** of Roald Dahl, a **publication** for children

wrong 1 *(The taxi went the wrong way.)* He was **mistaken** about the time. Your directions were **inaccurate**. He gave the police a **false** name. What he told you was **untrue**. She addressed the letter **incorrectly**. **2** *(the wrong sort of clothes)* **unsuitable** shoes for walking **3** *(It's wrong to steal.)* a **bad** person, a **dishonest** salesgirl, **criminal** behaviour, a **crooked** businessman, a **corrupt** politician, an **unethical** thing to do, an **immoral** way to behave, a **shocking** waste

w

Xx

Yy

x-ray a **photograph** of the inside of your body, a **picture** of a broken bone

yet 1 *(Have you eaten yet?)* I've **already** had tea. I had it **earlier**. **2** *(He's old, yet he's fit.)* I like it, **but** I don't want to buy it. She's been ill; **however**, she's better now.

young *(a young girl)* Don't shout at him; he's only **little**. a **small** boy, **childish** behaviour, **new** buds, an **immature** bird, **youthful** looks, a **babyish** way to behave, a **juvenile** court

yell *(Max yelled at his brother.)* He **shouted** for help. Lianne **screamed** at her sister. The old man **bellowed** at the children. The crowd **roared** with approval. Kay **called out**, 'Hi!' 'I'm coming!' she **cried**. 'You're here!' he **exclaimed**. 'Help!' they **screeched**.

yellow *(a bright yellow T-shirt)* **gold**, **honey**, **blonde**, **flaxen** hair, **sandy**, **lemon**, **primrose**, **butter**

yes *(Yes, I'm coming.)* **Of course! Sure!** '**Certainly**, Madam.' '**Affirmative**, Captain.'

A leveret is a **baby** hare.

Zz

zero *(room number three-zero-four)* A thousand is a one followed by three **noughts**. The winning ticket is six-**o**-seven-one. We lost four-**nothing**. How much did you win in the bingo? **Zilch**.

x
y
z

Word List

Use this list to
find the word you want.
The page number will tell you
where to look in the book.